Study Guide for

ELEMENTS OF PSYCHOLOGY

Fourth Edition

11/1/84

**David Krech, Richard S. Crutchfield,
Norman Livson, Allen Parducci,
and William A. Wilson, Jr.**

JANET LEONG

Prepared by
Donald Forgays
University of Vermont

Alfred A. Knopf New York

Contents

iv

HOW TO USE THIS STUDY GUIDE

The purpose of this Study Guide is to help you to learn the material in the text well and easily and to enable you to pass a variety of examinations based on the text. The material in the following two sections is designed to help you to be a better student in this course and in all the courses that you will take in your career.

After these first two sections, there are 30 brief sections, each corresponding to a unit in the text. Their format is the same, although their lengths may vary. Each section contains the following:

1. *Introduction:* In this section one or two of the central themes of the text unit is usually highlighted. This is done by presenting relevant historical information not contained in the text. The purpose is to motivate you, the reader, by including little-known facts about some of the persons involved in the central themes. Many of these introductory statements emphasize the role of the Zeitgeist in scientific discovery or, for that matter, in the suppression of science. The Zeitgeist is the spirit of the times. In light of the pertinent facts about mid-nineteenth-century science and philosophy, for example, it seems clear that something like the science of psychology was bound to develop. It did not occur spontaneously, but rather followed other developments that had been occurring for decades to some even for centuries. On the other hand, it seems equally clear that research on sexual behavior, such as that conducted by Masters and Johnson in the past 20 years, would not have been permitted early in this century.

It is important to understand that science is significantly influenced by the times. Sometimes, however, science is inappropriately influenced by the times, as when — usually in sociopolitical areas — external pressures and their attendant emotions are allowed to influence the selection of topics for study or the formation of conclusions.

Some of the units do not easily lend themselves to this approach. In these cases, more specific reference is made to concepts developed in the unit; elaborations of such material are also made, usually with reference to broad underlying themes or controversies.

2. *Issues and Concepts:* This section assumes the role of a "Study Objectives" section in other study guides. It attempts to pinpoint the important issues and concepts contained in the unit. For greater interest and clarity, the material is presented in statements, rather than in outline form. In some instances, not only is a question raised but the answer is also given. All of the central concepts of the unit are included, and in some cases, why you should know them is also discussed.

3. *Unit Review:* The unit review is a summary of the entire unit. All the central themes, concepts, and terms are included, although illustrative examples, elaborations, and repetitions are not given. In order to make the review a more intensive learning experience, a programmed instructional format is employed; that is, certain words are left out, and the reader is expected to supply them. This approach has been found to be one of the most effective study techniques for mastering material such as is presented in an introductory psychology text. We suggest that you write what you consider to be the missing word(s) in pencil in the spaces provided. Each of these is numbered, and at the end of the unit you will find a numbered list of words that best complete the sentences. A word of caution: In many cases the missing word will be the label for a concept or theme in the unit. In other cases it will not be a specific psychological term, but rather a term from ordinary use. Don't attempt to think of a psychological term each time. The same word may also be used several times in the review. Thus, the fact that you have already used a particular word does not preclude its being used again, even for the next blank. In the answer key, if you find two words given with a slash [/] in between, either word is acceptable. Also, if the correct

word is not a technical word and if your word has the same sense as that in the answer key, consider it correct. Try to enter the flow of the review and grasp the relation of the sentences to each other. Also, don't read too far ahead before penciling in your responses. While the following sentence probably won't contain the material missing from the sentence you're working on, the sentence or two after that may. For us to avoid this possibility, we would have had to make the review less complete on the one hand or unreadable on the other.

4. *Thought Questions:* This section contains four questions for each unit. In some cases the question is an attempt to get you to integrate material in the text. In other cases it attempts to get you thinking about alternative interpretations of material presented. In still other cases, you may be asked to provide some practical application of the material. In most cases there are no set answers for the question. You may wonder if you are capable of providing realistic answers to questions that have not yet been answered by science. This is not the point of this section. After a thorough reading of the relevant text material, we wish you to speculate about the question. We suggest that you use processes akin to the free-association technique of psychoanalysis. In this case the associations will be somewhat controlled and restricted by the question and by your background reading.

These questions are designed to encourage creativity on your part. Dealt with appropriately, they should prove to be provocative and, hopefully, fun in the bargain.

5. *Evaluation (Self-tests):* This section is designed to assess in a variety of ways the degree of your mastery of the unit material. To do this, it mimics in format the evaluations that you are likely to meet in your course. Since these formats will differ from course to course, we have provided four that are used in most courses. In each unit there are 10 fill-in-the-blank items. These are very much like the unit review material in which you provide the missing word. There are also 10 matching items and 10 multiple-choice questions. Finally, there are four brief essay-type questions. While there is some overlap, in many cases different test styles cover different terms and concepts. Recall memory and recognition memory are both tapped in these tests. Recall memory is required by the fill-in items and the short-answer questions, recognition memory by the matching and the multiple-choice items. As you will learn in the course, students usually do better on recognition than on recall tasks. You may find, then, that you make more errors on the recall tests. Perhaps you can gauge your level of learning by comparing your performance on the two forms. You can feel confident when your recall matches your recognition and both are high.

At the end of the unit, correct answers are provided for the fill-in, matching, and multiple-choice items. Page references are also given for each of these items to allow you to confirm the answer suggested or to review the material involved in case you gave an incorrect answer. Page references are also provided for material with which to answer the short-answer items. You will have to assume the instructor role and compare your answer with the indicated material to evaluate your responses to these items.

SUGGESTED ORDER OF STUDY

This Study Guide is designed to supplement the text as you work your way through the course. While you are free to develop your own style of using the guide effectively, we designed it to be used in the following way: First of all, read the introduction to a unit in the guide before you read the corresponding text unit. These introductory statements can be read in conjunction with the several Perspectives sections of the text. They serve similar purposes. Next read the Issues and Concepts section of the guide for a rapid introduction to what you will find in the text unit and what is deemed important to focus on. Then read the text unit, using appropriate reading and studying methods (see reading and studying suggestions in the next section of this guide). When you think you have learned the material well enough to be evaluated, return to the guide to complete the Unit Review. If you find that you are unable to complete many of the sentences or that you have made many errors, return to the text for additional study. An analysis of your errors should be made to see if you should emphasize one type of material or one section of the unit when you study. When you believe you have mastered the unit material, with or without additional study, respond to the self-tests. Complete all four types of tests before checking the answers at the end of the unit. Remember that these self-tests mimic course examinations, and respond to them as such; that is, take them in a quiet place without interruptions, and allow only a reasonable interval — say, 45 minutes — to respond to all of the items.

Each text unit contains a glossary at the end. In it are concept labels that the authors consider important enough to be learned by the student. It is likely that instructors will design examination questions around many of these terms. As an aid to learning them, we suggest that you make flash cards of these terms and their definitions or explanations. To do so, simply take 3- by 5-inch filing cards, available in any college bookstore, and put the term on one side and the definition or explanation on the other. You will then have a resource that can be used alone or with a review partner. Students have used this technique to good effect particularly in foreign language vocabulary, but it is a good method for learning any vocabulary. You may wish to undertake such a drill after reading the text but before responding to the Unit Review.

Learning can be enjoyable and rewarding in any field and certainly ought to be in the science of behavior. If you read and study the text effectively and use this study guide to advantage, you should be able to master the material. Additionally, the typical anxiety associated with evaluation episodes — that is, examinations — should be dissipated to some extent.

METHODS FOR EFFECTIVE STUDY AND EXAMINATION TAKING

This section of the guide describes a number of techniques that have been found to contribute to effective study, mastery of learning, and better examination performance. Included are brief sections on study methods, reading performance, lecture attendance, memory improvement, and control of test anxiety.

A. HOW TO STUDY THE TEXT

While excellent students may adopt widely different methods of studying — which is as it should be — the following are general rules for studying text material effectively. Excellent students inevitably use these rules, at least to some degree, even if they are unaware of it. These rules have been formalized at Ohio State University and given the label SQ3R, meaning that the steps to effective study are *s*urvey, *q*uestion, *r*ead, *r*ecite, and *r*eview. Each of these steps will be discussed in turn.

1. *Survey:* Making an effective survey of a learning unit means getting a complete overview of it. Your first learning unit is the entire text. To get an overview of the text, read the preface, the table of contents, the various Perspectives sections, and the 30 unit summaries. This should take no more than three to four hours and will be time well spent. You will obtain the general approach of the authors, understand the overall organization of the text, and even begin to pick up some detail.

An overview of each unit can be best obtained by reading the first page or two until you hit a main heading. This is introductory material designed to set the stage for the unit. Then read the first two sections of the study guide for that unit. Returning to the text, read the summary of the unit and then go over its various headings carefully. These headings constituted the original organization of the text before detail and illustrative material were added, so it is important for you to attend to them. Pay attention to the main headings that divide the unit into several principal themes. Then attend to the subheadings provided and, if necessary, the sub-subheadings. Different sizes and styles of type are usually used for these various headings, so you can spot them readily. It may be useful to record these headings and subheadings. Getting the overview of a unit is essential to studying it effectively. Failure to do so is usually associated with ineffective study habits and poor examination performance.

2. *Question:* The second step in effective study is asking questions of the material. For example, in assembling the outline of headings discussed above, you should already begin to ask questions, if only about the definitions of the terms used or how the terms are to be used. You will ask further questions after reading the summary. You should be asking additional questions after reading the first two sections of the study guide for the unit. You may wish to glance at the self-test material for the unit at this time to prompt still further questions. This kind of questioning is an important part of studying and learning because it points up what you're looking for: answers to your questions!

3. ***Read:*** Now you are prepared to read the material in the unit. You already have a good idea of the organization of the text as a whole and of the specific unit to be read. You also have a number of questions about the unit for which you will be seeking answers. You are ready to read. Never forget that this is the third step in effective study and not the first. Many students begin with reading, failing to recognize that reading is only one of the necessary steps — and perhaps not even the most important one. Read in an active manner, integrating the headings and other guideposts. Look for organization at all times. Look especially for answers to the questions you have already framed. Note any words or phrases in a different typeface, since these are the terms that the authors emphasize. Instructors pay attention to them, so you should too. Read the entire unit, including the boxes and figures and tables and their captions. These help to clarify statements made in the text. They sometimes summarize several pages of text.

4. ***Recite:*** Recitation is a necessary part of the study pattern because of the devastating effects of forgetting. If you simply read the material, much of it is forgotten by the time you have finished the unit. Further forgetting takes place between reading and review or between reading and examination. To avoid forgetting, you must recite. In other words, after reading a section of the unit, for example, a main heading section, sit back and review what you have just read. Pay attention to the main headings and the subheadings. Recite terms and their definitions, always trying to put information in order and to organize it effectively. Recitation should also be part of your review process later.

5. ***Review:*** The last phase of effective study is review. Most students do some kind of review before examinations, so it is not a new experience. The first review should occur right after the reading and recitation phases, however. You should make another survey at this time, now that you are familiar with the territory. Use the recitation technique, but include the entire unit this time. In effect, you recite material covered in the unit, definitions of terms, illustrative material, and so forth. You will probably find that some rereading is needed to check yourself or to improve clarity and detail. This first review should be a brief one. Section 3 of the study guide unit (the Unit Review) should be completed as part of this review. It should clarify what rereading needs to be done.

Between the first review immediately after the reading and the last one undertaken just before an examination, a second review or even a third one is generally useful. These interim reviews will highlight ideas that are unclear and indicate further rereadings that may be necessary. Notes that you have taken should be used at each stage of review. The final review should be more extensive; it should occur as close to examination time as possible and should review all the material. At this time you might find the last two sections of the study guide to be of greatest help. These contain the Thought Questions and the Self-tests. If you do not use these materials until the final review, make sure sufficient time remains before the examination is scheduled for any rereading still required.

These, then, are the five phases of effective study of textbook-type material. If you use them and coordinate the entire process with the study guide materials as indicated, you will be employing techniques known to contribute to both higher student course satisfaction and better grade attainment.

A word about note taking. There are two principal ways to take notes on a text. The first is to underline material in the text, and the second is to take notes on the material independently in a separate booklet. Many students do both. If you underline in the text, use a pencil, so that you can change your emphasis if you wish after you have studied the material. (The resale value of your book will also be increased if you are able to erase the underlinings.) When you underline, don't underline large sections of the book. The book is always available for you to study; what good does it do to underline half or more of it? The note should be a *cue* to the material, not all the material.

Taking independent notes is a good idea for a number of reasons. One is that notes can be combined with your initial survey of the unit. When you overview the unit's organization, take active notes on the headings and subheadings. Leave plenty of space between entries so that you can add detail later. A second reason is that note taking is an active process involving a good deal of thought and motor behavior, both of which will be involved in the examinations to come. The kind of summarizing you do in note taking will enable you to recall it later, and the entire activity will become rooted in your memory.

For years we have recommended to students that they limit their text underlining but that they take more notes. To students who take too elaborate notes, we suggest that you make notes on your notes. This may sound somewhat facetious. It is not. The additional summarizing practice and active writing behaviors will add appreciably to your memory of the material. These notes, of course, will be invaluable at the review stage.

B. HOW TO IMPROVE READING SKILLS

In this section we will review the three different kinds of reading that you should be doing with the text; we will then discuss the most common problems that influence students' reading speed and comprehension along with some suggested solutions.

You should do three kinds of reading: the survey type of reading, reading for specific detail, and then reading for review. Each involves a different reading speed and skill. The survey type of reading has already been detailed above. You remember that in the survey you scan the unit for organization, headings and subheadings, and so forth. This can be done very rapidly, and it is usually associated with taking notes in outline form, as was discussed. When surveying, you don't read every word — you are looking for organization and main ideas only. Surveying an entire unit may take only 30 or so minutes.

Once you have this organizational base, you read for specific details. This is slower reading, because you have to read very word. But you do not want to get bogged down here, and so, if you don't understand a specific word, note it for further study but try to grasp the passage anyway, so that you can continue reading at a good level of speed. If your survey reading has given you a good grasp of the principal ideas in the passage, the specific details related to the main ideas should also be clear. Here, you must guard against paying too much attention to relatively trivial material. Effective survey reading should prevent this. Depending on the student's reading speed and comprehension and on the unit (some are quite brief, with less detail, and some are much longer, with a lot of detail), this second type of reading for details may require from one to four hours per unit. Most details are closely associated with a principal idea. They may be used to illustrate the main idea or as evidence of it. Other details may provide additional support or illustration. While added details may be interesting and important, the main ideas and specific details will earn you the high grade on the examination.

The third type of reading is for review purposes. Here you read, again rather quickly, to assess your knowledge of the principal ideas and the more important specific details. Such a review should take no more than 30 to 90 minutes, depending on the unit.

A college student must have an adequate reading speed to accomplish the required amount of reading in the time available. Your speed should be at least 200 words a minute for material such as your text and several times that for easier material. Your university will probably have a resource center where your speed can be checked, and it may even provide a course to ameliorate reading difficulties. If so, take advantage of it.

In this section we will suggest techniques to incorporate and practices to avoid if you wish to improve your reading speed and comprehension. First of all, your reading should be silent. You may have started to read aloud as a child, but doubtless you now want a reading speed faster than that of a typical five-year-old! Not only should your reading be silent, but you should not move your lips while you read. Moving one's lips is usually associated with reading every word, or at least more than you need to. Increases in reading speed depend on reading groups of words. To check on lip movement, put a finger on your lips while you read. If they move, continue to practice reading with your lips immobilized until the behavior is extinguished. One way to do this is to develop a more rapid reading speed, so that there is no time for lip movements to occur.

Increasing reading speed is not mysterious. It simply requires a great deal of practice each day. Using a watch that indicates seconds, you should time the number of words you read per minute each day. Starting with relatively easy material, such as a novel, proceed to more difficult material, such as a weekly newsmagazine, and on to material such as the textbook for this course. In each case spend about 10 minutes reading a passage and then 2 or so minutes reviewing it, to check your comprehension, that is, to see if you are learning what there is to be learned in the passage. Force yourself to read faster and faster. Spending about 40 minutes a day over several weeks should yield a large improvement in your speed; comprehension should also be improved. Once you have increased your reading speed, use a practice routine to maintain your new, higher level of skill. This can be done with your regular study material by occasionally timing your reading speed and then reviewing for comprehension.

Another means of increasing reading speed and comprehension is to develop a better vocabulary. Often an unfamiliar word will disturb your reading flow and decrease your speed dramatically. It has already been suggested that you read around such words but note them. Return to them to check their meaning, either in the text or in a good dictionary, which should be by your side when you read. As you do with glossary terms, you may wish to put some of these words on flash cards.

Finally, try to avoid backtracking when you are reading. Many of us read a passage and then immediately reread it because we fear we didn't understand it. Backtracking wastes a great deal of time, so try to avoid it and to maintain a constant reading pace. Remember that you will be going back to the material for review. At that time you can reread any passages about which you felt doubtful.

Incidentally, there is no reason to read different kinds of material at the same rate. Some of your academic reading will be no more difficult than the weekly newsmagazine. In this case you should read it at your top speed— say, 500 words a minute. More difficult material can be read at a much slower but still adequate speed — say 200 words a minute. When you make your survey of the reading task, you will learn to judge the appropriate speed.

C. HOW TO ATTEND LECTURES AND TAKE NOTES

The first point about attending lectures properly is to learn to be a good listener. This will be easier with some lecturers than with others; but it can be done with all. Sit erect, be alert, and adopt appropriate sets. The two most important sets correspond to the two items you look for in reading a text — main ideas and specific details. Since you don't have a book to refer to in a lecture, you must use every indication of main ideas and key details that the instructor provides. If the instructor follows the text, this should not be difficult. If the instructor does not — and most probably don't — then attend carefully to his or her cues. Frequently the lecturer will say what the lecture will be on, will deliver it, and will then say what the lecture was on. Attend to these important cues. You can almost make a game of discovering the point of the lecture. If you listen in this manner, even a less-than-sparkling lecture will become absorbing. Listening actively will also help you to respond to questions based on the lectures.

Often you will know the topic of the lecture in advance. Either it will be part of the course syllabus, or the topic will have been announced at the end of the last lecture. If the lecture is a continuation of the previous one, prepare for it by going over your notes from the last one. If it is not a continuation but the topic is known to you, go over the topic in the text. Either procedure should help you both   understand the lecture and to take better notes.

Your lecture notes should correspond to the lecturer's organization, which will appear provided either formally in some sort of outline or informally in the way that the material is presented. Learn to set up your notes in an organized fashion, and to record the main ideas and the specific details related to them.

You will recognize that this process is much like the study and reading process. First you survey to find the organization, and then you watch for the main points and the specific details. When the lecture is over, review your notes and reorganize them if necessary. If you have questions, bring them to the next meeting and get them clarified during class or privately. Your final review of your lecture notes should occur shortly before any examination based on the material.

Perhaps the most critical part of the lecture-attending and note-taking process is the mental set suggested earlier. It is critical that you adopt and maintain a set to learn what the lecturer is trying to communicate.

D. HOW TO REMEMBER MORE EFFECTIVELY

In your text you will be reading quite a bit about memory processes. Please refer to Unit 11 in the text for this information. Here, we will suggest general ways of studying and reviewing course material for optimal retention. We have already observed that learning is an active process. We stress that fact here. Approach all your readings and lectures in an active manner. Ask questions of the material, establish its organization, its main facts and specific details, take notes, and review everything.

For material such as your text, the methods of whole learning and distributed practice are probably most effective. Whole learning means that the material to be studied is an intact whole. While there will be parts and subparts, one or more central themes underlie them all. You read in wholes, then, rather than bits and pieces. You stop to ponder or take notes only when you have a *chunk* of material to ponder or note.

Distributed practice means that you don't study — say, for an examination — in a single trial. That is, you don't spend 20 hours immediately before an examination preparing for it, but instead distribute the 20 hours as 10 sessions of 2 hours each, scattered over several weeks. Such a pattern allows for review and rehearsal between sessions. On many occasions students are not even aware of the rehearsal that occurs. It is important, then, to distribute your study periods over substantial intervals of time and to pursue the study effort in terms of units or wholes of material. Much research indicates that your learning will be more effective and your retention greatly improved if you use these methods.

Repetition is also related to memory improvement. We have already recommended several reviews of reading and lecture material. We reemphasize the idea here and recommend even additional repetitions. These repetitions allow for overlearning. You pass the point at which you feel you know the material. You keep reviewing and practicing: you overlearn. This will serve you in good stead when on your next examination you feel completely prepared — even after you see the questions!

E. HOW TO ATTEMPT TO CONTROL TEST ANXIETY

All evaluations in life are tinged with anxiety, and course tests are no exception. Grades are greatly influenced by examination performance. Many students become overwhelmed by such stress and "draw a blank," responding in a random manner, including irrelevant material, and otherwise performing poorly. A student who is soundly prepared will not experience these stresses, on the whole, and many instructors suspect that the "blank" is a rationalization for a lack of preparation. There is no substitute for preparation. Thus, if you follow the procedures outlined above, you probably won't be highly stressed by examinations.

No matter how well prepared, some students still find examinations an ordeal. This can be ameliorated. Approach the examination in an unhurried way. Get to the room a few minutes early. Don't use this time to look over your notes. This is not the time for such review. If you followed the procedures above, you have reviewed enough. Try to think cheerfully and don't argue with fellow students about course material or what will be on the test. Above all, be relaxed. Take a few deep breaths and do some progressive muscle relaxation, starting with your toes and working up your body to your head. These efforts will take only a minute or two and should put you in the appropriate set to respond well to the examination.

A final word. During the course of these suggestions for improving study performance you may have been wondering: How in the world can I find time to study in this way? The answer is that these techniques take no more time that the methods you already use. In fact, per item of material learned, they take less time. You will determine how much time you will spend on a particular course. You may decide that it will be the "traditional" six hours a week for a three-credit course, or you may decide to spend double that — or half that. We trust that it will be about six hours a week, although these matters vary greatly among students who achieve the same grade. Whatever time you spend will be better spent if you follow our study suggestions. The only exception is the student who spends a token amount of time studying. For that student, no study method is better than any other, for effective study cannot be accomplished in a token amount of time.

Unit 1

INTRODUCTION: PSYCHOLOGY AS A SCIENCE

---

1. INTRODUCTION TO STUDY OF THIS UNIT

Psychology is a field with a long past but a relatively short history. This is to say that some of the idea systems that have attracted the attention of psychologists over the past 100 years have been around for some time — some even among the early Greek philosophers. Modern psychology dates from about the middle of the nineteenth century, when the field of psychophysics began to develop with the work of Weber and Fechner in Germany. Any such dating scheme is arbitrary, of course, since ideas have not only a present and perhaps a future but also a past. What happened with some of these ideas in Germany in the mid-nineteenth century is that they were pursued experimentally. Weber and Fechner collected data on certain subjects, ordered their data, and speculated about it — that is, formed theories. This approach blended philosophy with a methodology, which came from the science of physiology. It is not surprising that the first experimental psychologists were frequently trained as physiologists and as philosophers. Wundt, a physiologist at the University of Leipzig in Germany, followed up earlier work in psychophysics and founded the first psychology laboratory in 1879. This dating, too, is arbitrary, since quite a bit of experimental psychology was going on in various places in the world by that time. However, Wundt was dedicated, prolific in his publications, and eager to train graduate students and send them around the world to carry on his traditions. For these reasons it is understandable that he earned the title of "father of experimental psychology."

Experimental psychology involves the application of scientific procedures to questions of interest to psychologists, either to develop information for its own sake or because the information can be applied in the solution of problems that are considered important. These scientific procedures are shared with all the other sciences, including physics, chemistry, and biology. What constitutes a science is not the questions asked — that is, the content of the field — but rather how practitioners try to answer them. Reliance on one's own convictions, the authority of others, or folklore for explanations of natural phenomena is not acceptable. The scientist must collect data under rigorously prescribed conditions. The scientist's objective is to be able to predict and control the occurrence of a phenomenon and ultimately to understand it better that it had been understood before.

1

2. ISSUES AND CONCEPTS

The most important thing to learn in this unit is that psychology is a science and why this is so. Psychologists employ the same kinds of research procedures as other scientists and are bound by the same rules of evidence; in addition, they work in a wide variety of areas. You must learn an acceptable definition of psychology and have an idea of the range of topics in the field.

In order to rule out improper causal interpretations of what they are studying, scientific psychologists use experimentation whenever possible. You must know what an experiment is and the role of hypotheses, independent and dependent variables, and controls in experiments. Understand the double-blind procedure and the placebo, since they are important in some experimental designs, especially those investigating drug effects. Be aware that scientists use statistical tests to help them make decisions about experimental effects. Know what a mean and a standard deviation are.

Know why some scientists use correlational studies even though they are less desirable than experimental studies. Be clear on the difference between these two types of studies and why one is less preferred. Know what a correlational coefficient is and what its numerical expression means in terms of relationships.

Learn about the basic goals of all science, including psychology. Be able to differentiate understanding, prediction, and control, and know how the three are interrelated.

Finally, be aware of the distinction between experimental and applied psychology and how these are interrelated.

3. UNIT REVIEW

Correct answers are given at the end of the unit.

Psychology is a science because psychologists apply the same (1)_____ employed by scientists in other fields and are bound by the same rules of (2)_____. Psychologists work with a great variety of problems that sometimes overlap the domains of many other fields.

Definitions of psychology appear to have changed over the years; a common current definition of psychology is the science of (3)_____. Psychologists study both humans and (4)_____ and may study individuals or (5)_____.

Psychologists employ experimentation when possible to rule out improper (6)_____. Experiments begin usually with hunches, or (7)_____, about some aspect of nature. To investigate your hunch experimentally, you manipulate — that is, vary systematically — a variable called the (8)_____. It is called this because the experimenter controls it totally by varying it independently of other environmental features. Usually you apply the different conditions of this variable not to the same subjects but to different groups of subjects who are (9)_____ to conditions. One or more groups will be untreated and they are referred to as the (10)_____, called so because they provide a check on the possible effects of (11)_____ that could be responsible for an observed effect. The measure of the outcome of the influence of the independent variable is called the (12)_____. It is

thought to be dependent on the systematic variation of the (13)_____. This outcome measure is usually used to differentiate the experimental group(s) from the
(14)_____ group. Measures of the outcome variable should be as
(15)_____ as possible. Ways of maintaining objectivity of the dependent variable
include keeping the provider of the scores ignorant of what group the subject has been assigned to and also
keeping the subject so unadvised. This procedure is referred to as the (16)_____.
To achieve this in drug studies and some other studies, an inert substance is frequently used that looks like the
drug, and this is called a (17)_____. Frequently scientists use statistical tests to
evaluate the influence of the independent variable, usually by comparing the mean value of the dependent
variable for the (18)_____ with that of the (19)_____.
In addition to the mean value, which is the (20)_____ of a set of scores, scientists
usually measure variability or dispersion of those scores around the mean value with a statistic called
(21)_____.

A single experiment rarely settles an issue completely, even if it has been repeated, or
(22)_____. There is also the problem of (23)_____, or
extending the results to other subjects or situations.

It is sometimes impossible to test an hypothesis using the preferred experimental method, and a second
method in which relationships are studied, called the (24)_____, is used. In this
method one uses the correlation (25)_____ to study the relationship of interest.
This statistic is based on the ordering of scores in the two distributions. If the ordering is exactly the same on
both measures, the coefficient will be (26)_____. If the ordering is exactly
reversed, the coefficient will be (27)_____. If there is no relationship between the
two measures, the coefficient will be (28)_____. Many studies in psychology use
the correlational method, and this is associated with many problems in (29)_____. The
presence of (30)_____ factors may make it difficult to rule out competing interpretations of observed relationships. Such correlational studies should perhaps be viewed as sources of, rather
than tests of, (31)_____.

The first goal of science is (32)_____, that is, having a better explanation of
an aspect of nature. A test of this is whether you can state the conditions under which a phenomenon will or
will not occur, which is called (33)_____. With increased knowledge should come
the ability to cause the phenomenon to occur or not to occur, or (34)_____. While
there are many psychologists doing experiments and advancing knowledge, most psychologists today are
(35)_____ psychologists. These practitioners apply knowledge already learned.
They usually do not undertake formal (36)_____.

4. THOUGHT QUESTIONS

a. What are some of the problems associated with the extensive content of the field of psychology, ranging all the way from the basic sciences to literature and touching most of the social sciences in between?

b. Can a field limited to the method of correlational analysis be viewed as a science? If so, and what kind of a science could it be?

c. What kind of experiments would you undertake to test the hypothesis that eating tuna fish will improve IQ? How would you select your subjects, and what kinds of controls would be necessary?

d. The three definitions of psychology given in the text are: (1) the science of the mind; (2) the science of behavior; and (3) the science of behavior and experience. Are these definitions really different?

5. EVALUATION (SELF-TESTS)

Correct answers and text page references are given at the end of the unit.

a. Fill-in-the-blanks Items

Write the word(s) that best complete(s) the sentence in the space provided.

1. Psychology is a science because psychologists make use of _scientific methods_.

2. Psychology is commonly defined as the science of behavior and _experience_.

3. In an experiment, the variable that is a measure of outcome is called the _dependent_ variable.

4. A control group usually contains subjects who are _untreated_.

5. The double-blind procedure has both the data collector and the subject ignorant of what group the _subject_ is in.

6. The average of a number of scores is called the _mean_.

7. The preferred method of science is the _experiment_.

8. Correlational analysis cannot preclude the possibility of _____ of the data.

9. Having an improved explanation of an aspect of nature is referred to as _understanding_.

10. Control is demonstrated when the scientist can _cause_ a phenomenon to occur.

b. Matching Items

Write the number of the correct item from the right column in front of the matching item in the left column.

3	ethologists	1. measure of dispersion
6	experimentation	2. index of relationship
4	independent variable	3. study instincts in animals
7	dependent variable	4. controlled by the experimenter
10	placebo	5. state conditions for phenomenon appearance
1	standard deviation	6. done to rule out improper interpretations
9	replication	7. outcome measure
2	correlation coefficient	8. done if causal assessment is difficult
5	prediction	9. doing an existing experiment again
8	correlational studies	10. control in a drug study

c. Multiple-choice Items

Circle the letter in front of the answer that best completes the stem.

1. The preferred method of science is:
   a. case history
   b. the experiment
   c. correlational analysis
   d. objective approach

2. In an experiment, the variable that is controlled by the experimenter is the:
   a. independent variable
   b. dependent variable
   c. control variable
   d. treatment variable

3. The outcome measure in an experiment is called the:
   a. independent variable
   b. dependent variable
   c. control variable
   d. treatment variable

4. The measure(s) of the outcome variable should be:
   a. extensive
   b. simple
   c. variable
   d. objective

5. A placebo in a drug study is usually:
   a. given to all subjects
   b. provided by a physician
   c. an inert substance
   d. as effective as the drug

6. Statistics used most frequently in evaluating the influence of the independent variable are the:
   a. mean and correlation
   b. correlation and dispersion
   c. dispersion and standard deviation
   d. standard deviation and mean

7. A correlation coefficient of +1.0 indicates that the ordering of the two measures is:
   a. exactly the same
   b. reversed
   c. not related
   d. unknown

8. Correlational studies should be viewed as:
   a. equal to experimental studies
   b. sources of tests of hypotheses
   c. sources of hypotheses
   d. controlled causal interpretations

9. Scientific explanation is typically demonstrated through:
   a. understanding
   b. prediction
   c. control
   d. applied psychology

10. Causing a phenomenon to occur illustrates:
    a. understanding
    b. prediction
    c. control
    d. applied psychology

d. Short-answer Items

Answer the following questions with short, concise statements. Reference pages for the material are given at the end of the unit.

1. What are the principal differences in the approaches of the psychologist and the sociologist to the study of group behavior?

2. Why do scientists usually employ statistical analysis in their experimental studies?

3. What is the function of the double-blind procedure in drug studies?

4. Why should a person wishing to become a clinical psychologist be trained in scientific methodology and statistical analysis?

ANSWER KEY FOR UNIT 1

Unit Review

1. research methods
2. evidence
3. behavior and experience
4. lower animals
5. groups
6. causal interpretations
7. hypotheses
8. independent variable
9. randomly assigned
10. control group(s)
11. other factors
12. dependent variable
13. independent variable
14. control
15. objective
16. double-blind
17. placebo
18. experimental group

19. control group
20. average
21. standard deviation
22. replicated
23. generalization
24. correlational method
25. coefficient
26. $+1.0$
27. -1.0
28. 0
29. interpretation
30. confounding
31. hypotheses
32. understanding
33. prediction
34. control
35. applied
36. experiments

Evaluation (Self-tests)

a. **Fill-in-the-blanks Items**

   1. scientific methods (pp. 5–6)   6. mean (p. 8)
   2. experience (p. 4)   7. experiment (pp. 6,8)
   3. dependent (p. 7)   8. alternative interpretations (p. 9)
   4. untreated (p. 7)   9. understanding (p. 9)
   5. subject (p. 8)   10. cause (p. 10)

b. **Matching Items: Correct order and page references are:**

3 (p. 4); 6 (p. 6); 4 (p. 6); 7 (pp. 7–8); 10 (p. 8);
1 (p. 8); 9 (p. 8); 2 (p. 9); 5 (p. 9); 8 (p. 9).

c. **Multiple-choice Items: Correct answers and page references are:**

1—b (p. 6); 2—a (p. 6); 3—b (pp. 7–8); 4—d (p. 8); 5—c (p. 8);
6—d (p. 8); 7—a (p. 9); 8—c (p. 9); 9—b (p. 9); 10—c (p. 10).

d. **Short-answer Items: Page references for answer material are:**

1. pp. 4–5; 2. p. 8; 3. p. 8; 4. p. 10.

Unit 2

HEREDITY AND ENVIRONMENT

1. INTRODUCTION TO STUDY OF THIS UNIT

The issue of the relative contributions of heredity and environment to important human characteristics has been raised for a good many years. As you read in the text, some of the early Greek philosophers wondered about the variation of some behaviors across generations. The issue assumed greater importance over the last 100 years or so and became known as the nature-nurture controversy. The debate was heavily influenced by the theory of evolution proposed by Charles Darwin and by the work of his half cousin, Sir Francis Galton, on individual differences and the inheritance of important psychological characteristics, including intelligence. On the one hand, Darwin proposed that the evolution of species occurred through the operation of the principles of natural selection and survival of the fittest. That is, those members of a species best suited to survive in particular environments would survive longer and would be more likely to pass on their genes to enhance the survival of future generations in those environments. This process naturally selects the fittest members of a species; it can also lead to the extinction of an entire species. Genetic factors are clearly emphasized here, albeit as operating interactively with particular environmental characteristics. Galton emphasized even more strongly the probable contribution of genetics to behavior, including the intellectual behavior of humans. He suggested that genius was hereditary and outlined the twin-study method for examining the relationship between heredity and environment. Clearly, the European tradition has been more nativist than empiricist, and the Galtonian emphasis is seen later in the work of Sir Cyril Burt and of Hans Eysenck.

In contrast, many psychologists in this country have been more empiricistic than nativistic, emphasizing the contribution of experience and sociocultural variables in the development of most human behaviors. The pendulum swings, of course, and usually comes to a rest in the middle. Thus we now tend to talk about the interaction of heredity and environment, rather than to establish the proportional contribution of each. If you understand that the effects of environment occur as early as those of heredity — that is, at conception — and that all kinds of environmental inputs, including chemical and physical events, occur even before birth, it is not difficult to see why the interactive position is currently accepted and why attempts to sort heredity from environment have largely failed with respect to human behavior. One even begins to wonder if, whether deliberately or otherwise, sociocultural biases have been responsible for some of the which-is-important? inquiries raised about heredity and environment. It does appear that historically the question has been more often raised by those espousing an hereditarian point of view, although this may be only an historical accident.

2. ISSUES AND CONCEPTS

Learn the three answers possible to the question of the origin of a psychological trait, and which seems to be the preferred answer today. Know about selective breeding studies in lower animals, especially the important study by Tryon and the limited generalizability of his findings. Remember that heredity always works within an environmental context.

Know a definition of heritability and some criticisms of the concept. Know also why lower animals are usually the subjects of research into heredity and environment, and the finding in studies with dogs that specific behavioral traits could be bred but no overall trait for brightness discovered.

Know of the limitations of human-behavior genetic studies and the confounding factors usually inherent in them. Learn what confounding means, why twin studies were designed to reduce confounding, and why these designs do not really unconfound the heredity and environment variables, even when identical twins are reared in different environments. Conclude that behavior always reflects a mixture of genetic and environmental factors.

Learn that traits attributed largely to genetic origin can still be significantly modified by environmental change, and know two examples of this kind of interaction.

Know what *regression toward the mean* means as a statistical tendency and how it relates to studies of heredity and environment.

Learn about the recent field of sociobiology and how this position differs from traditional Darwinian theory. Learn that this model is highly speculative and that it presently appears to be an unfalsifiable theory, and what this means.

3. UNIT REVIEW

Correct answers are given at the end of the unit.

Three answers are possible to the question of the origin of some psychological traits: 1. (1)_____, 2. (2)_____, and a 3. (3)_____ of these two. The framework for thinking about the effects of heredity and environment comes from (4)_____ theory, which states that species evolve by (5)_____.

Selective breeding has been used for years to produce (6)_____ traits. Tryon did this with rats to produce two groups with differing abilities on a (7)_____ problem. Subsequent study indicates that the differential ability was specific to the original (8)_____. In other situations the performance of the two groups was not (9)_____ and might even be reversed. So, heredity always works within an environmental (10)_____. Because of this, today we emphasize the (11)_____ of heredity and environment.

Heritability refers to the proportion of observed trait differences that are attributable to (12)_____. However, if heritability is dependent on specific environments, then overemphasizing any single value would seem to be (13)_____. Skepticism about the application of heritability to human psychological traits is strong because it is so difficult to separate the influences of (14)_____ and (15)_____ upon such traits.

We can control heredity and environment experimentally only by using

(16)_____ as subjects. Selective breeding studies using a variety of animals

have been done, and they show an increase or a decrease of certain traits across

(17)_____. Studies involving the selective breeding of several types of dogs

showed the genetic bases of various behavioral traits but did not find trans-situational differences in

(18)_____.

The impossibility of achieving effective experimental control over human genetics opens the door to

(19)_____ of heredity and environment studies. In most of these studies,

heredity and environment are (20)_____, that is, they always seem to vary

(21)_____. One way possibly to unconfound these variables in human studies is

to examine as subjects (22)_____, since they have the same

(23)_____ structure. Any observable differences in their behavior might be at-

tributable to (24)_____ differences. We could compare them with

(25)_____, who ae the same age but no more similar in genetic structure than

(26)_____. With fraternal twins, we can assume environmental similarity but

(27)_____ difference. This does not appear to be a reasonable assumption,

however, since it is likely that identical twins share more environmental

(28)_____ than fraternal twins. Examining identical twins reared in different

homes does not appear to unconfound these studies because adoption agencies tend to match foster homes to

the (29)_____ in important characteristics. Studying other family

relationships does not solve the confounding problem since closer genetic relationship is typically

associated   with   closer   (30)_____   relationship.   Behavior   always

reflects a (31)_____ of genetic and environmental factors.

Certain traits that are attributable to genetic origin can be modified by

(32)_____ change. For example, PKU disease, an enzyme deficiency that

can lead to severe (33)_____, can be modified greatly by selective

(34)_____. As another example, those cases of depression for which there

is the strongest evidence of heritability are most amenable to treatment with

(34)_____. In both examples, the treatment is an

(36)_____ change.

Although children tend to resemble their parents in both physical and psychological traits, extreme

scores in one generation are no (37)_____ of extremes in the next.

Parents who deviate from the average on an attribute produce offspring who tend to deviate

(38)_____ on that attribute. This statistical tendency is

called (39)_____.

Two recent theoretical approaches have directed increased attention to the role of heredity in the determination of behavior. First, Chomsky says that universal (40)_____ is embedded in the nature of the human (41)_____. The second is sociobiology, which hypothesizes that complex social behavior often reflects the (42)_____ of the genes that control the behavior. This ensures the future production of the same (43)_____. The ultimate goal is for these genes to survive and (44)_____. The sociobiologists emphasize the survival of an (45)_____ genes, rather than the survival of the (46)_____, as Darwin did. A term used by sociobiologists to refer to the amount of energy a parent devotes to the survival of offspring is (47)_____. On the basis of such concepts, the sociobiologists have attributed some of the differences in sexual behavior between female and male to (48)_____. This approach has been partly successful in explaining the behavior of lower animals but has not been successful at the human level in accounting for the (49)_____ that take place in human culture, since genetic change over time is so (50)_____ and genetic differences among human populations are so (51)_____.

It is clear that sociobiological interpretations of human social institutions are highly (52)_____, and there seems to be no way to (53)_____ them. This model, then, seems to be an (54)_____ that does not really account for anything.

4. THOUGHT QUESTIONS

a. How would you design a human heredity and environment study so that these two factors were not confounded? Is it possible to accomplish this within our ethical system?

b. When do genetic influences and when do environmental influences first occur in the organism? If they occur at the same time, how could we ever hope to separate their relative contributions to the development of most psychological traits?

c. Why are the speculations of the sociobiologists about human social behavior so difficult to refute?

d. Why do we demand of a scientific explanation that it be able to predict specifically what will occur under some conditions and not under others?

5. EVALUATION (SELF-TESTS)

Correct answers and text page references are given at the end of the unit.

a. Fill-in-the-blanks Items

Write the word(s) that best complete(s) the sentence in the space provided.

1. The origin of most psychological traits is probably based on the _____ of heredity and environment.

2. Heredity always works within an _____ context.

3. Heritability refers to the _____ of a trait attributable to genetic variation.

4. We typically use lower animals as subjects in these studies because we can then _____ the action of heredity and environment.

5. In human studies heredity and environment are always _____.

6. Identical twins have been studied frequently because this allows the possibility of studying the relative contribution of _____.

7. Even for traits that are basically genetically determined, much modification can occur through _____ change.

8. Regression toward the mean means that short parents are likely to have _____ children.

9. Sociobiology suggests that one's behavior tends to guarantee the _____ and multiplication of one's genes.

10. The general theory of sociobiology appears to be very difficult to _____

b. Matching Items

Write the number of the correct item from the right column in front of the matching item in the left column.

_____ heritability	1. child is average height, parent is tall
_____ animal experiments	2. predicts what will occur under specific conditions
_____ Tryon	3. proportion of trait due to genetic variation
_____ confounding	4. control hereditary and environment experimentally
_____ identical twins	5. universal grammar
_____ fraternal twins	6. maze-bright and maze-dull animals
_____ regression toward the mean	7. share exactly the same heredity
_____ Chomsky	8. two or more variables vary simultaneously
_____ scientific explanation	9. consistent with all possible occurrences
_____ unfalsifiable theory	10. share heredity to same extent as any siblings

c. Multiple-choice Items

Circle the letter in front of the answer that best completes the stem.

1. Modern psychological thinking accepts that the origin of most psychological traits is:
   a. heredity
   b. environment
   c. interaction of heredity and environment
   d. heredity or environment depending on conditions

2. Heritability refers to how much of a trait is due to:
   a. heredity
   b. environment
   c. interaction of heredity and environment
   d. heredity or environment depending on conditions

3. The variables of heredity and environment can be controlled in experiments by studying:
   a. identical twins
   b. fraternal twins
   c. siblings
   d. lower animals

4. Every study of heredity and environment at the human level has suffered because of:
   a. the small number of subjects studied
   b. confounding of the two variables
   c. difficulty in controlling heredity
   d. difficulty in controlling environment

5. Pairs that have the same degree of genetic similarity as fraternal twins are:
   a. identical twins
   b. brothers and sisters
   c. cousins
   d. mothers and fathers

6. Studies of identical twins reared in different homes have not unconfounded heredity and environment because:
   a. they were not identical twins
   b. identical and fraternal twins act the same
   c. the subjects are not selected randomly
   d. foster homes are not selected randomly

7. For traits that are of genetic origin, environmental change can have:
   a. no influence
   b. an overwhelming influence
   c. only a minor influence
   d. an unknown influence

8. Very bright parents are likely to have offspring who are:
   a. less bright
   b. more bright
   c. exactly the same brightness
   d. of no relationship to the parents

9. Sociobiology is different from basic Darwinian theory in that it emphasizes the survival of:
   a. individual genes
   b. group genes
   c. the species
   d. the culture

10. The theory of sociobiology appears to be an unfalsifiable theory because it:
    a. makes specific predictions
    b. can be verified
    c. can incorporate any outcome
    d. is an experimental theory

d. Short-answer Items

Answer the following questions with short, concise statements. Reference pages for the material are given at the end of the unit.

1. Explain briefly the following statement: Heredity always works in an environmental context.

2. Why is it not a good assumption that fraternal twins will share as common an environment as identical twins?

3. What kind of influence can the phenomenon of regression toward the mean have on studies of the relative contributions of heredity and environment on some psychological trait?

4. Contrast the position of sociobiology with that of classical Darwinian theory with respect to survival mechanisms and purposes.

ANSWER KEY FOR UNIT 2

Unit Review

1. heredity
2. environment
3. combination
4. Darwin's
5. natural selection
6. stable
7. maze
8. test situation
9. different
10. context
11. interaction
12. genetic variation
13. misleading
14. heredity
15. environment
16. lower animals
17. generations
18. brightness
19. alternative explanations
20. confounded
21. together
22. identical twins
23. genetic
24. environmental
25. fraternal twins
26. siblings
27. genetic
28. similarities
29. biological parents
30. environmental
31. mixture
32. environmental
33. mental retardation
34. diet
35. lithium
36. environmental
37. guarantee
38. less
39. regression toward the mean
40. grammar
41. nervous system
42. natural selection
43. genes
44. multiply
45. individual's
46. species
47. parental investment
48. biological selection
49. rapid changes
50. slow
51. small
52. speculative
53. refute
54. unfalsifiable theory

Evaluation (Self-tests)

a. **Fill-in-the-blanks Items**

1. interaction (p. 17)
2. environmental (p. 18)
3. proportion (p. 18)
4. control (p. 18)
5. confounded (p. 21)
6. environment (p. 22)
7. environmental (p. 23)
8. taller (p. 24)
9. survival (p. 25)
10. refute (pp. 26–27)

b. **Matching Items: Correct order and page references are:**

3 (p. 18); 4 (p. 18); 6 (p. 18); 8 (p. 21); 7 (p. 22);
10 (p. 22); 1 (p. 24); 5 (p. 25); 2 (p. 26); 9 (p. 26).

c. **Multiple-choice Items: Correct answers and page references are:**

1—c (p. 17); 2—a (p. 18); 3—d (p. 18); 4—b (p. 21); 5—b (p. 22);
6—d (p. 23); 7—b (p. 23); 8—a (p. 24); 9—a (p. 25); 10—c (p. 26).

d. **Short-answer Items: Page references for answer material are:**

1. p. 18; 2. pp. 22–23; 3. p. 24; 4. p. 25.

Unit 3

A LIFE-SPAN OVERVIEW OF HUMAN DEVELOPMENT

1. INTRODUCTION TO STUDY OF THIS UNIT

An important concept you will meet in this unit is that of developmental staging. A number of theorists have suggested that human development, especially in the preadult years, follows a set of predictable and separate stages and that one must deal with earlier-stage tasks before one can deal with those that come later. Such a model has been applied to motor behavior, such as locomotion, and to cognitive behavior, such as reasoning ability. A second concept you will find in this unit is that of maturation. This notion suggests that many aspects of development involve an unfolding of physical and mental characteristics that accompany the growth of the body. Nativists commonly accept the concept of maturation, although they recognize the importance of experience as well. Nativists also accept the concept of staging. The nativist regards development as largely following a built-in design, supplied by heredity, but with environmental stimulation underlying some aspects of individual differences. The extent of the environmental contribution is usually unstated, but it is seemingly low, relative to the influence of inheritance.

Some of the early studies done by Arnold Gesell and his colleagues in the 1920s used identical twins as subjects. The experiment was designed to pit heredity against environment by providing one twin with extensive motor experience in early life while giving the other much less. The experience was provided during a period preceding "normal" appearance of these motor functions. The usual finding was that the experience produced no long-term benefits, and the researchers suggest this was so because it had occurred before appropriate maturation had taken place. Here you see the staging and maturational concepts work hand in hand, as they usually do. Some of these researchers have invested much energy in research seemingly designed to emphasize the genetic contribution to development, and in some cases, at least, it turned out to be a waste of time. For example, in 1935 M.B. McGraw did a study similar to that of Gesell. She provided one identical twin with a lot of motor experience and the other with much less, but during a time preceding "normal" maturation of the motoric behaviors. She found only a small and nonlasting difference in the motor behavior of the twins. (She also found later that the twins were not identical, but fraternal. C'est la vie!)

Piaget's theory is the best known of contemporary approaches to the concept of stages. Again, although Piaget views genetically based potential as always interacting with the environment to determine cognitive ability, his view does seem to be at least a bit on the nativistic side. Your authors suggest in this unit and throughout the text that the two factors contributing so importantly to development — heredity and environment — always interact — and in many cases, very intricately and not very obviously.

2. ISSUES AND CONCEPTS

In this unit, first learn a definition of development and how heredity and environment almost always interact to determine the process. Know the point of view of the developmental staging theorists and of those who are critical of this approach. Learn what happens in the transitions between stages and the possible role of these gap fillers. Learn which human characteristics seem to be continuous over the life-span and which don't. Be able to differentiate clearly among the three methods of studying development: cross-sectional, retrospective, and longitudinal. Know the assets and liabilities of each approach. Learn that the child is very different from the adult in many ways. With respect to body growth in infancy and childhood, be able to compare the overall growth rates and the differential growth rates for various body parts and for the two sexes. Learn the factors that influence the rate of growth, including seasonal variation. Learn about variation in the onset of menarche throughout history and the possible explanations for it.

Learn about the different growth rates for various parts of the body, and be able to distinguish cephalocaudal from proximodistal developmental directions. Know of the general pattern of sensorimotor development in white and black children and the possible explanations for it. Know how the brain grows over the first few years after birth and how this growth may be encouraged. Learn a definition of maturation.

Know that maturation and learning interact and that learning occurs very early in life. Learn how differentiation of action begins shortly after birth.

Learn that activity level is a persisting characteristic and that it, along with other characteristics, appears to be significantly influenced by the interaction between parent and child. Understand the special problem of the premature infant in this regard. Know that there are large individual differences in the timing and rates of all aspects of development.

Learn the physical and psychological changes that occur in adolescence and that the beginning of this period is determined by physiological factors while the end is defined — usually loosely — by cultural factors. Know of the changes in sexual activity and attitudes in Western society in recent years and that the notion of adolescent turmoil may be a myth.

Know why the adult years may be viewed as a developmental period and that several stage theories refer to this period; be aware of the kinds of stages that these theories propose. Learn that the notion of a necessary midlife crisis in the male is apparently a myth, and that suicide occurs more frequently in males than females at this time, and why this may be so. Learn the several stereotypes about the aged and that these, too, appear to be unsupported by evidence.

3. UNIT REVIEW

Correct answers are given at the end of the unit.

Development can be broadly defined as any sequential and continued process of

(1)_____, both qualitative and quantative, in any physical or psychological

structure or function in any (2)_____. Change may be abrupt or gradual

but most changes are (3)_____. Each of these changes is to some

extent determined by hereditary factors influenced by the (4)_____ in

which they occur. With only rare exceptions, nature and nurture are in a continual process of

(5)_____, and this process is unique to each

(6)_____. The stage of development during which an environmental

force occurs can be (7)_____.

Advocates of stage theory define a stage as a developmental phase during which a single theme or task dominates behavior and in which progression to the next phase requires mastery of the tasks of the (8)_____. An essential requirement of a true stage is that there be a distinct (9)_____ between it and the next one. Stage theorists typically emphasize the (10)_____ level of the individual as a factor influencing progress from one stage to the next. Changes in stage take place (11)_____, according to Piaget's theory. Critics of stage theory may accept stages as convenient (12)_____ but regard the developmental process as proceeding (13)_____, reflecting the interaction of experience and the maturationally determined abilities of the individual.

Transitions between stages are times of instability and (14)_____. The essence of a transition is (15)_____. Because change is (16)_____, each transitional period has a unique set of adaptive challenges and stresses. The need to change is an impetus to psychological (17)_____.

Some human characteristics are continuous over the life span, for example, (18)_____. There is less continuity in (19)_____ characteristics. For example, while intelligence level may be fairly stable, much (20)_____ may occur throughout the life span. Longitudinal studies reveal that (21)_____ personality traits remain stable over long intervals during development, although introversion, warmth, expressiveness, irritability, and (22)_____ seem to be durable traits. To observe that personality is highly modifiable is not to assert that its development is (23)_____. Behaviors that appear to be different over the life span but that serve much the same purpose are referred to as showing (24)_____.

A requirement for a developmental study is that measures of the characteristics under study be available at a number of (25)_____ in the developmental span. The method most used to study development is to study groups of individuals of different ages, called the (26)_____ method. It is convenient and, for some purposes, adequate — except to portray trends that are subject to (27)_____ change. Such change can (28)_____ the true trend of a trait when this method is used. A second method, called (29)_____, compares current measurements for an individual with (30)_____ values for such measurements. This method avoids the errors inherent in (31)_____, but it is subject to errors associated with the fallibility of (32)_____. Retrospective inaccuracies include a bias toward reporting things as more (33)_____ than they were. Psychologically (34)_____ mothers are more prone to these errors. Since mothers have a significant role in determining the (35)_____ of a family, they tend to shape the nature of retrospective findings, including reports by the other parent and the (36)_____ themselves. Because of the difficulties in these first two methods, psychologists must employ the third approach, called the (37)_____. In this method, the same group of individuals is observed and measured (38)_____ over the period of development being investigated. This method has problems beyond the need for funds and (39)_____. They include sample (40)_____, problems inherent in (41)_____ measurements, and the generalization of study results to individuals born during (42)_____ periods.

The child is very different from the (43)_____. To assess body growth during infancy and childhood, we must measure (44)_____ by measuring the total height and total weight and also (45)_____ to discover the different times and rates of growth of different parts of the body. The most rapid of the overall body growth periods are the (46)_____ period and the first (47)_____ years of life. There is another spurt of growth in late childhood and (48)_____. After puberty the rate (49)_____ until final height is reached. On average, girls mature (50)_____ years earlier than boys. Factors influencing the rate of growth include nutritional level, physical and psychological health, and, most important, (51)_____. There are also seasonal variations, with (52)_____ growth nearly twice that of the (53)_____.

During the 1980s, the first menstrual period in females may occur at an average age as young as (54)_____ years, and childbearing capacity may begin by (55)_____ years of age. Menarche at about (56)_____ years of age occurred between 400 B.C. to 700 A.D. and also in the eleventh century, but after that it began to be later, about (57)_____ years of age in the 1800s, at which point the accelerating trend began.

There are very different growth rates for the (58)_____ of the body. Shortly after conception, the (59)_____ starts growing rapidly. At birth it is about (60)_____ of its adult size. The trunk is next in rate, reaching (61)_____ of its final length by the end of the (62)_____ year of life. At that time the arms and legs begin to grow more rapidly, reaching the (63)_____ percent point at about the fourth year. Progressive growth in the head-to-foot direction is called (64)_____. The body also grows in a (65)_____ direction from center to periphery.

The (66)_____ behavior of the infant also shows a head-to-foot and center-to-periphery developmental pattern. There has been (67)_____ change over recent years in the average age at which various motor skills occur in the first year of life, and

(68)_____ children show more rapid development than (69)_____

children in this period. This latter difference seems to be based on (70)_____.

In the first few days after birth, female infants show more (71)_____ movement

than males, who in turn exceed females in (72)_____ movement and use

of (73)_____ muscles. At birth the central nervous system has all the neural

cells it will ever have. In the first six months the sensory and motor brain areas are (74)_____

over the rest of the brain. The cortical (75)_____ areas develop later.

Brain growth and brain function go hand in hand, and brain growth may be (76)_____

by increasing the amount and complexity of early experience. The successive, natural unfolding of

function that seems to depend exclusively on the development of body structures is called

(77)_____.

The development of behavior reflects maturation through growth as well as the cumulative effects

of (78)_____ through experience. These two elements (79)_____

upon each other. The newborn shows (80)_____, a primitive form of

learning. Within the first few weeks after birth, infants begin to produce responses

(81)_____. Only a few weeks after birth, (82)_____

learning occurs. Behavior after birth changes from massive responses to precise and specialized actions,

a process called (83)_____.

The activity level of the infant is evident from birth, and it tends to persist at least into

(84)_____. Activity level and other infant characteristics affect the

(85)_____ influences between parent and child. Such influences occur differ-

ently with (86)_____ infants, and parents are (87)_____

of the infant's physical conditions and needs. This may be due to improper (88)_____

by the infant or by the mother's (89)_____, which affects her perception;

there may be a greater tendency for (90)_____ mothers to give birth

to (91)_____ infants.

There are very large (92)_____ in the timing and rates of all aspects of

development, and these differences have profound effects on personality development.

Adolescence refers to the period between (93)_____ and

(94)_____, during which there are both quantitative and qualitative

changes in various characteristics of the organism. This period is controlled by physiological factors

that are largely (95)_____. These physical changes signal the beginning

of adolescence, while its end is a more or less ill-defined (96)_____

phenomenon. There are wide variations within and across countries in criteria for attainment of

(97)_____ status. An important psychological characteristic of adolescence is (98)_____ interest. In recent years in Western society, there seems to be little relationship between sexual activity and (99)_____ maturity. "Adolescent turmoil" may be a (100)_____, along with the notions of a "sexual revolution" and a "generation gap," and may well occur largely in those who show (101)_____ before and after adolescence, as well.

The adult years can be viewed as developmental in the sense that ongoing changes such as marriage, child rearing, and vocational choice and achievement all generate a continuing flow of (102)_____ demands. There are a number of stage theories of adult development, and they all emphasize that new challenges occur at all times and the way they are dealt with influences the course of (103)_____ development. The notion of the necessary male mid-life crisis appears to be a (104)_____, although (105)_____ occurs more frequently in male than in female adults. This difference may be due to a difference in (106)_____ of the two sexes.

Several stereotypes about the aged appear to be (107)_____, including the notion that old age is a time of deepening depression, that old people are less intelligent, that all old people eventually become senile, and that sexual activity eventually vanishes in old age. While there is some evidence that people become more introverted as they grow older, there seem to be no necessary personality changes with age, except possibly for the changes associated with physical (108)_____ problems.

4. THOUGHT QUESTIONS

a. Why do you suppose that developmental stage theorists typically emphasize biological, maturational, and genetic factors in development and that their critics tend to assume a more behavioral point of view?

b. Think what the requirements would be to use the cross-sectional method of developmental study in a completely meaningful way, that is, as a substitute for the longitudinal method. Do you think it will ever be possible to accomplish such a study with human subjects? What would be the limitations of using lower animals as subjects in such studies?

c. There are very large individual differences in physical and behavioral growth. What kinds of problems would be likely to occur for three male children, all 10 years old and all in the same fourth grade class? One is 44 inches tall and weighs 50 pounds, one is 52 inches tall and weighs 64 pounds, and the third is 62 inches tall and weighs 85 pounds. How will other persons, both young and older, probably respond to them? Based on stereotypes, what expectations will others have of their behavior?

d. Stereotypes have recently developed about the adult years and old age. The male adult is supposed to have a midlife crisis, and old persons are presumed to lose intelligence and interest in sex. Meaningful studies conclude that these expectations are essentially myths. Why do you suppose such myths arose, and why were they so well accepted by many people?

5. EVALUATION (SELF-TESTS)

Correct answers and text page references are given at the end of the unit.

a. Fill-in-the-blanks Items

Write the word(s) that best complete(s) the sentence in the space provided.

1. Development essentially refers to _____.

2. Developmental stage theorists typically expect that stage changes occur _____.

3. Transitions between stages are seen as times of _____.

4. Of the three methods discussed, the one most subject to errors of memory is

_____.

5. The folklore of a family is largely determined by the _____ of the family.

6. The most rapid of the overall body growth periods occurs _____.

7. Proximodistal growth occurs from _____.

8. Between black and white children, _____ children show less rapid motor-skill development in the first year after birth.

9. The beginning of adolescence is signaled by _____ changes.

10. A myth about the male in midlife is that a _____ will probably occur.

b. Matching Items

Write the number of the correct item from the right column in front of the matching item in the left column.

_____ development	1. most subject to secular change error
_____ stage	2. predictable developmental transformations
_____ transitions	3. myth about the aged
_____ genotypic continuity	4. sequential and continuous change
_____ cross-sectional method	5. times of instability and stress
_____ longitudinal method	6. sexual awakening
_____ neonate	7. developmental phase
_____ differentiation	8. sample attrition problems
_____ adolescence	9. increasingly greater precision of function
_____ loss of intelligence	10. newborn infant

c. Multiple-choice Items

Circle the letter in front of the answer that best completes the stem.
1. Most developmental changes:
   a. are difficult to perceive
   b. occur gradually
   c. occur abruptly
   d. do not occur in premature infants

2. Stage theorists typically emphasize:
   a. biological and maturational factors
   b. cognitive factors
   c. experiential factors
   d. learning

3. A human characteristic that is continuous over the life span is:
   a. intelligence
   b. personality
   c. activity level
   d. eye color

4. The developmental study method most subject to secular change error is:
   a. cross-sectional study
   b. retrospective study
   c. longitudinal method
   d. periodic study

5. Which of the following are the most rapid of the overall body growth periods?
   a. before birth and after puberty
   b. after puberty and during adolescence
   c. the first two years after birth and during adolescence
   d. before birth and the first two years after birth

6. Girls, on the average, mature _____ year(s) earlier than boys.
   a. one
   b. two
   c. three
   d. four

7. A characteristic of the infant that tends to persist into late childhood at least is:
   a. use of larger muscles
   b. facial movement
   c. activity level
   d. fine muscle movement

8. The beginning of adolescence is signaled by _____ factors and the end by _____ factors.
   a. societal and experiential
   b. experiential and physical
   c. physical and cultural
   d. cultural and societal

9. Which of the following is a myth about adolescence?
   a. turmoil always occurs
   b. there has been a sexual revolution
   c. there is a generation gap
   d. all three are myths

10. Which of the following is a myth about old age?
    a. this is a time of deepening depression
    b. old people become less intelligent
    c. all old people eventually become senile
    d. all three are myths

d. Short-answer Items

Answer the following questions with short, concise statements. Reference pages for the material are given at the end of the unit.

1. Define development and differentiate physical from psychological development.

2. Contrast the cross-sectional and the longitudinal methods of developmental study. Specify the assets and liabilities of each method.

3. Differentiate between cephalocaudal and proximodistal aspects of development.

4. Discuss briefly, pro and con, the issue that the period of adolescence in Western society is a period of much stress.

ANSWER KEY FOR UNIT 3

Unit Review

1. change
2. direction
3. gradual
4. environment
5. interaction
6. individual
7. critical
8. preceding one
9. demarcation
10. biological and maturational
11. abruptly
12. labels
13. gradually
14. stress
15. change
16. forced
17. growth
18. eye color
19. psychological
20. change
21. very few
22. activity level
23. unpredictable
24. genotypic continuity
25. different ages
26. cross-sectional
27. secular
28. distort
29. retrospective study
30. recalled
31. the cross-sectional approach
32. memory
33. favorable
34. warm
35. folklore
36. children
37. longitudinal method
38. repeatedly
39. time
40. attrition
41. repeated
42. different
43. adult
44. overall growth rates
45. differential growth rates
46. prenatal
47. two
48. adolescence
49. slows
50. two
51. heredity
52. spring
53. fall
54. 12
55. 13
56. 13 or 14
57. 17
58. different parts
59. head
60. 60 percent
61. half
62. second
63. 50
64. cephalocaudal
65. proximodistal
66. sensorimotor
67. little
68. black
69. white
70. experience
71. facial
72. overall
73. larger
74. far advanced
75. association
76. encouraged
77. maturation
78. learning
79. act
80. habituation
81. voluntarily
82. complex
83. differentiation
84. later childhood
85. reciprocal
86. premature
87. less aware
88. signaling
89. anxiety
90. anxious
91. premature
92. individual differences
93. childhood
94. adulthood
95. hormonal
96. cultural
97. adult
98. sexual
99. psychological
100. myth
101. disturbance
102. environmental
103. subsequent
104. myth
105. suicide
106. adaptability
107. myths
108. health

Evaluation (Self-tests)

a. Fill-in-the-blanks Items

1. change (p. 30)
2. abruptly (p. 32)
3. instability/stress (pp. 35–36)
4. retrospective study (p. 39)
5. mother (p. 39)
6. prenatally (pp. 43–44)
7. center to periphery (pp. 45–46)
8. white (p. 46)
9. physical (p. 54)
10. crisis (pp. 57–59)

b. Matching Items: Correct order and page references are:

4 (p. 30); 7 (p. 32); 5 (p. 36); 2 (p. 37); 1 (p. 38);
8 (p. 42); 10 (p. 46); 9 (p. 50); 6 (pp. 54–55); 3 (p. 59).

c. Multiple-choice Items: Correct answers and page references are:

1—b (pp. 32, 36); 2—a (p. 32); 3—d (p. 36); 4—a (p. 38); 5—d (pp. 43–44);
6—b (p. 44); 7—c (pp. 50–51); 8—c (pp. 53–54); 9—d (p. 55); 10—d (pp. 59–60).

d. Short-answer Items: Page references for answer material are:

1. pp. 30–31; 2. pp. 38–43; 3. pp. 45–46; 4. pp. 53–55.

Unit 4

BIOLOGICAL MECHANISMS RELATED TO BEHAVIOR

1. INTRODUCTION TO STUDY OF THIS UNIT

One of the important areas to be studied in this unit is that of genetics and the hereditary mechanisms that determine bodily structure and function, including some aspects of behavior. One early well-accepted theory of heredity was that offered by Charles Darwin in 1868. It contained the hypothesis of pangenesis, which sought to explain how offspring could be quite like their parents and also quite unlike them, a puzzle that had mystified scientists for years before Darwin. His theory satisfied many — but not his half cousin, Sir Francis Galton, who did not accept the central hypothesis nor the fact that the theory allowed for acquired characteristics, that is, the experiential modification of inherited characteristics.

Even before Darwin produced his theory, more fundamental information about the genetics of inheritance had already been provided by Mendel. Gregor Mendel was an Augustinian monk who worked in a monastery in Moravia (present-day Czechoslovakia). His classic experiments on pea plants were done in the monastery garden. While many animal-breeding studies had preceded Mendel's work, his study was advantageous because it dealt with simpler material and focused on dichotomous characters. He also counted *all* the progeny, a simple but important experimental innovation in such study. Mendel reported the results of these studies orally in 1865, and they were published somewhat later. Neither Darwin nor Galton were aware of this more advanced information, and, in fact, it was not until 1900 that Mendel's work was rediscovered and a great deal of research undertaken, leading to the foundation of modern genetics.

A second area you will be studying in this unit is the structure and function of the nervous system. As you examine the material you will appreciate the tremendous complexity of the nervous system — and the complexity of the information that has been acquired about it. It is difficult to believe that virtually all this information has been gathered over the past 100 years — most of it over the past 50 years. It was only a little over 100 years ago that Paul Broca subjected to autopsy a patient whose chief difficulty was an inability to speak. He found clear evidence of damage in the left frontal lobe, and this was the beginning of the development of scientific information about localization of function in the human nervous system, a topic that had previously been of more anecdotal concern. Again, it was little more than 100 years ago that Fritsch and Hitzig brought localization studies into the experimental laboratory by working out a technique for electrical stimulation of the living brain.

2. ISSUES AND CONCEPTS

The first area to study in this unit is that of hereditary mechanisms. Know a definition of genetics, and the basic process of the genetic development of an individual, including fertilization, division, and the differentiation of cells, including those parts of cells called chromosomes. Learn how genes, the carriers of hereditary messages, are arranged, how they are made up partly of DNA, and how they work in terms of controlling certain proteins. Know how heredity produces individual differences and similarities in families, and how the different kinds of multiple births are produced genetically. Learn about gene action and interaction in the production of specific traits.

The second area of content of this unit concerns the evolution of human beings. Learn here about the ways of producing evolutionary variation, mutation, and gene combination, and the underlying principle of natural selection. Know how speciation takes place. Learn the characteristics of primates and how the human being is supposed to have evolved from Australopithecus through Homo to Homo sapiens and finally to Homo sapiens sapiens. Know the rough time scale associated with this evolution and the differences in important characteristics among these four stages.

The third area of content to learn in this unit is the nervous system. Know the structure of the basic unit of the nervous system, and how neural conduction takes place. Learn about the threshold of the neuron, the refractory period after firing, and the meaning of the all-or-none law. Know what a synapse is and how the neural impulse crosses this gap by means of transmitter substances. Know that neurons are not passive and inactive in a resting state and that a stimulus that starts a pattern of activity can have widespread effects throughout the nervous system. Know what an EEG is, at least one kind of wave which it can measure, and what kind of measure is called an evoked potential. Know the principal methods for studying the structure and function of the nervous system (Box 4.3). Be able to differentiate clearly between the central nervous system, the peripheral nervous system, and the autonomic nervous system. Learn the three basic divisions of the brain, the structures found in each, and the functions of these various structures. Learn why stimulation of different sensory nerves produces different sensory experiences. Finally, learn how the effects of stimulation of the organism and the ongoing activity in the nervous system can influence behavior through the control of neural responses in motor nerves.

3. UNIT REVIEW

Correct answers are given at the end of the unit.

Humans share many features in which they are quite (1)_____ even from their closest nonhuman relatives. On the other hand, there are many ways in which each of us (2)_____ from every other human being. The science that studies how characteristics of bodily structure and function, including some aspects of behavior, are determined in part by the action of gene transmission to each child from its (3)_____ is called (4)_____.

Life begins when the (5)_____ from the male penetrates the (6)_____ from the female. Two cells become a single cell called the (7)_____, which divides into nerve cells, bone cells, etc. The developing organism is now called an (9)_____. With further differentiation at 6 to 8 weeks, the developing organism is called a (10)_____, and retains this label until (11)_____. Carriers of heredity are (12)_____ in the (13)_____ of cells. In most cells, there are (14)_____ pairs of them, and these are duplicated in each multiplied cell. However, the sex cells, called

(15)_____, randomly receive only one from each pair or

(16)_____ in all.

Each chromosome is thought of as constructed from (17)_____ which carry

the specific heredity messages. They are partially made up of (18)_____, and

these molecules have subunits of (19)_____ different types that determine

how an individual differs from and (20)_____ all other organisms. The

DNA sequence does this by determining the structure of a (21)_____; two

genes work together to determine the structure of the protein that determines (22)_____

anatomical or physiological (23)_____ in the organism. The number of dif-

ferent gametes possible from a given person is almost (24)_____ large

because of the large number of chromosomes-pairing possibilities and also the (25)_____

of genes.

Heredity produces both individual differences and also (26)_____ within

families. Sometimes, separation takes place and two or more embryos develop from the same

(27)_____. Since they have the same chromosomes, they are genetically

(28)_____, and we call them identical (29)_____,

triplets, and so on. When the female parent produces two eggs and both are fertilized by (30)_____

sperm cells, (31)_____ twins are produced, and they are no more alike

genetically than are (32)_____. One in 86 births in the U.S. are twins and

(33)_____ of these are identical twins.

Any one gene will affect the production of only one (34)_____, but

any such chemical will enter into the structure of (35)_____ of the body or

control other substances, thereby influencing a number of (36)_____ or

functions. Also many traits are determined by the action of many factors from several genes, a characteristic

called (37)_____. The two members of a pair of genes may be identical and

have the same effect on the traits they produce; here the person is said to be (38)_____

for the gene and the trait it produces. If the pair of genes is different in structure, they would tend to

produce different (39)_____, and therefore different effects with respect to

a certain (40)_____. This person is said to be (41)_____.

Thus, the person's characteristics of body structure and function, or (42)_____,

are only a partial indication of the actual genes that have been transmitted from his or her parents,

called the (43)_____. The parent and child share (44)_____%

of their genes, as do fraternal twins and (45)_____, while cousins and grand-

parent-grandchild pairs share (46)_____% of their genes.

Genetic accidents caused by chemicals or radiation are called (47)_____.

They, plus the results of different gene (48)_____, produce the variability necessary for evolutionary changes in organisms. According to a principle which Darwin called (49)_____, certain genes will increase in (50)_____ within a group because they produce organisms better (51)_____ for survival. If the environment of a species does not change, natural selection leads to a (52)_____ genetic balance within the species and little (53)_____ change. If the environment changes, individuals of a species who survive will pass on that (54)_____. If a species is separated into different environments, the opportunity for genetic (55)_____ becomes great and interbreeding becomes (56)_____. If the difference becomes so great that the members of the two subgroups will not or cannot (57)_____, then (58)_____ is said to have taken place, and the two groups are considered two separate species.

Human beings are all of one species but we belong to a group of 200 living species called (59)_____, which includes apes, monkeys, and (60)_____. Apes are more closely related to humans than to (61)_____. Compared to other mammals, primates depend more on (62)_____ than on olfaction; their brains are (63)_____; they use their hands for (64)_____ as well as locomotion; they have single births or small (65)_____; and the young remain with adults for a relatively (66)_____.

·The characteristics of primates have developed slowly over (67)_____ million years. Australopithecus appeared about (68)_____ million years ago. Their brains were about (69)_____ the size of the modern human's but the bodies of their largest were about (70)_____ as modern humans. They walked on their (71)_____ and ate (72)_____. Homo appeared about (73)_____ million years ago, had a (74)_____ brain, and its (75)_____ was completely modern. Homo evolved into (76)_____ man and other first groups of Homo (77)_____. They had (78)_____ as large as ours but were probably less (79)_____ and had larger (80)_____. In this group there is more evidence of (81)_____ and (82)_____. Modern humans are sometimes called Homo sapiens sapiens and they began to appear about (83)_____ years ago.

Perhaps the most important change in human evolution has been the development of a larger (84)_____. It consists of over (85)_____ billion nerve cells, or (86)_____. Each contains a nucleus in which are found

the determinants of (87)_____ activity. The nucleus is embedded in the

cell body where cell respiration and metabolism take place, and the entire cell is covered with a

(88)_____ which is involved in neural (89)_____.

A neuron has an area of great sensitivity called the (90)_____. The long

portion of a neuron is called an (91)_____ and it is able to produce action in

a relatively (92)_____ part of the organism. In the resting state, there are

positively charged (93)_____ ions outside of the cell. When the cell is

stimulated the membrane becomes temporarily (94)_____, and the

(95)_____ rush into the cell, producing an increase in

(96)_____ at the region of stimulation. As this process continues along the

neuron we refer to it as the (97)_____.

The critical size of stimulus necessary for production of the impulse is called the

(98)_____ of the neuron. The size of the impulse is

(99)_____ by increasing the stimulus above the threshold, and this

relationship is called the (100)_____. After firing, the neuron is in a

(101)_____ period during which its threshold is (102)_____.

The end of an axon has several branches or (103)_____ which come

very close to the dendritic zone of other neurons, this small space being called the

(104)_____. Within each axon terminal are vesicles which release chemicals

called (105)_____ which carry the impulse to the next neuron, or else may

sometimes inhibit the impulse.

Neurons are not passive or inactive in a resting state; (106)_____ occurs

continuously. A stimulus, then, does not start a pattern of activity in the nervous system but rather

(107)_____ it, and it may have (108)_____

effects throughout the nervous system.

Electrical activity of the nervous system can be measured from outside the head, using a recording

device called the (109)_____. When the organism is resting quietly, a

rhythmic pattern of (110)_____ cycles per second, called the

(111)_____, is found. Different waves are found for different conditions.

As seen in EEG measurements, change in neural activity, produced by a stimulus, is called an

(112)_____.

The principal methods for studying the structure and function of a nervous system are electro-

physiological methods, stimulation methods, and (113)_____ methods.

Other more molecular techniques have been developed in recent years (Box 4.3).

The brain and (114)_____ form the central nervous system. The peripheral nervous system includes the (115)_____, which carry sensory and motor impulses between the spinal cord and the trunk and limbs, and the (116)_____, which carry impulses to and from the brain. The autonomic nervous system is concerned with the control of (117)_____, and is also involved in the production of (118)_____ responses.

Some structures in the central nervous system are concentrations of cell bodies called (119)_____. A layer covering the brain also consists of cell bodies and is called the (120)_____. Large groups of axons coursing together are called (121)_____. The forebrain contains the (122)_____, the thalamus, and the hypothalamus. The thalamus and hypothalamus are sets of nuclei. In the thalamus, for example, the lateral geniculate and the medial geniculate nuclei are involved in the senses of (123)_____ and (124)_____, respectively. The hypothalamic nuclei are involved in the control of (125)_____, motivation, and related behaviors. The cerebrum contains the two (126)_____, several movement-control nuclei called (127)_____, and tracts called (128)_____ running from one hemisphere to the other, the largest called the (129)_____.

The midbrain contains a large part of the (130)_____, involved in controlling the level of (131)_____. The hindbrain contains the (132)_____, which plays a role in coordinating and regulating (133)_____, the pons, involved in the control of (134)_____, and the medulla, involved in the control of (135)_____.

All of the brain structures except the cerebral hemispheres and the (136)_____ are referred to as the (137)_____. The spinal cord is the continuation of the central nervous system down the (138)_____. Its core consists of (139)_____ covered with fiber tracts for carrying sensory and motor impulses between the rest of the body and the (140)_____.

Stimulation of different sensory nerves produces different sensory experiences not because of differences in (141)_____ cells or because of differences in impulses in the various (142)_____, but because different nerves terminate in (143)_____ of the brain which are called (144)_____, and these are responsible for producing the appropriate sensation.

The effects of stimulation of an organism and the ongoing pattern of activity in the nervous system can influence behavior only through their control of (145)_____. The reticular formation and other midbrain structures and the cortical (146)_____ connect to motor-control cell groups in the (147)_____, thereby producing the muscle and (148)_____ activity that constitutes behavior.

4. THOUGHT QUESTIONS

a. How could parents have produced a redheaded baby even though there don't seem to be any redheads in either family, at least for several generations? Consider your possible answer to this question in terms of genetic pairing and the important differences between phenotypes and genotypes.

b Homo sapiens sapiens began to appear about 40,000 years ago. Since there is no reason to believe that the process of evolution has stopped, what kinds of evolutionary changes do you think may occur in the human over the next, say, 25,000 years? Base your thinking on expectations about the changing environments, world population change, planetary travel and colonization, and possible speciation.

c. The organism is always quite active 24 hours each day. What does this statement imply about nervous system activity? Can you imagine ways in which we may someday be able to take advantage of this high level of neural activity, especially during rest or sleep?

d. When we finally understand fully the functioning of the nervous system, do you think that we will then be able to make a robot which will be able to think, problem-solve, and dream?

5. EVALUATION (SELF-TESTS)

Correct answers and text page references are given at the end of the unit.

a. Fill-in-the-blanks Items

Write the word(s) that best complete(s) the sentence in the space provided.

1. Identical twins occur in approximately one out of every _____250_____ births.

2. Genes have their influence on heredity by controlling a _____protein_____.

3. The group called primates includes apes, monkeys, prosimians, and _____human beings_____.

4. Neanderthal man belongs to a group called _____Homo sapiens_____.

5. In a neuron the dendrite carries the impulse _____towards_____ the cell body.

6. In a neuron the axon carries the impulse _____away from_____ the cell body.

7. In a resting state, the neuron has a _____positive_____ charge on the outside.

8. Transmitter substances carry an impulse across the _____synapse_____.

9. The central nervous system consists of the brain and _____spinal cord_____.

10. The cerebellum is importantly involved in the regulation of _____motor activity_____.

b. Matching Items

Write the number of the correct item from the right column in front of the matching item in the left column.

_3_	zygote	1. spinal and cranial nerves
_5_	gamete	2. appeared 250,000 years ago
_10_	phenotype	3. fertilized ovum
_7_	genotype	4. threshold of neuron is very high
_9_	Homo	5. sex cell
_2_	Homo sapiens	6. neurons always fire with the same energy
_6_	all-or-none law	7. one's genes that can be transmitted
_4_	refractory period	8. control of the heart
_1_	peripheral nervous system	9. appeared 4 million years ago
_8_	autonomic nervous system	10. characteristics of body structure and function

c. Multiple-choice Items

Circle the letter in front of the answer that best completes the stem.

1. Sex cells contain _____ chromosomes.
   a. 23
   b. 23 pairs of
   c. 26
   d. 24

2. Fraternal twins are about as alike genetically as:
   a. identical twins
   b. identical triplets
   c. siblings
   d. cousins

3. Compared to other mammals, primates make more use of:
   a. feet and vision
   b. vision and hands
   c. hands and olfaction
   d. olfaction and feet

4. Homo sapiens sapiens began to appear about _____ years ago.
   a. 6 million
   b. 4 million
   c. 250,000
   d. 40,000

5. The longest part of a neuron is the:
   a. axon
   b. dendrite
   c. cell body
   d. terminals

6. If a stimulus twice as large as the threshold is applied to a neuron, the size of the impulse will be:
   a. the same as usual firing
   b. twice the size of the usual
   c. one/half the size of the usual
   d. an unknown relationship

7. An impulse crosses a synapse through the aid of:
   a. refractory periods
   b. increased stimulation
   c. transmitter substances
   d. EEG

8. Change in neural activity produced by a stimulus and seen on the electroencephalogram is called:
   a. an Alpha Wave
   b. an evoked potential
   c. a refractory period
   d. a Delta Wave

9. The hypothalamic nuclei are chiefly concerned with:
   a. circuiting sensory impulses
   b. respiration
   c. movement control
   d. motivation and emotion

10. The basal ganglia are chiefly concerned with:
    a. circuiting sensory impulses
    b. respiration
    c. movement control
    d. motivation and emotion

d. Short-answer Items

Answer the following questions with short, concise statements. Reference pages for the material are given at the end of the unit.

1. Genetically, what are the differences between identical and fraternal twins?

2. Compare Homo and Homo sapiens with respect to at least two different and important *behavioral* characteristics.

3. What does the EEG measure and how is this information productively used?

4. Contrast the functioning of those two very important forebrain nuclei, the thalamus and the hypothalamus.

ANSWER KEY FOR UNIT 4

Unit Review

1. different
2. differs
3. parents
4. genetics
5. sperm cell
6. ovum
7. zygote
8. differentiated
9. embryo
10. fetus
11. birth
12. chromosomes
13. nuclei
14. 23
15. gametes
16. 23
17. genes
18. DNA (deoxyribonucleic acid)
19. four
20. resembles
21. protein
22. one
23. trait
24. infinitely
25. crossing-over
26. similarity
27. zygote
28. identical
29. twins
30. different
31. fraternal
32. siblings
33. one-third
34. protein
35. many parts
36. traits
37. polygenic
38. homozygous
39. proteins
40. trait
41. heterozygous
42. phenotype
43. genotype
44. 50
45. siblings
46. 25
47. mutations
48. combinations

49. natural selection
50. frequency
51. adapted
52. stable
53. evolutionary
54. genotype
55. divergence
56. unlikely
57. mate
58. speciation
59. primates
60. prosimians
61. monkeys
62. vision
63. larger
64. manipulation/exploration
65. litters
66. long time
67. 70
68. six
69. one-third
70. the same size
71. hind limbs
72. grass/seeds
73. four
74. larger
75. gait/walk
76. Neanderthal
77. sapiens
78. brains
79. tall
80. faces/teeth
81. cognitive ability
82. sociocultural relationships
83. 40,000
84. brain
85. 10
86. neurons
87. cellular
88. membrane
89. conduction
90. dendritic zone
91. axon
92. distant
93. sodium
94. open/permeable
95. sodium ions
96. negativity

97. nerve impulse
98. threshold
99. not increased
100. all-or-none law
101. refractory
102. very high
103. terminals
104. synapse
105. transmitter substance
106. spontaneous activity
107. changes
108. widespread
109. EEG (electroencephalogram)
110. 8 to 12
111. alpha waves
112. evoked potential
113. lesion
114. spinal cord
115. spinal nerves
116. cranial nerves
117. internal organs
118. emotional
119. nuclei
120. cortex
121. tracts
122. cerebrum

123. vision
124. audition
125. emotion
126. hemispheres
127. basal ganglia
128. commissures
129. corpus callosum
130. reticular formation
131. arousal
132. cerebellum
133. motor activity
134. sleep and waking
135. respiration
136. cerebellum
137. brain stem
138. back
139. cell bodies
140. brain
141. receptor
142. nerves
143. different parts
144. sensory projection area
145. motor nerves
146. motor area
147. spinal cord
148. gland

Evaluation (Self-tests)

a. Fill-in-the-blanks Items

1. 250 (p. 69)
2. protein (p. 70)
3. human beings (p. 73)
4. Homo sapiens (p. 74)
5. toward (p. 77)
6. away from (p. 77)
7. positive (p. 77)
8. synapse (p. 78)
9. spinal cord (p. 81)
10. motor activity (p. 87)

b. Matching Items: Correct order and page references are:

3 (p. 65); 5 (p. 66); 10 (p. 70); 7 (p. 70); 9 (p. 74);
2 (p. 74); 6 (p. 78); 4 (p. 78); 1 (p. 87); 8 (p. 87).

c. Multiple-choice Items: Correct answers and page references are:

1—a (p. 66); 2—c (p. 69); 3—b (p. 73-74); 4—d (p. 75); 5—a (p. 77);
6—a (p. 78); 7—c (pp. 78-79); 8—b (p. 81); 9—d (p. 85); 10—c (p. 85).

d. Short-answer Items: Page references for answer material are:

1. pp. 67-70; 2. pp. 74-75; 3. pp. 80-81; 4. p. 85.

Unit 5

PERCEPTUAL EXPERIENCE AND SENSATION

1. INTRODUCTION TO STUDY OF THIS UNIT

It is customary to say that modern experimental psychology began with the formation of the psychology laboratory by Wilhelm Wundt at the University of Leipzig in 1879. This is an arbitrary date, of course, and many others could have been chosen. In actuality, experimental psychology began with the birth of psychophysics, and this birth took a long time, certainly at least 50 years. Psychophysics eventually became a group of methods concerned with the measurement of sensation and experience. Wundt importantly used these methods in his training and research programs. Many aspects of sensation, however, had been studied for years before. The new emerging experimental physiology, which was not much older than experimental psychology, was very much concerned with sensation, since it appeared to be an important function of the peripheral nervous system. In 1815, research specified the intensities of two spectral lights for the colors to be seen as equally bright. In 1760 — anticipating Weber's work by many years — a man named Bouguer showed that if a shadow is to be just noticeably different from the surrounding light, the relative illuminations had to be just so. This kind of relationship was just what Ernst Weber had studied in many experiments and then had presented systematically in 1834. More specifically, Weber had discovered that two sensations are just noticeably different on the basis of a constant ratio of the two stimuli. This was later to be called Weber's law by Gustav Fechner.

Fechner graduated from medical school at Leipzig in 1822. Interested in humanism for many years, he reacted to the materialism of his medical training by publishing under a pseudonym a series of articles poking fun at medicine and science. He also began to be interested in physics and made a considerable reputation in this field, assuming the chair in physics at Leipzig. He initiated systematic research in sensation and damaged his eyes by looking into the sun while studying afterimages. Not being able to work, he resigned his post as a result of a "nervous breakdown." Upon his recovery, he became even more mystical, focusing much attention on the issue of the relationship between material and immaterial — the old mind-body problem. He began to promote a philosophy of panpsychism, a view that mind and matter are one and that mind was therefore all. Weber's research fit well into this scheme because it had demonstrated a rather exact relationship between matter — the physical stimulus — and mind — the experience of sensation. Fechner vigorously pursued the development and refinement of psychophysics and published the monumental *Elements of Psychophysics* in 1860; and all of this was incidental to his philosophical interest. These methods, with Wundt and others, were to become *the* methods of psychological science for the school of Structuralism, several of which are still used frequently today.

Such was only some of the background of Wundt's "initiation" of experimental psychology. The Zeitgeist rides again!

2. ISSUES AND CONCEPTS

Learn how the two approaches to sensation, the physiological and the phenomenological, relate to each other and why they are both necessary to understand sensation fully. Be able to trace the chain of perception from the physical stimulus in the environment to reception of the response in the projection area. Know the difference between a stimulus and a stimulus object, and learn a working definition of psychophysics. Know what the physical stimulus for vision is, and what are the three principal dimensions of vision, and the important characteristics of these dimensions. Know the basic rules of color mixture, what complementary colors are, and how the three primary colors and white and black can produce any hue, brightness, and saturation. Be able to distinguish total color-blindness from red-green color-blindness, and what colors someone with the latter perceives and for what wavelengths. Learn about the sensitivity of brightness and hue and their relationship to intensity and the retina, and know what visual acuity means and how it is measured.

Know what the physical energies are for hearing, tasting, smelling, and feeling, and how these sensations occur. Learn also the physical energy for kinesthesis and how that sensation occurs.

Be able to define the absolute threshold and know how it is influenced by so many factors that this concept was eventually cast out by the signal detection approach. Be able to define the differential threshold and be able to state Weber's law and write its formula. Know what a j.n.d. is.

Be able to describe temporal summation and know how the flicker and fusion of light signals occurs. Learn about the important concept of sensory adaptation and learn that light and dark adaptation and afterimages are illustrations of this notion. Learn also about spatial summation and spatial fusion and how these phenomena occur. Finally, learn how simultaneous contrast is demonstrated, how it takes place with brightness, hue and saturation, and the conditions under which it does not occur.

3. UNIT REVIEW

Correct answers are given at the end of the unit.

How we sense our world has intrigued man for thousands of years, and the study of perception is one of the oldest concerns in psychology. The (1)_____ approach is indispensable in providing essential information about the nature of sensory processes. It is necessary, however, to add the technique of (2)_____, in which the subject provides a detailed account of how things (3)_____. A phenomenological description of perception establishes facts that physiological and (4)_____ analysis are challenged to explain. The relationships between data derived from the various approaches are not always obvious, as illustrated in the "facial vision" of blind persons which is really based on (5)_____ cues, cues even the experiencer was (6)_____, or by the vestibular system in the (7)_____, or by the (8)_____ limb phenomenon.

The chain of perception starts with the (9)_____ and its properties. The second link is the (10)_____ by which these properties are transmitted to our (11)_____. The third is the interaction of these stimuli with the (12)_____ of our perceptual systems. The fourth is the

(13)_____ leading from the receptor organs to the (14)_____,

while the fifth is the (15)_____ areas in the brain. Nerve paths

(16)_____ the brain can also influence the sensory messages received and

transmitted. Other impulses from the brain affect (17)_____ which move the

body. Difficulties arise when any link is (18)_____. If the chain is complete

and we are accurate in our perception, we are perceiving (19)_____.

Physical energy that can excite a sense organ is called a (20)_____,

while the source of that stimulus in the environment is called a (21)_____.

For many reasons, a given stimulus object can give rise to many different stimuli on the

(22)_____, and the same stimulus there can be produced by very different

(23)_____.

The study of how different sensory experiences are related to different forms of physical energy is

called (24)_____. Part of the electromagnetic wave spectrum, the

(25)_____ rays, are the physical stimuli for producing

(26)_____. Color perception has three principal dimensions; hue, brightness

and (27)_____. Hue is what we call (28)_____

in everyday language. Wavelengths of about 700 nanometers (a nm is about (29)_____

of a meter) are usually seen as (30)_____ light, while those of 400 nm

are seen as (31)_____ light. Each other hue has its own

(32)_____ between these two extremes. White light is a

(33)_____ and has no single (34)_____

that produces it.

Brightness corresponds closely with the (35)_____ of the light

energy. When it is greater, colors are (36)_____, and vice versa.

Saturation refers to the (37)_____ of the color. A completely desaturated

color is called an (38)_____ color, such as (39)_____.

Desaturation of hues can be produced by mixing many (40)_____,

higher saturation by cutting down on the number. Wavelength and (41)_____

interact to determine hue and brightness.

The light that strikes your eye is almost always a (41)_____ of

many wavelengths. There are specific rules by which we can predict the hue, brightness, and

saturation of a color produced by (42)_____. One rule is that every

color has its own (43)_____ color. When two such colors are mixed in equal

amounts, the product is an (44)_____. Adding two noncomplementary

wavelengths will produce a hue that corresponds to an (45)_____ wavelength. All hues can be produced by mixing the primary colors of red, blue, and

(46)_____. Adding (47)_____ and

(48)_____ to these, we can produce any hue, brightness and saturation.

A totally color-blind person, which is rare, sees only shades of (49)_____.
The most common type of partial color-blindness involves an inability to distinguish red and

(50)_____. Such a person sees only (51)_____
if the wavelength is from the long end of the spectrum and (52)_____ if

the wavelength is from the short. Around 500 nm, which is (53)_____ for

normals, these people see (54)_____ but only (55)_____

Sensitivity is defined as how easily a receptor can be stimulated to produce a (56)_____,

measured by amount of (57)_____. Brightness sensitivity depends on

the (58)_____, on the eye's state of (59)_____,

and by the part of the (60)_____ being stimulated. You need more

(61)_____ to see hue than brightness, and hue sensitivity is greatest

in the (62)_____ of the retina and seen (63)_____

at the edges of the retina. Visual acuity refers to the ability to detect (64)_____

in the sizes and shapes of objects. Conventionally tested with (65)_____,

the measure is expressed as a comparison with the (66)_____ person.

Thus, 20/20 means that one can see at 20 feet what the average person can see at 20 feet, and 20/40

means one can see at (67)_____ what the average person can see at

(68)_____. Visual acuity is much better in the (69)_____

of the retina.

When an object is set into vibration, (70)_____ are transmitted in

air; the impact of these on the (71)_____ is the stimulus for hearing. Pitch is

mostly determined by the (72)_____ of these signals; the greater it is, the

(73)_____ the pitch. Loudness varies primarily with the

(74)_____ of these waves. Sound waves that reach our ears are almost always

(75)_____, leading to timbre, beats, and the like. Only a certain frequency

band is capable of producing sound; in humans it is between a low of (76)_____

hertz and a high of (77)_____.

Substances dissolved on the tongue give rise to taste. The four basic components of taste, along with

some chemical substances which produce them, are: sweet (78)_____,

(79)_____ (hydrochloric acid), bitter (80)_____,

and (81)_____ (sodium chloride). Food flavor is usually a combination of

taste and (82)_____.

The stimuli for smell are (83)_____ particles that contact the receptors in the nose. We have not been able to discover a basic set of (84)_____.

For skin senses, objects that move the skin directly or which disturb the (85)_____ give rise to the sensations of touch or (86)_____; (87)_____ is produced when the skin is injured, and (88)_____ is the stimulus for temperature experience. Not all skin areas are (89)_____ sensitive.

Sensitivity to body structure movement is called (90)_____. The physical stimuli for these sensations are mechanical forces that affect receptors in body (91)_____.

The level of intensity of physical energy which separates awareness of the signal from non-awareness is called the (92)_____. It is influenced by many factors, and because of this, psychologists have agreed that it is the lowest stimulus intensity which is perceived (93)_____ of the time. The signal-detection approach leads to the determination of measures of (94)_____ and sensitivity, and (95)_____ with the concept of a threshold. The absolute thresholds for various stimuli differ widely and some are very (96)_____.

The differential threshold is the physical energy difference between two stimuli which can be seen (97)_____ of the time. The value of this threshold varies widely depending on the nature of the stimulus and the condition of the (98)_____. That differential threshold is a constant fraction of the stimulus intensity is a statement of (99)_____, and it is written as (100)_____. Another way of expressing this relationship is to say that the increment needed to produce a j.n.d., or (101)_____, is relative to the (102)_____ of the original stimulus.

When a succession of stimuli arrives on a given receptor organ, they may interact and there appears to be a kind of (103)_____ of each momentary stimulation over time, leading to an (104)_____ in receptor response. This process is called (105)_____. If we turn a light on and off at one-second intervals, we see it as such; if we shorten the intervals, the light is seen to (106)_____. If we shorten the intervals still further, (107)_____ occurs. When a succession of identical stimuli falling on the same receptor leads to a (108)_____ in the effectiveness of later stimuli, we call it (109)_____. This process occurs in all the other senses as well, but to a (110)_____ degree.

Whether a light is seen or not depends, among other things, on the number of (111)_____ points stimulated, a phenomenon called (112)_____. Spatial fusion occurs when one perceives a single impression originating from a number of spatially

(113)_____ stimuli. This phenomenon has been found with many visual stimuli

and for some (114)_____.

    A given gray stimulus seems lighter to us in (115)_____ surroundings

and darker in (116)_____ surroundings, an effect known as

(117)_____. This effect can be found not only with brightness stimuli,

but also for (118)_____ stimuli. If there are, however, only

(119)_____ between neighboring areas, you may not get this effect

but rather its opposite, (120)_____.

4. THOUGHT QUESTIONS

a. Think about all of the adjustments which would have to be made by a person who is totally color-blind in order to adapt to the world. Which problem areas do you think would cause the most trouble?

b. Similarly, think of all of the adjustments which would have to be made by a person who is red-green color-blind to adapt to the world. In this case, which problem areas do you think would cause the most trouble?

c. There are persons who are not able to experience typical pain stimulation because of physiological deficit. What kinds of survival problems might such a person have, especially in early life? How long do you think such a person would survive and under what circumstances?

d. Imagine yourself to abruptly put on a blindfold and to wear ear plugs, each device effective in cutting out all stimulation. You wear them for a week. How would the lack of these stimuli influence your daily life? What kinds of problems would arise and what kinds of adjustments would you likely make to them?

5. EVALUATION (SELF-TESTS)

Correct answers and text page references are given at the end of the unit.

a. Fill-in-the-blanks Items

Write the word(s) that best complete(s) the sentence in the space provided.

1. When a subject details how things appear to him, we call this a ___phenomelogical___ account.

2. Psychophysics is concerned with relationships between physical energy and ___sensory exp.___.

3. What we call color in everyday language is what technically is called ___hue___.

4. An achromatic color is one which is completely ___desaturated___.

5. All hues can be produced by mixing ___colors___.

6. A typical red-green color-blind person sees only the colors of ___red green blue___.

7. Hue sensitivity at the edges of the retina is ___absent___.

8. By and large, frequency of waves determines the ___pitch___ of auditory signals.

9. By and large, amplitude of waves determines the _____loudness_____ of auditory signals.

10. Your noticing a very slight cooling when the sun goes down is an example of the _____differential_____ threshold.

b. Matching Items

Write the number of the correct item from the right column in front of the matching item in the left column.

_____ veridical 4	1. 700 nm
_____ nanometer 6	2. adding up of momentary stimulation
_____ red light 1	3. sensitivity to body structure movement
_____ violet light 8	4. accurate perception
_____ saturation 10	5. quinine
_____ brightness 9	6. one-billionth of a meter
_____ bitter 5	7. fusion
_____ kinesthesis 3	8. 400 nm
_____ temporal summation 2	9. intensity of light energy
_____ movies 7	10. concentration of color

c. Multiple-choice Items

Circle the letter in front of the answer that best completes the stem.

1. Physical energy which can excite a sense organ is called a:
   a. light ray
   b. sound wave
   c. stimulus
   d. stimulus object

2. The study of how different sensory experiences are related to different forms of physical energy is called:
   a. physics
   b. psychophysics
   c. phenomenology
   d. physiology

3. A totally color-blind person can see only:
   a. edges
   b. hues
   c. saturation
   d. brightness

4. Mixing two noncomplementary colors results in a color which is:
   a. in between the two mixed
   b. achromatic gray
   c. acromatic black or white
   d. nonpredictable

5. With light at 500 nm, a red-green color-blind person will see:
   a. yellow
   b. blue
   c. bluish-green
   d. no color

6. Brightness sensitivity depends on the _____ of the stimulus.
   a. intensity
   b. amplitude
   c. wavelength
   d. adaptation

7. Hydrochloric acid on the tongue leads to which of the following tastes?
   a. sweet
   b. sour
   c. bitter
   d. salty

8. That level of intensity of physical energy which separates awareness from nonawareness is called the:
   a. absolute threshold
   b. differential threshold
   c. Weber's law
   d. j.n.d.

9. Temporal summation is associated with some _____ in the response of the receptor.
   a. shift
   b. adaptation
   c. decrease
   d. increase

10. Seeing a given gray stimulus as darker when the surround is light is an example of:
    a. Weber's law
    b. assimilation
    c. simultaneous contrast
    d. fusion

d. Short-answer Items

Answer the following questions with short, concise statements. Reference pages for the material are given at the end of the unit.

1. Trace the chain of perception from physical energy in the environment to a response to the physical energy by the organism.

2. Specify the physical energy involved in stimulation of five different senses.

3. Define and contrast the absolute threshold and the differential threshold.

4. Define and contrast temporal summation and spatial summation with respect to visual stimuli.

ANSWER KEY FOR UNIT 5

Unit Review

1. physiological
2. phenomenology
3. appear
4. psychological
5. auditory
6. not aware of
7. ear
8. phantom
9. environment
10. medium
11. senses
12. receptors
13. sensory nerves
14. brain
15. sensory projection
16. leaving
17. muscles
18. disrupted
19. veridically
20. stimulus
21. stimulus object
22. receptor surface
23. stimulus objects
24. psychophysics
25. light
26. vision
27. saturation
28. color
29. one-billionth
30. red
31. violet
32. wavelength
33. mixture
34. wavelength
35. intensity
36. brighter
37. concentration
38. achromatic
39. white/gray/black
40. wavelengths
41. mixture
42. mixing
43. complementary
44. achromatic
45. intermediate
46. green
47. white/black
48. black/white
49. white-gray-black/brightness
50. green
51. yellow
52. blue
53. bluish-green
54. no color
55. white or gray
56. sensation
57. physical energy
58. wavelength
59. adaptation
60. retina
61. light
62. center
63. not at all
64. small differences
65. reading charts
66. average
67. 20 feet
68. 40 feet
69. center
70. sound waves
71. eardrum
72. frequency
73. higher
74. amplitude
75. complex
76. 20
77. 20,000
78. sugar
79. sour
80. quinine
81. salty
82. smell
83. gaseous
84. odors
85. skin hairs
86. pressure
87. pain
88. thermal energy
89. equally
90. kinesthesis
91. muscles, tendons, and joints
92. absolute threshold
93. one-half
94. criterion level

95. dispenses
96. low
97. one-half
98. organism
99. Weber's law
100. $\dfrac{\Delta I}{I} = K$
101. just noticeable difference
102. intensity
103. adding up
104. increase
105. temporal summation
106. flicker
107. fusion

108. decrease
109. sensory adaptation
110. different
111. retinal
112. spatial summation
113. separated
114. tastes
115. dark
116. light
117. simultaneous contrast
118. hue and saturation
119. small differences
120. assimilation

Evaluation (Self-tests)

a. Fill-in-the-blanks Items

1. phenomenological (p. 100)
2. sensory experience (sensation) (p. 107)
3. hue (p. 107)
4. desaturated (p. 107)
5. red, green, and blue (p. 109)

6. yellow and blue (p. 109)
7. absent (p. 109)
8. pitch (p. 111)
9. loudness (p. 111)
10. differential (p. 113)

b. Matching Items: Correct order and page references are:

4 (p. 105); 6 (p. 107); 1 (p. 107); 8 (p. 107); 10 (p. 107);
9 (p. 107); 5 (p. 112); 3 (p. 112); 2 (p. 115); 7 (p. 116).

c. Multiple-choice Items: Correct answers and page references are:

1—c (p. 105); 2—b (p. 107); 3—d (p. 109); 4—a (p. 109); 5—d (p. 109);
6—c (p. 109); 7—b (p. 112); 8—a (p. 112); 9—d (p. 115); 10—c (p. 119).

d. Short-answer Items: Page references for answer material are:

1. p. 105; 2. pp. 107, 111–112; 3. pp. 112–113; 4. pp. 115, 117.

Unit 6

PERCEPTION OF SPACE, TIME, AND MOTION—AND OF PERCEPTION

1. INTRODUCTION TO STUDY OF THIS UNIT

For many years, the perception of motion or movement was thought to involve the production of successive visual images as the moving object stimulated the eye (now we would say the retina) in various places. But this is not the case. Max Wertheimer demonstrated early in this century that these successive images were not needed to perceive movement, or, at least, what appeared to be movement. He employed a manual tachistoscope, which is an apparatus for exposing visual material for very short periods of time. He exposed a line or a curve first at one location and then at another, a short distance away, and varied the time between the two presentations. If the time was very short (about 1/30th of a second), the two members were seen together, i.e., as simultaneous presentations. When the time interval was very long (about 1/5th of a second), the members were seen as in a succession, first one, then the other. When the timing was in-between (about 1/15th of a second was optimal), movement from one member to the other was reported. This is *seen movement* or *apparent movement,* where no movement actually had occurred. This occasioned the birth of Gestalt Psychology after Wertheimer reported this, the phi phenomenon, in a well-known 1912 paper. Incidentally, the two observers (subjects) in his experiment in Frankfurt, Germany were K. Koffa and W. Kohler, who, along with Wertheimer, are viewed as the early Gestalt pioneers. At about the same time H. Helmholtz, a physicist who was a giant in research on sensation and perception, reported the autokinetic effect; that is, a pinpoint of light in a dark room will frequently be seen as moving. No actual movement occurred in the experiment, of course, and the effect appeared to be due to the lack of a frame of reference.

(We have emphasized the importance of the Zeitgeist and the steady growth of information as important to scientific findings and acceptance. So, too, here, was the case for the phenomenon of seen movement. Seen movement had been reported far earlier than Helmholtz and Wertheimer. Well before the end of the nineteenth century, it had been reasonably well accepted that seen movement was not a result of actual eye movements but rather it was a direct sensory effect. This was confirmed by Thomas Edison in his invention of the kinetoscope, which later developed into the motion picture. These were the backdrops for the early twentieth century observations.)

Much of what we know about space and motion perception was importantly influenced by experiments like those of Wertheimer and Helmholtz, experiments demonstrating what is *not* involved in specific phenomena such as movement perception. In so doing, these researchers caused the rejection of some existent theories and also demonstrated certain minimal conditions for a particular phenomenon.

In this unit, you will first examine a number of theories of perception because they help to set the stage for the data presentations following. The data then presented indicate what we actually know about space perception, including sound localization and the perception of visual direction and distance, time perception, and motion or movement perception.

2. ISSUES AND CONCEPTS

Initially in this unit, you will learn six theoretical approaches to perception. Know the original position of the structuralists and be able to contrast this with the Gestalt position, the information processing approach, constructionism, adaptation-level theory, and Gibson's position which emphasizes stimulus qualities. Be able, of course, to contrast each of these latter five models with one another.

In the perception of space, learn how the two binaural cues (differences in time and intensity of signals at the two ears) coupled with movements of the head localize sound for us. In visual localization, know how the two binocular cues of retinal disparity and convergence contribute to our perception of depth. Learn the monocular cues to depth perception including movement parallel, interposition, and relative size, and how each contributes to this perceptual process. Learn the additional depth cues which depend on stimulation pattern —including perspective, texture gradients, and shadow patterning and how they may contribute to perception. Know that space perception cannot be explained adequately by an extreme empiricistic nor an extreme nativistic point of view.

Learn the two presented explanations of time perception, the first based on sensory filling of the interval in question and the second suggesting the existence of an internal clock based on body rhythms.

Learn that movement perception is not explained simply by real movements in the world, as shown by the phenomena of apparent movement, induced movement, and the autokinetic effect. Know what each of these effects is and what they tell us about motion perception. Finally, be able to state what the perception of motion *does* depend on.

3. UNIT REVIEW

Correct answers are given at the end of the unit.

The different theoretical approaches to perception offered over the past 75 years are a development of, or a response to, the early (1)_____ view. The Gestalt position was presented by groups of psychologists in Germany who felt that we naturally perceive (2)_____ forms and objects in terms of the (3)_____ stimulus pattern present. This was in sharp contrast to the structural view that discrete sensory experiences are later (4)_____ into perceptions. The structuralists believed that (5)_____ was very important in determining what is seen as a whole. In place of this influence, the Gestaltists offered the laws of form or (6)_____ to explain what is perceived. For them, past experience plays a (7)_____ role. They spoke of good continuation, or the tendency for elements of the stimulus (8)_____, thus permitting the continuation of a straight line or curve. They believed in innate laws of brain (9)_____, wherein a stimulus pattern activates brain processes and the equivalent (10)_____. A basic tenet for Gestalt psychology is that the (11)_____ is different from the sum of its parts, an idea clearly opposed to (12)_____ view.

In the information-processing approach to perception, stimulation of the receptors provides information which is changed as it goes through the (13)_____, leading to perception. A great deal of information is perceived in a very brief exposure, although one can report only a (14)_____. This shows that one had perceived for a short time a

(15)_____ amount of the total stimulus. An early stage of perception

is the (16)_____ store which holds a good deal of information which reaches

the eye; for audition, it is the (17)_____ store. This stage lasts for

about (18)_____. In this first-storage system, the information is really

a (19)_____ of the sensory input. This is the basis over time for our

(20)_____ world. From this brief store or from the perceptual image, informa-

tion is transferred into (21)_____. Most psychologists today accept the view

that there are different (22)_____ in the entire perception-cognition sequence.

The constructionist approach is an information-processing view which emphasizes the role of

(23)_____ and other processes in perception. A percept is constructed

out of stimulus-induced sensations and the memory of (24)_____.

According to the template-matching theory, a new symbol is compared with a set of internal

(25)_____ and whichever best fits will win out and provide the percept.

The constructionists reject this approach, saying that the recent memory of the stimuli just viewed will

influence the (26)_____, that is, we add material from memory into our

(27)_____ perceptions. Memory may be supplying

(28)_____ rather than detail to perception.

In Helson's Adaptation Level approach, a distinction is made between the (29)_____

stimulus which is being perceived and the (30)_____ stimuli in which

the first stimulus is encountered. Perception of the (31)_____ stimulus

is influenced by all the background stimuli and all other focal stimuli present. Perception is also

influenced by (32)_____ stimuli which reflect past experience, motivation,

and other psychological effects. Effects of all these stimuli are pooled to produce a reference value,

or (33)_____, against which a given focal stimulus will be judged. All

stimuli are perceived in relation to the appropriate (34)_____, which itself

defines two sets of stimuli, those (35)_____ it and those (36)_____ it.

While all the theories mentioned above include internal processes in perception, Gibson emphasizes

the total (37)_____ available to the organism. He feels that the stimulus

(38)_____ has all the information necessary to allow us to perceive the

world if we can select that aspect of the (39)_____ that provides the information

we seek. For example, he emphasizes the function of (40)_____ in the

stimulus for the perception of depth. A gradient arises on the retina when the surface

(41)_____ from us, and this provides information about the

(42)_____ of various points as well as about the (43)_____

and slants of objects and surfaces. Gibson feels that the perceptual system has evolved over time which results

in our being able to find the (44)_____ stimulus variables that lead to

(45)_____ knowledge of the world. He also feels that our experiments must

(45)_____ knowledge of the world. He also feels that our experiments must

have (46)_____; that is, they must be able to be generalized to the actual

environment which has shaped the individual and the species.

It is clear that all of our (47)_____ help provide information about

spatial location and organization. Some aspects of a stimulus may tell us the direction of a stimulus

object in relation to the (48)_____ and some other aspects may tell us how far

away it is, and it is possible that some perceptual mechanisms determine both direction and

(49)_____.

In auditory localization, sounds may be accurately localized if sound waves reach both eardrums,

thereby providing (50)_____ cues. One important cue is the

(51)_____ difference between the sound reaching the two ears, even with very

samll differences. This difference is beyond (52)_____ recognition and

the effect occurs through an (53)_____ integrating system. A second

binaural cue is the (54)_____ difference to the two ears when the sound is

(55)_____. However, these two important binaural cues are not sufficient

by themselves to enable us to localize sounds from all possible (56)_____,

especially sound in the (57)_____ plane, nor do they tell us

(58)_____. Normally, when we try to localize sounds, we move our

(59)_____, often imperceptibly. These movements plus changes of

stimulus pattern at the (60)_____ localize exactly the location of a sound

source. However, these factors play only a small role in sound (61)_____

perception, which is more influenced by sound (62)_____ and by

the number of (63)_____ waves.

Visual direction is perceived rather directly because light from different directions in the external

world gets sent to different parts of the (64)_____ and from there to

different parts of the (65)_____. Depth perception is dependent upon a

pattern of stimulation. An object provides a different image to each of the two eyes, and this difference

is known as (66)_____. These images are fused into a

(67)_____ image. Another binocular cue to depth is (68)_____

of the two eyes; if muscular movement tells you the eyes have turned toward each other, the viewed

object must be (69)_____ than if the muscle movement tells you the

eyes have turned away from each other. So, this is a (70)_____ cue

to visual perception, and it operates without conscious awareness and only for objects at a relatively

(71)_____ distance. One powerful monocular cue to depth involves relative

(72)_____. This arises when head movements change the position of

different objects on the retina relative to each other and near objects are displaced to the

(73)_____ and farther objects to the (74)_____

of one another. Other binocular cues to depth include (75)_____, in which an object that partly covers another is seen as being (76)_____, and (77)_____, in which one of two objects of identical shape and presumably the same real size which covers a larger part of the retina will be perceived as (78)_____.

Other cues to depth which depend on stimulation pattern include perspective, texture gradients, and different patterns of (79)_____. Those that come directly from stimulus characteristics, possibly interacting with past experience, include familiar size, relative clarity, and (80)_____, the latter being a (81)_____ cue to depth of near objects.

The most full-bodied experience of depth occurs when both (82)_____ and (83)_____ cues work together simultaneously. The perceptual process weighs the various cues and derives a percept of space, emphasizing the more (84)_____ cues.

It is clear that neither extreme empiricism nor extreme nativism provides a total explanation of the phenomenon of spatial perception. Our experience of space depends on some interplay among innate, (85)_____, and experiential factors.

One explanation for the perception of the passage of time suggests that it is dependent upon how much (86)_____ is processed during the interval being considered. Adding more signals to the interval will (87)_____, inaccurately, its perceived duration. A second explanation is based on the fact that biological and psychological events vary greatly in their (88)_____. Many of these are about 24 hours in duration and are called (89)_____. Others are different from this value and area mainly (90)_____. It has been suggested that these cycles act as a kind of internal (91)_____ mechanism.

The perception of movement is not explained simply by real physical movement in the world, as shown by several phenomena. For example, if two lights a few inches apart are exposed successively with a brief duration between them, (92)_____ movement of one light to the other will occur. A common example for us is the (93)_____. The Gestalt psychologists label this phenomenon (94)_____. When we see the moon gliding swiftly behind a stationary cloud, this effect is called (95)_____ movement, because in reality the moon is (96)_____ or nearly so and the cloud (97)_____. The experience of movement depends upon the inter-action between eye movements and the position of images on the (98)_____. When the eyes move to follow an object, an image that stays in the same position on the retina is seen, correctly, to be in (99)_____. When the eyes move in the stationary world, eye movement and change in image position interact precisely to counteract each other and leave the perceptual world (100)_____, as it is. The instructions to the eye muscles by the (101)_____ are a necessary part of this perceived stability or motion.

When one sees movement of a tiny dot of light in a dark room when no movement actually exists, it is called (102)_____. This self-generated movement occurs only in the absence of any visual (103)_____ for the dot of light. Also, importantly involved in this phenomenon are eye movements, postures of the body, and the (104)_____ of the perceiver.

The perception of motion, then, depends on changes in the relative position of (105)_____ from one moment to another, and on their interaction with the ''commands'' for changes in eye position that are sent to the (106)_____ by the (107)_____.

4. THOUGHT QUESTIONS

a. Can you think of a way of integrating the Gibsonian approach to perception with the information-processing approach? Are they really far apart as models, or do they largely emphasize different aspects of the perceptual process?

b. In recent wars, some infantry personnel became quite expert in judging the direction and distance of certain sounds, even in jungle environments. What special talents do you think they had? What specific processes were they likely using?

c. You recall reading about circadian and other biological and psychological periodicities which humans display. How might these operate in the perception of time? Do you suppose it might be possible for a person to become so aware of some of these signals that he could tell accurately the time of day (clock time) without a watch or clock?

d. Where is the movement in a motion picture? An important difference between early ''movies'' and contemporary films is in what kinds of timing adjustments? What would happen if we decreased these important timing relationships to, say, one-half their present value? What would we see?

5. EVALUATION (SELF-TESTS)

Correct answers and text page references are given at the end of the unit.

a. Fill-in-the-blanks Items

Write the word(s) that best complete(s) the sentence in the space provided.

1. The structuralism view of perception emphasized the ____combination____ of unorganized experiences into a precept.

2. The Gestalt position on perception emphasizes that seeing a complete form directly and immediately is ____natural____.

3. The Gibsonian position suggests that all of the information we need for a percept exists in the ____stimulus____.

4. Two important binaural cues to auditory localization are time and ____intensity____ differences between the two ears.

5. In addition to the two binaural cues, accurate auditory localization requires _____head movement_____

6. Binocular cues to visual localization include retinal disparity and _____convergence_____.

7. The most powerful monocular cue to depth involves _____relative movement_____.

8. Other monocular cues to depth include relative size and _____interposition_____.

9. A motion picture is a good example of the Gestalt notion of _____phi phenomenon_____.

10. Autokinetic movement will only occur when the visual framework for the light dot is _____absent_____.

b. Matching Items

Write the number of the correct item from the right column in front of the matching item in the left column.

__5__ iconic or echoic image	1. Gibson's theory of depth
2 ✗ 9 information-processing approach	2. distinct stages in perception
__10__ constructionism	3. small light dot in a dark room
__1__ texture gradients	4. phi phenomenon
9 ✗ 2 ecological validity	5. stimulus image for about 1 second
__8__ retinal disparity	6. kinesthetic cue to depth
__6__ convergence	7. rhythms of about 24 hours
__7__ circadian periodicities	8. each eye gets a different image of an object
__4__ apparent movement	9. can be generalized to actual environments
__3__ autokinetic movement	10. importance of memory in perception

c. Multiple-choice Items

Circle the letter in front of the answer that best completes the stem.

1. That theoretical position which emphasizes the stages in the perceptual processes is:
   a. information-processing
   b. constructionism
   c. adaptation-level
   d. Gibson

2. That theoretical position which emphasizes the role of memory in perception is:
   a. information-processing
   b. constructionism
   c. adaptation-level
   d. Gibson

3. That theoretical position which emphasizes the role of focal and background stimuli in perception is:
   a. information-processing
   b. constructionism
   c. adaptation-level
   d. Gibson

4. That theoretical position which emphasizes the information in the stimulus itself for perception is:
   a. information-processing
   b. constructionism
   c. adaptation-level
   d. Gibson

5. Binaural cues for sound localization are differences in:
   a. time and distance
   b. distance and source
   c. source and intensity
   d. intensity and time

6. Which of the following is not a monocular cue to depth?
   a. movement parallax
   b. relative distance
   c. relative size
   d. interposition

7. Which of the following is not a stimulus-oriented cue to depth?
   a. convergence
   b. accommodation
   c. relative clarity
   d. familiar size

8. Which of the following has not been suggested as a possible explanation of time perception?
   a. amount of sensory information processed
   b. biological rhythms
   c. counting
   d. internal timing mechanism

9. The motion picture is a good example of:
   a. apparent movement
   b. stroboscopic movement
   c. phi phenomenon
   d. all of the above

10. Seeing a light dot move in a dark room is an example of:
    a. apparent movement
    b. induced movement
    c. autokinetic movement
    d. phi phenomenon

d. Short-answer Items

Answer the following questions with short, concise statements. Reference pages for the material are given at the end of the unit.

1. Contrast the earlier structuralist's view of perception with that of Gestalt psychologists.

2. Contrast Gibson's approach to perception with that of the information-processing approach.

3. List two binocular and two monocular cues to visual depth perception and describe how each operates.

4. Contrast two different explanations of time perception.

ANSWER KEY FOR UNIT 6

Unit Review

1. structuralist
2. complete
3. whole
4. compounded
5. past experience
6. organization
7. minor
8. go together
9. organization
10. perception
11. whole
12. structural
13. stages
14. limited amount
15. much larger
16. iconic
17. echoic
18. one second
19. replica
20. perceptual
21. memory
22. stages
23. memory
24. previous experience
25. models
26. percept
27. constructed
28. context
29. focal
30. background
31. focal
32. residual
33. adaptation level/AL
34. adaptation level/AL
35. above/below
36. below/above
37. stimulus energy
38. pattern
39. stimulus
40. texture gradients
41. slants away
42. relative distance
43. sizes
44. higher-order
45. accurate
46. ecological validity
47. senses

48. perceiver
49. distance
50. binaural
51. time
52. conscious
53. automatic
54. intensity
55. to one side
56. directions
57. median
58. distance
59. head
60. two ears
61. distance
62. intensity
63. reflected
64. retina
65. brain
66. retinal disparity
67. three-dimensional
68. convergence
69. closer
70. kinesthetic
71. near
72. movement
73. right
74. left
75. interposition
76. closer
77. relative size
78. nearer
79. shadowing
80. accommodation
81. kinesthetic
82. binocular/monocular
83. monocular/binocular
84. accurate
85. maturational
86. sensory information
87. lengthen
88. rhythms/periodicities
89. circadian
90. longer
91. timing
92. apparent/stroboscopic
93. motion picture/movies
94. phi phenomenon

95. induced
96. stationary
97. moves
98. retina
99. motion
100. stable
101. brain

102. autokinetic movement
103. framework
104. set
105. retinal images
106. eye muscles
107. brain

Evaluation (Self-tests)

a. **Fill-in-the-blanks Items**

1. compounding (p. 123)
2. natural/innate (p. 123)
3. stimulus (p. 129)
4. intensity (p. 132)
5. head movements (pp. 133–134)

6. convergence (p. 134)
7. relative movement (pp. 134–135)
8. interposition (p. 135)
9. phi phenomenon (p. 141)
10. absent (pp. 142–143)

b. **Matching Items: Correct order and page references are:**

5 (p. 126); 2 (pp. 124–126); 10 (pp. 126–127); 1 (p. 130); 9 (p. 130);
8 (p. 134); 6 (p. 134); 7 (p. 140); 4 (p. 141); 3 (p. 143).

c. **Multiple-choice Items: Correct answers and page references are:**

1—a (p. 124); 2—b (p. 126); 3—c (p. 128); 4—d (p. 129); 5—d (p. 132);
6—b (p. 135); 7—a (p. 135); 8—c (pp. 140–141); 9—d (p. 141); 10—c (p. 143).

d. **Short-answer Items: Page references for answer material are:**

1. pp. 123–124; 2. pp. 124–125; 129–130; 3. pp. 124–135; 4. pp. 140–141.

Unit 7

PERCEPTUAL ORGANIZATION: THINGS AND PATTERNS

1. INTRODUCTION TO STUDY OF THIS UNIT

For most of the history of modern psychology, the perceptual field has been of experimental concern to psychologists, and it was the central focus for that group called Gestalt psychologists. Years ago, they identified figure-ground as the basic organization of the perceptual field, and they proposed that form perception was a much more complex process. They also proposed the notion of closure and the principles of organization outlined in this unit. It is important to recognize that these early perceptionists were nativistic in their explanations of these and other phenomena; that is, they believed that the organization of these basic processes occurred spontaneously and innately and not on the basis of specific past experiences. The various constancy phenomena were also proposed to be spontaneously organized, further supporting the position that the environment contributed relatively little to these very important systems. The Gestaltists were also holistic in their approach, emphasizing that the organism perceives in terms of the entire field and not in terms of bits and pieces of it. Of course, this nativistic and holistic approach was the antithesis of the behavioristic group, against whom the Gestaltists ''battled,'' usually in the form of conducting ingenious experiments attempting to discredit the Behaviorists by demonstrating the limitations of the specificity, muscle-twitch approach.

Since the heyday of this battle earlier in this century, a great deal of data have been collected which indicate, once again, that neither the extreme nativistic nor the extreme empiricistic position is an adequate explanation of behavioral phenomena — including perception. While the figure-ground relationship does appear to be organized spontaneously, there is little else in perception which does not reflect the important inroading of experience, and this is especially true when one examines the more complex perceptual phenomena.

In reading this unit, then, always keep in mind the kinds of experiential factors which may contribute to the processes described, for example, the constancies, the influence of set, and the process of attention, including selective attention.

2. ISSUES AND CONCEPTS

Initially in this unit, learn what a perceptual field is, and learn that a field with only a small amount of variation in it will be perceived as homogeneous. Perception, then, depends on a certain level of change. Know figure-ground differentiation, since it is the basic organization of the field, and also what a contour is. Perceptual grouping is based on the principles of organization, including proximity, similarity, and good figure. Be able to define these principles, and know the components of good figure and the difficulty of defining goodness. Learn about the influence of change in stimulation upon perception. Also, learn that perceptual change can occur without stimulus change, as in the reversible figures. Be aware of the theoretical notion of neural satiation and the authors' suggestion that adaptation is a more plausible process.

Know of the various perceptual constancies such as the tendencies to perceive in the same way, even though the stimulus pattern has changed, including its size, brightness and hue, and shape. Know on what kinds of information each type of constancy is based, and that the entire pattern of stimulus information is necessary for complete understanding. Remember that differences in perceptual functioning exist, although the nativists tend to downplay them in terms of threshold factors and the like. Be aware that there may well be important sex differences in perception, what those differences appear to be, and why they may exist. Possible perceptual differences attributable to cultural, experiential variation are still unclear due to design problems in the study of them. Be aware of how perceptual set may influence at least the content of perception and that the stimulus appears to be preeminent as a determinant of what will be perceived. Know that individual needs, emotions, attitudes and values also influence perception.

Learn about vigilance and its possible relationship to arousal. Know of selective attention and its subprocesses and the two kinds of theories proposed to explain this phenomenon. Be aware of the implications of the ability to change one's focus of attention quickly and efficiently.

3. UNIT REVIEW

Correct answers are given at the end of the unit.

Perception includes the awareness of the qualities of space, time, and of movement that takes place without (1)_____ direction and at great speed. The two basic theoretical approaches to perceptual organization are the nativist and the (2)_____. If a perceptual field has little variation in it, we perceive it as (3)_____, which is an example of (4)_____. So perception depends on the presence of an (5)_____ of change through space or over time. Such change has to be greater than the necessary (6)_____. The basic organization of a perceptual field is in terms of (7)_____ differentiation. If we perceive a figure, we see (8)_____ separating it from the ground. Camouflage deliberately tries to add lines and edges to the original contours. We tend to see a more closed area as a (9)_____. The reverse is also true: we tend to see figures as more (10)_____ than they really are. Closure is illustrated in the extreme by the example of (11)_____ contours. You usually see such "figures" when their presence helps to (12)_____ a complex percept. Where there are multiple figures to be perceived, principles of organization become important. They include grouping objects which are close together, or (13)_____, which occurs for figures (spatial) as well as for sounds (14)_____, similarity, or grouping in terms of

(15)_____ visual, auditory, or other stimuli, and (16)_____.
The latter grouping principle, itself, is illustrated by the examples of (a) the tendency for a line, curve,
or movement to proceed in an established direction, or (17)_____; (b) the
favoring of balanced wholes, or (18)_____; (c) the tendency to make a more
complete figure, or (19)_____, and (d) the grouping of elements that
change or move in a common direction, or (20)_____. In this regard the
general definition of goodness is certainly not obvious, but it may have something to do with
(21)_____.

Some changes in perceptual organization occur because of a change in expectations, attitude, or
attention. Some appear to occur more spontaneously, and may flip back and forth as in
(22)_____. These flip-flop characteristics can be controlled to some
extent by the perceiver, and the characteristics which cause this figure to be seen in a reversible
pattern also cause the figure to be seen in an (23)_____ scene.
An early theory suggested that figure reversibility may be due to neural (24)_____,
but there is little evidence for this. A better explanation of such phenomena may be in terms of the
general notion of (25)_____.

In many cases where the actual physical stimuli change, the perception does not change, and this
phenomenon is called (26)_____. By maintaining this stable perception
of objects and their properties, we can cope more (27)_____ with the
environment. This process operates for a number of perceptual characteristics. They include: size
constancy, which seems to be due to the interaction of the size of the (28)_____
with the (29)_____ of a given object; brightness and hue constancy,
which seems to be a function of an intensity and/or wavelength change from (30)_____
other parts of the field; and shape constancy, which appears to reflect the overriding influence of
knowledge of the (31)_____ of the object. It appears clear that the entire
pattern of stimulus information is necessary before a complete understanding of the
(32)_____ can be achieved.

Evidence in support of individual and group differences in perceptual ability seems to be accumulating.
This includes sex differences, since it appears that (33)_____ have lower
thresholds for olfactory, auditory, pressure and pain stimulation, while (34)_____
seem to be able to perceive better in some visual functions. These differences may be a function of
(35)_____ differences between the sexes. Importantly, evidence of cultural
differences influencing perception is unclear because such evidence could reflect real such differences
or else (36)_____ in experimental design. Perceptual set also influences
perception, but is different from sex and group differences in that it affects the (37)_____

of perception rather that whether a stimulus is perceived or not. When a perceptual set is produced by prior experience, experimentally, (38)_____ seems to be more important than frequency in determining its effect. In general, it appears that the (39)_____ is preeminent in determining what is perceived. However, we should keep in mind that the needs, emotions, attitudes and values of the perceiver will also (40)_____ perception. Attention varies widely; one is more or less alert at any given time. The ability to maintain accurate perception, especially over sustained periods is called (41)_____. All tasks require varying degrees of such a factor, and at times, too much arousal may produce a (42)_____ in it. However, changes in this factor over longer periods are associated with a change in (43)_____ rather than with a change in sensory sensitivity.

Selective attention is, perhaps, the most important aspect of attention. It involves a series of (44)_____ which lead to better clarity and differentiation of the center of attention. Information-processing theories of selective attention suggest that nonattended material is (45)_____, or that the (46)_____ is limited and only some stimuli are attended to. The focus of attention is quite brief. Change of focus suggests that the organism was paying attention to (47)_____ all along and this accounted for most change. On other occasions, deliberate scanning reveals that fixations are located at (48)_____ parts of pictures, where most (49)_____ is to be found. This means that such scanning does not proceed randomly, but rather in terms of a presighting in the (50)_____ of what is important and then moving the eyes to that spot.

The level and direction of attention is determined by stimuli currently impinging on the organism and by (51)_____, which in turn, can be determined by intentions, or instructions, or by (52)_____.

4. THOUGHT QUESTIONS

a. Many of the principles of perceptual organization have been incorporated into "works of art." Is this really art or simply a type of pseudoscience?

b. What difficulties might you have in living your typical day if the principles of perceptual constancy did not operate as they do?

c. If you wished to study experiential influence on basic aspects of perception, what kinds of well-controlled studies would you carry out? What would you have to control and what are several potential confounds in such studies?

d. If you were training persons to work in an early-warning military center and you wished to take account of what you know about vigilance effects, what kinds of environmental conditions would you suggest during actual work and what kinds of special training would you provide the personnel?

5. EVALUATION (SELF-TESTS)

Correct answers and text page references are given at the end of the unit.

a. Fill-in-the-blanks Items

Write the word(s) that best complete(s) the sentence in the space provided.

1. The two basic theoretical approaches to perceptual organization are the empiricist and the _____*nativist*_____.

2. Deliberately trying to disguise a figure by adding lines and edges to the original contour is called _____*camouflage*_____.

3. If we perceive a figure, we perceive _____*contour*_____ separating it from ground.

4. We tend to see complete figures rather than partial ones due to the principle of _____*closure*_____.

5. Emmert's law states that the perceived size of an _____*afterimage*_____ will change with perceived distance of the projection surface.

6. Hue remains constant under most conditions because light has changed not only from the observed patch but from _____*other parts*_____ of the field.

7. Relative to males, females appear to have lower thresholds for pressure, pain, and _____*auditory*_____ stimulation.

8. Relative to females, males appear to have lower thresholds for _____*visual acuity*_____.

9. The ability to maintain accurate perception especially over a sustained period of time is called _____*vigilance*_____.

10. Selective attention seems to always involve certain _____*motor adjustment*_____.

b. Matching Items

Write the number of the correct item from the right column in front of the matching item in the left column.

_4_	contour	1. see figure as more bounded than it is
_5_	figure-ground differentiation	2. spontaneous change in perceptual organization
_1_	closure	3. better clarity in perception
_7_	temporal proximity	4. edge
_8_	good figure	5. part of the field stands out
_2_	reversible figure	6. too much arousal
_10_	satiation	7. grouping of sounds close together
_9_	set	8. symmetry
_6_	decrease in vigilance	9. readiness to achieve a percept
_3_	motor adjustments	10. neural "fatigue"

c. Multiple-choice Items

Circle the letter in front of the answer that best completes the stem.

1. Perceiving homogeneity even though the perceptual field differs somewhat illustrates:
   a. accommodation
   b. assimilation
   c. constancy
   d. satiation

2. The fact that there is no change in perceptual quality even though there has been a change in the stimulus is an example of:
   a. accommodation
   b. assimilation
   c. constancy
   d. satiation

3. The perceived size of an after-image changes with the perceived distance of the projected surface. This is:
   a. good figure
   b. symmetry
   c. Emmert's law
   d. impossible

4. Perceptual grouping is based on all but which one of the following?
   a. assimilation
   b. proximity
   c. closure
   d. common fate

5. The phenomena explained on the basis of neural satiation seem to be better explained on the basis of:
   a. assimilation
   b. accommodation
   c. constancy
   d. adaptation

6. That constancy which is based on the interaction of size of retinal image with the apparent distance of the object is:
   a. size
   b. brightness
   c. shape
   d. pattern

7. That constancy which is based on the uniformity of light coming from various parts of the field is:
   a. size
   b. brightness
   c. shape
   d. pattern

8. Perceptual set most influences:
   a. whether stimulus is perceived at all
   b. what your past experience determines
   c. what your personality dictates
   d. the content of perception

9. The most important aspect of attention is:
   a. set
   b. vigilance
   c. arousal
   d. selective

10. Evidence that the organism is paying attention to the periphery at all times is provided by information from:
    a. focus of attention
    b. vigilance
    c. constancy
    d. sex differences

d. Short-answer Items

Answer the following questions with short, concise statements. Reference pages for the material are given at the end of the unit.

1. On what perceptual phenomena is the art of camouflage based?

2. What does the evidence concerning individual differences in perception tell us about the relative importance of heredity and environment in perception?

3. What are the principal functions of motor adjustment in selective attention?

4. One tends to see the important parts of pictures where most of the information is. What does this phenomenon tell us about the efficiency of perceptual processing and the role of peripheral scanning?

ANSWER KEY FOR UNIT 7

Unit Review

1. conscious
2. empiricist
3. homogeneous
4. assimilation
5. adequate amount
6. threshold value
7. figure-ground
8. contour
9. figure
10. closed/bounded
11. subjective
12. simplify
13. proximity
14. temporal
15. similar
16. good figure
17. good continuation
18. symmetry
19. closure
20. common fate
21. simplicity/predictability
22. reversible figures
23. unambiguous
24. satiation
25. adaptation
26. constancy

27. effectively
28. retinal image
29. apparent distance
30. many
31. shape
32. perceptual outcome or field
33. females
34. males
35. hormonal
36. difficulties
37. content
38. recency
39. stimulus
40. influence
41. vigilance
42. decrease
43. criterion-cutoff value
44. motor adjustments
45. filtered out
46. capacity
47. the periphery
48. important
49. information
50. periphery
51. peceptual set
52. past experience

Evaluation (Self-tests)

a.   **Fill-in-the-blanks Items**

1. nativist (p. 146)
2. camouflage (p. 148)
3. contour (p. 148)
4. closure (p. 149)
5. after-image (p. 155)

6. other parts (p. 157)
7. auditory/olfactory (p. 160)
8. visual functions/acuity (p. 160)
9. vigilance (p. 164)
10. motor adjustments (p. 165)

b.   **Matching Items: Correct order and page references are:**

4 (p. 147); 5 (p. 147); 1 (p. 149); 7 (p. 151); 8 (p. 151);
2 (p. 153); 10 (p. 154); 9 (p. 161); 6 (p. 165); 3 (p. 165).

c.   **Multiple-choice Items: Correct answers and page references are:**

1—b (p. 146); 2—c (p. 155); 3—c (p. 155); 4—a (pp. 149–151); 5—d (p. 154);
6—a (p. 155); 7—b (p. 157); 8—d (p. 161); 9—d (p. 165); 10—a (p. 166).

d.   **Short-answer Items: Page references for answer material are:**

1. pp. 147–149; 2. pp. 159–161; 3 p. 165; 4. p. 166.

Unit 8

PHYSIOLOGICAL BASES OF PERCEPTION

1. INTRODUCTION TO STUDY OF THIS UNIT

Your goal in this unit is to discover how the organism responds to incoming stimuli and to learn what is known about the physiological basis of conscious human perception. This kind of inquiry has had a long history. The Stoics, who first had the notion of a *tabula rasa*, the blank tablet of the mind on which experience wrote, felt that sensations were impressions made on the mind by things outside the body. Other early Greek philosophers like Empedocles, Democritus, and Epicurus felt that objects give off effluvia, or image projections, from their surfaces; they are then conducted to the mind of the observer to provide a knowledge of the objects they represent. Aristotle identified five senses and studied them in some detail. It is interesting that this identification, by so important a personage as Aristotle, actually delayed the identification of the sixth sense that you will be studying in this unit: the sense of position and movement of one's body, or kinesthesis.

Over the years scholars in a variety of fields have contributed much to our knowledge of sensation and perception. Leonardo da Vinci studied color combinations, as did Sir Isaac Newton. Newton contributed the first important theory of color based on his studies of optics. Physicists, physiologists, artists, and others had been studying such areas for many years before psychologists became interested in them.

Certainly a central issue in this unit concerns the relationship between sensation and perception. Where does sensation end and perception begin? This is not an easy distinction to make. Sensation clearly involves the impingement of energy on receptor surfaces, which are thereby activated. These, in turn, may convert the energy into a different form for transmission deeper into the organism and finally to the higher nerve centers, where we may become aware of the original stimulation and respond to it. The latter adjustment certainly seems to be perception. But keep in mind that the original stimulation may not start the process going at all, or the process may be modified at one or more junction points along the line of transmission. Where, then, is perception? There are other instances where the organism seems to be unaware of the sensation aspect of a stimulus but can demonstrate perception of it in a way that cannot be laid to chance alone.

A second issue of importance in the study of this material is the ever-present nativism-empiricism controversy. As you read about the rather exact relationship between receptor activity and activity in the cortical projection area for a particular sense, you may be tempted to conclude, as have people for over 100 years, that these processes must be part of the normal functioning of the organism and not based on specific experiences. While all agree that labeling such experiences clearly is learned, many still feel that the very organization of these processes into even elementary perceptions is a function of experience. The controversy goes on.

2. ISSUES AND CONCEPTS

In this unit, there are two types of information to be learned. The first type has to do with the general reception of information by one of the senses and its transmission further into the organism, leading to perception and possible response. The second type has to do with the molecular level of an organism and involves learning in detail the various physiological and neurological mechanisms and submechanisms involved in sensation and perception. Both types of information must be learned for each of the most important human senses. For example, in studying the visual sense from the first point of view, you should know that light rays impinge on the eye, are processed there, and then stimulate the nerve fibers in the retina in the back of the eye; there, the electrical stimulation created goes through various connections and passes through subcortical areas to arrive finally at the primary sensory or projection areas in the cortex of the brain. From the second, or molecular, point of view, you will have to learn the various parts of the optical, retinal, and central mechanisms, how they function, and how they interact.

For the visual system and the auditory system, there is quite a difference between the two types of information to be learned. For both, however, it is probably important to learn the general, or molar, information, before attempting to add on the molecular detail. For the senses of taste and smell, as well as the somesthetic senses, the task will be less difficult since either the systems are more direct (that is, involve less processing), and simpler, or we know less about their detailed functioning.

The Unit Review will be of substantial help in learning the molar information and some of the molecular. Of course, it is impossible to review all of the text, and this would not be a good idea even if it were possible. As an aid in studying, you should develop a set of study flash cards, as described in the introduction to this guide. These should be based on the glossary items and on other material found in various diagrams in this unit. Coupled with the Unit Review below, they should be very helpful in learning information relevant to this unit at both a molar and molecular level.

3. UNIT REVIEW

Correct answers are given at the end of the unit.

Unless the (1)_____ is functioning properly, a stimulus will not be effective in producing a (2)_____. The nervous system selects, modifies, and transmits the (3)_____, sometimes seeking out new (4)_____, when necessary.

Light entering the eye passes through the (5)_____ and then through the (6)_____. Light rays are bent so that they will be focused on the (7)_____. As the observer changes fixation across different distances, the shape of the lens changes to maintain focus, a process called (8)_____. Normal vision depends on tiny, (9)_____ eye movements. If special apparatus is used to stabilize the retinal image, the image will probably (10)_____ in a short time.

The retina has two kinds of photoreceptors, or light-sensitive cells. The (11)_____ are most numerous at the fovea (the center of the (12)_____). Rods are absent in the (13)_____ but are common some distance away. Both of these receptors are connected to (14)_____, which in turn are connected to

(15)_____, the axons of which make up the (16)_____.
Rods and cones contain pigments which (17)_____ upon light stimulation.
This chemical reaction produces an (18)_____ in the bipolar and ganglion
cells. Pigment breakdown and (19)_____ occur simultaneously.

Cones give rise to the sensation of hue, or (20)_____. There are
(21)_____ different kinds of cones. While each is sensitive to a wide range of
wavelengths of light, each has a different region of greatest (22)_____,
in the red, green, and (23)_____ parts of the spectrum. Many ganglion cells
apparently receive input from two kinds of cones and respond in (24)_____
ways, depending on which kind of cone is active. Color-blindness represents some kind of defect in the
(25)_____ or their (26)_____.

Another type of ganglion cell depends on light intensity regardless of wavelength. The greater the light
intensity, the greater the perception of (27)_____.

The retina is more sensitive at the (28)_____ than at the fovea, probably
because of the greater concentration of (29)_____ there and their connections
with relatively few (30)_____ cells. Rods contain more
(31)_____ than do cones and are more (32)_____
than cones. Form vision and acuity is best in the (33)_____, where there are
tightly packed receptors. Half of the neurons in each optic nerve cross over to the opposite side of
the brain at the (34)_____, forming the optic tracts, in which fibers from
the two retinas go to the other side of the brain. The optic tracts end in the (35)_____
of the (36)_____, and from there other neurons carry impulses to
the (37)_____.

The receptor fields of cells in the primary visual cortex are complex, each one representing a line,
a length, a corner, or the like. This suggests that the perception of a given visual form depends on
stimulation of the appropriate cortical cells along the (38)_____ complex
pathways.

The secondary visual cortex receives input from the primary visual cortex and from the
(39)_____. The cortex's various subareas analyze sensory information such
as the distance, color, or (40)_____ of stimuli.

Sound travels through air in the outer ear to the (41)_____, where
vibrations occur in three small bones of the middle ear, called (42)_____.
The last bone causes a pressure wave in the (43)_____ within the
(44)_____ of the inner ear. The auditory hair cells rest upon the
(45)_____ of the cochlea and have microscopic projections into the
(46)_____. These latter structures move, producing an (47)_____

called the (48)_____. This movement, in turn, causes activity in the auditory

(49)_____. Loudness depends on the (50)_____

of neural impulses reaching the brain, which depends on the (51)_____ of

the original stimulus. Sound waves of different frequencies produce their maximum amount of movement

in cochlear structures at (52)_____ points, and thus the brain receives

different neural messages representing different frequencies, which results in our discrimination of

(53)_____. The auditory sensory pathway starts with 30,000 spatially

organized neural elements, then leads through the subcortical nuclei, including the cochlear nuclei,

the (54)_____, and the (55)_____ of the

thalamus, with partial crossover along the way, and finally ends in the auditory cortex. The auditory

cortex does not appear to be necessary for perception of pitch and (56)_____.

Localization of sound involves a process of (57)_____ of sounds coming

from the two ears. This takes place first in the (58)_____ and then in the

(59)_____. Complex sounds, such as speech, seem to be based on a complicated

interaction of neurons each carrying simple messages, and perception of these sounds is dependent upon

a functioning (60)_____.

Taste depends on the activation of receptor cells in the (61)_____ by

chemicals. A single taste cell responds to stimuli of more than one of the four basic taste qualities of

sweet, sour, bitter, and (62)_____. Nerve fibers from taste buds combine into

bundles and travel by way of three (63)_____ nerves to the hindbrain and

the thalamus. From there, other neurons take the taste message to the (64)_____.

Ablation of this area results in a (65)_____ but not in the

(66)_____ of taste sensitivity. Perception of a particular taste depends

on the brain's receiving a distinctive pattern of response from (67)_____

neurons in the taste nerve. Olfactory receptors are neurons in the nasal cavity; they also operate as

connecting cells to the (68)_____. The size and shape of odor molecules

that stimulate these receptor sites may determine odor (69)_____. The

olfactory sensory fibers go through the skull, enter the (70)_____, and

from there by way of the olfactory tracts go to subcortical and (71)_____ centers.

These centers can act to enhance or (72)_____the experience of smell.

The skin, or cutaneous senses, functions in the perception of touch, temperature, pressure, and

(73)_____. Light touch seems to depend on receptors around the body hair

follicles, and there are specialized receptors for (74)_____ tissue. Skin

sensation begins with stimulation of (75)_____ and from there goes by

cranial nerves to the (76)_____ or else enters the (77)_____

and then goes to the brain. There are three somatosensory areas of the parietal lobe of the cortex — one for cutaneous pressure, one for deep pressure, and one for (78)_____. Signals

to these areas arrive from the spinal cord and the thalamus over the (79)_____.

The extralemniscal system sends fibers to the reticular formation, the colliculi, and the cortex, and

seems to be concerned with the sensation of temperature and (80)_____.

Evidence for the cortical representation of temperature and pain is (81)_____.

According to the information in Box 8.4, pain can be controlled through a (82)_____

system, perhaps on the basis of the release of (83)_____.

The receptors for kinesthesis are found in the capsules and ligaments associated with

(84)_____. Complete perception of body movement and position also depends

on input from the (85)_____ of the inner ear. This apparatus responds

to wave motions of fluid in the (86)_____ and to the position of hairs

in the (87)_____ organs. The vestibular nerve carries impulses from

the sensory cells to the (88)_____; from there, some fibers go to the

cerebellum but most go to the (89)_____, and from there to some eye

muscles, the viscera, the cerebellum, and the cortex. Motion sickness is caused by

(90)_____ stimuli received from two sensory systems.

Conscious awareness of a stimulus may require (91)_____ cortical

activation. This requirement might preserve consciousness from transient and insignificant activation.

There are many connections between the various sensory systems and the limbic system, association

cortex, basal ganglia, and the cerebellum. All of these structures have connections with the reticular

formation and the (92)_____. In this way signals may finally get to

the (93)_____, resulting in response.

4. THOUGHT QUESTIONS

a. On the basis of your knowledge of the visual system, do you think that it might be possible to train persons who are born blind (e.g., because of an inoperable, detached retina) to actually "see"? How might this be done?

b. Assume that you are completely color-blind and can experience no sensations of color at all, only brightness. Think of the many ways that this deficit would interfere with your everyday living patterns.

c. Assume that a baby is born without the sensation of pain. How might this deficit interfere with everyday living? What special difficulties could such a person have in the areas of learning and motivation? Do you think there would be any specific survival problems for him or her?

d. What kinds of advice, other than the use of drugs, would you give to friends who tend to suffer from motion sickness?

5. EVALUATION (SELF-TESTS)

Correct answers and text page references are given at the end of the unit.

a. Fill-in-the-blanks Items

Write the word(s) that best complete(s) the sentence in the space provided.

1. Visual accommodation involves changing the shape of the _____*lens*_____ to maintain focus.

2. In the retina, cones are most numerous at the _____*fovea*_____.

3. Photoreceptors called _____*cones*_____ give rise to color sensation.

4. Rods and cones connect to bipolar cells, which, in turn, connect to _____*ganglion*_____ cells.

5. The primary visual cortex is located in the _____*occipital*_____ lobe.

6. The physical vibrations that are involved in sound change to an electrical potential in the _____*cochlea*_____.

7. The pitch of a sound is sensed because the brain receives different neural messages representing different _____*frequency*_____.

8. Sensation of the four basic tastes is a function of _____*the same*_____ taste buds.

9. The size and shape of _____*odor molecules*_____ are the effective stimuli for the sensation of smell.

10. The primary somatosensory cortex is in the _____*parietal*_____ lobe.

b. Matching Items

Write the number of the correct item from the right column in front of the matching item in the left column.

_4_ rods	1. secondary visual cortex
_6_ cones	2. middle ear
_7_ corner cells	3. inner ear
_1_ distance information	4. involved in brightness sensation
_8_ cornea	5. taste quality
_2_ ossicles	6. fovea
_3_ cochlea	7. occipital cortex
_10_ loudness	8. first structure involved in vision
_5_ bitter	9. vestibular apparatus
_9_ kinesthesis	10. number of effective neural impulses

c. Multiple-choice Items.

Circle the letter in front of the answer that best completes the stem.

1. Which of the following is *not* an appropriate order of signal transmission in vision?
   a. cornea, lens, retina
   b. lens, retina, bipolar cell
   c. retina, bipolar cell, ganglion cell
   d. bipolar cell, ganglion cell, medial geniculate nucleus

2. Which of the following is primarily involved in color sensation?
   a. rods
   b. cones
   c. pigment
   d. geniculate nucleus

3. Which of the following is primarily involved in brightness sensation?
   a. rods
   b. cones
   c. pigment
   d. geniculate nucleus

4. Pigment decomposition in the photoreceptors is a(n):
   a. physical reaction
   b. electrical reaction
   c. chemical reaction
   d. simple reaction

5. The most sensitive area of the retina is in the:
   a. fovea
   b. blind spot
   c. lens
   d. periphery

6. Environmental sound waves become liquid waves in the:
   a. ear canal
   b. middle ear
   c. inner ear
   d. auditory nerve

7. The auditory hair cells are found in the:
   a. ear canal
   b. middle ear
   c. inner ear
   d. auditory nerve

8. Binaural interaction is involved in the sensation of sound:
   a. localization
   b. loudness
   c. intensity
   d. pitch

9. The extralemniscal systems appear to be involved in the sensations of:
   a. touch and temperature
   b. temperature and pain
   c. pain and pressure
   d. pressure and touch

10. The receptors for kinesthesis are found around the:
    a. otolith organs
    b. bones
    c. vestibular apparatus
    d. semicircular canals

d. Short-answer Items

Answer the following questions with short, concise statements. Reference pages for the material are given at the end of the unit.

1. What are the implications of the fact that "seeing" appears to be possible in humans whose primary visual cortex has been lost?

2. Stimulation coming down the spinal cord from the cortex and/or brain stem can block pain reception. How could this information be used in the treatment of persons who suffer intractable pain?

3. What appear to be the mechanisms underlying motion sickness?

4. What are the possible functions of mechanisms in the organism that inhibit the perception of some of the stimuli impinging on that organism?

ANSWER KEY FOR UNIT 8

Unit Review

1. nervous system
2. perception
3. sensory messages
4. information
5. cornea
6. lens
7. retina
8. accommodation
9. involuntary
10. disappear
11. cones
12. retina
13. fovea
14. bipolar cells
15. ganglion cells
16. optic tract
17. decompose
18. impulse
19. restoration
20. color
21. three
22. sensitivity
23. blue
24. opposite
25. cones
26. interconnections
27. brightness
28. periphery
29. rods
30. ganglion
31. pigment
32. sensitive
33. fovea
34. optic chiasm
35. lateral geniculate nuclei
36. thalamus
37. occipital cortex
38. correct/specific
39. superior colliculi
40. movement
41. eardrum
42. ossicles
43. fluid
44. cochlea
45. basilar membrane
46. tectorial membrane
47. electrical potential
48. cochlear microphonic
49. neurons
50. number
51. intensity
52. different
53. pitch
54. superior olive
55. medial geniculate nuclei
56. loudness
57. binaural interaction
58. superior olive
59. auditory cortex
60. auditory cortex
61. taste buds
62. salt
63. cranial
64. cortex
65. reduction
66. absence
67. several
68. olfactory nerve
69. perception
70. olfactory bulbs
71. cortical
72. inhibit
73. pain
74. deeper
75. free nerve endings
76. brain
77. spinal cord
78. body movement
79. lemniscal pathways
80. pain
81. not impressive
82. descending inhibitory
83. endorphins
84. bones
85. vestibular apparatus
86. semicircular canals
87. otolith
88. brain stem
89. vestibular nuclei
90. conflicting
91. prolonged
92. motor cortex
93. spinal cord

Evaluation (Self-tests)

a. **Fill-in-the-blanks Items**

1. lens (p. 171)
2. fovea (p. 173)
3. cones (p. 174)
4. ganglion (p. 172)
5. occipital (p. 182)

6. cochlea (pp. 188–189)
7. frequencies (pp. 189–190)
8. the same (pp. 193–194)
9. odor molecules (p. 194)
10. parietal (p. 195)

b. **Matching Items: Correct order and page references are:**

4 (p. 174); 6 (p. 173); 7 (p. 182); 1 (p. 185); 8 (p. 169);
2 (p. 187); 3 (p. 187); 10 (p. 189); 5 (p. 193); 9 (p. 197).

c. **Multiple-choice Items: Correct answers and page references are:**

1—d (pp. 169–182); 2—b (p. 174); 3—a (p. 174); 4—c (p. 174); 5—d (p. 176);
6—c (p. 188); 7—c (p. 188); 8—a (p. 192); 9—b (p. 197); 10—b (p. 197).

d. **Short-answer Items: Page references for answer material are:**

1. p. 184; 2. p. 198; 3. p. 197; 4. pp. 199–201.

Unit 9

CLASSICAL CONDITIONING

1. INTRODUCTION TO STUDY OF THIS UNIT

The systematic study of learning phenomena has almost as long a history as the field of general experimental psychology. It dates back to the pioneering studies of verbal learning done by Hermann Ebbinghaus in Germany nearly 100 years ago. While these studies had an important influence on academic psychology, it was the later work in Russia of Ivan Pavlov that heavily influenced psychologists in the United States to undertake learning research and to develop broad theories of behavior based on relatively simple conditioning phenomena. Thus in the second decade of this century, John Watson, dedicated to driving consciousness and introspection out of Western psychology, presented a new and important movement called behaviorism. It was based on the earlier work of Pavlov but extended that theory to account for the learning of all behavior.

The basic phenomena which Pavlov had described are now called classical conditioning, and they are the topic of this unit. It is important to understand them because they remain with us to the present time. In recent years there has been a resurgence of interest in the experimental investigation of classical conditioning. It is equally important to understand that many psychologists have criticized the simplistic nature of classical conditioning and the seeming lack of cognition involved in such learning. How could the elementary process described by classical conditioning account for rich and complex human behavior? This area remains controversial, but the controversy may reflect (1) emotional attachment to different theoretical approaches, (2) a comparison of data based on different subjects collected under different conditions, (3) the possibility that classical conditioning may account very well for the learning of certain behaviors and not at all for others, or (4) a combination of these possibilities. It is entirely possible that classical conditioning and other theoretical explanations of learning phenomena are not really in opposition: all may reflect a single, broader explanation of learning.

2. ISSUES AND CONCEPTS

The most important concept for you to understand in this unit is the experimental paradigm (pronounced *"paradime"*) of classical conditioning, which refers to the pattern of procedures used. An experimenter with an effective stimulus (UCS) that regularly elicits a response (UCR), and then applies a new stimulus that does not elicit that response (CS) in association with the UCS; finally the CS may come to elicit a response (CR) similar to or almost the same as the UCS. You should be aware that the time relationship (temporal patterning) of the CS and UCS is important for optimal learning and why. The interesting phenomenon of higher-order conditioning should be clear to you since it represents a possible explanation for very complicated human behaviors in terms of classical conditioning principles.

The basic principles and concepts of classical conditioning have become essential to nearly all learning models and include the notions of reinforcement (which in classical conditioning refers only to the pairing of the CS and the UCS); the learning curve (a growth-function display of learning); extinction (the experimental procedure of removing the UCS and repeatedly eliciting the CR by the CS); and its subsidiary, counter-conditioning (a way of getting rid of a response by having the subject learn a quite different response in the presence of the same stimuli); spontaneous recovery (a reappearance of an extinguished response without further training); stimulus generalization (responding similarly to somewhat different stimuli); and discrimination (responding differently to somewhat similar stimuli).

Finally, in this unit you should attend to the possible interpretations of classical conditioning. Is this process really just the mechanical substitution of one stimulus for another in the eliciting of a particular behavior? If so, why should the CR be somewhat different from the UCR on occasion? Or, why, then, should sensory preconditioning take place? Can this simple model of learning account for all learning? Not all learning appears to follow this design, nor are all behaviors learned equally easily using this approach. The automaticity of the model has been challenged by more cognitive approaches, which suggest that the organism pays attention to *what leads to what*, which seems to be a lot less automatic than classical conditioning suggests.

3. UNIT REVIEW

Correct answers are given at the end of the unit.

A response to a sudden change in stimulation involving behavioral and physiological reactions to increasing information flow is called the (1)_____. This response is an important part of the learning procedures of Ivan Pavlov now labeled (2)_____. This experimental design first finds an (3)_____ stimulus that will regularly elicit an (4)_____ response. It then finds a neutral stimulus for that response, or a (5)_____ stimulus, and associates it regularly with the effective stimulus, or (6)_____, until the formerly neutral stimulus comes to elicit a similar behavior, now called the (7)_____.

Time relationships, or temporal patterning, between the conditioned stimulus (CS) and the unconditioned stimulus (UCS) are important. For optimal conditioning, the CS usually (8)_____ the UCS, by approximately (9)_____ sec.; this interval is referred to as the (10)_____ interval. Other time relationships — including beginning the CS and US exactly together, called (11)_____ or having the UCS precede the CS, called (12)_____—typically lead to less learning or very little learning at all.

A fascinating conditioning phenomenon is one in which the CS used in one sequence becomes the UCS in a second sequence involving the same CR but a different CS. This process is called (13)_____ conditioning and may help to explain how quite complex human behaviors may be acquired through the simple classical conditioning paradigm.

Some dozen years or so after Pavlov's early discoveries, John Watson, the founder of (14)_____, used similar notions to explain *all* learning.

The basic principles of classical conditioning have largely become essential to all learning models. They include the repeated pairing of the CS and the UCS, or (15)_____; the growth function associated with changes in response strength after repeated pairings, or the (16)_____; the phenomenon of (17)_____, in which the CS is repeatedly presented without the UCS; and the phenomenon of (18)_____, in which the CR reappears without additional training after an extinction series. A concept related to extinction that involves training the organism to respond differently in the presence of the same stimuli is called (19)_____. This procedure has been used by J. Wolpe and others in the modification of anxiety and fear responses.

Another important principle of classical conditioning is that of (20)_____, in which a behavior (the CR), originally conditioned to a particular stimulus (the CS), can now be elicited by other stimuli (especially those similar to the original CS). A final principle involves training the organism to respond to certain stimuli (CSs), and not to other stimuli that are similar; it is called (21)_____ and is based on differential reinforcement, or the application of the UCS only with certain CSs and not with other related stimuli.

Questions have been raised about the simplicity and mechanical nature of this mode. If the process of learning is so mechanical, why is it that sometimes the UCR and CR are quite (22)_____? Or why is it that associating two stimuli ahead of time without reinforcement leads to some learning of the nonreinforced stimulus later on, a phenomenon called (23)_____? Finally, critics have suggested that organisms appear to attend to *what leads to what,* which seems to be less automatic and more (24)_____ than the model proposes.

4. THOUGHT QUESTIONS

a. You have never eaten oysters in your life, but you are certain that you would not like them so you avoid them. Explain this behavior on the basis of the classical conditioning paradigm, employing the concept of stimulus generalization.

b. How does the phenomenon of higher-order conditioning account for the learning of very complicated human social and emotional behavior?

c. How does the notion of stimulus generalization account both for much efficiency and for much inefficiency in human learning and behavior?

d. Mechanistically oriented psychologists are attracted to the simplicity and automatic nature of the classical conditioning paradigm in accounting for important learning. Other more cognitively oriented psychologists are dismayed by attempts to use this model to account for complicated human behavior. What are the essential differences between the two approaches? Can these differences be reconciled? If so, how?

5. EVALUATION (SELF-TESTS)

Correct answers and text page references are given at the end of the unit.

a. Fill-in-the-blanks Items

Write the word(s) that best complete(s) the sentence in the space provided.

1. The function of the orienting reflex appears to be to increase _____information flow_____ to the organism.

2. The critical feature of a UCS at the beginning of training is that it regularly ___elicited___ a particular response.

3. The critical feature of a CS at the beginning of training is that it is ___neutral___ for the response in question.

4. When the UCS precedes the CS in a conditioning sequence, this form of learning is called ___backward conditioning___.

5. Strictly speaking, in classical conditioning reinforcement refers to the pairing of the ___cs___ and the ___ucs___.

6. The experiments of Ivan Pavlov were important to the work of John Watson, the father of ___behavorism___.

7. The experimental procedure of eliciting the CR without the presence of the UCS is referred to as ___extinction___.

8. Opening the door of an automobile that you think to be your own but that is not might be an example of ___stimulus generalisation___.

9. Learning not to open the doors of automobiles that are similar to your own is an example of ___discrimination___.

10. In contrast to a more cognitive approach to behavior, classical conditioning is usually thought of as ___mechanistic___.

b. Matching Items

Write the number of the correct item from the right column in front of the matching item in the left column.

_8_	orienting reflex	1. systematic desensitization
_9_	habituation	2. UCS precedes CS
_7_	Pavlov	3. coordinated automatic response to stimulation
_3_	tropism	4. founder of behaviorism
_6_	interstimulus interval	5. pairing of CS and UCS
_2_	backward conditioning	6. time between CS and UCS
_4_	Watson	7. discovered classical conditioning
_5_	reinforcement	8. response to a sudden change of illumination
_1_	Wolpe	9. adaptation to repetitive stimulation
_10_	discrimination	10. responding differently to similar stimuli

c. Multiple-choice Items

Circle the letter in front of the answer that best completes the stem.

1. Conditioning in which the CS is one sequence becomes the UCS in a second sequence involving the same CR is called:
   a. trace conditioning
   b. higher-order conditioning
   c. simultaneous conditioning
   d. backward conditioning

2. Conditioning in which the UCS occurs after the CS has been removed is called:
   a. trace conditioning
   b. higher-order conditioning
   c. simultaneous conditioning
   d. backward conditioning

3. Conditioning in which the UCS precedes the CS is called:
   a. trace conditioning
   b. higher-order conditioning
   c. simultaneous conditioning
   d. backward conditioning

4. In an extinction procedure, the experimenter repeatedly elicits the _____ without the presence of _____.
   a. UCR, UCS
   b. UCR, CS
   c. CR, UCS
   d. CR, CS

5. Reappearance of an extinguished response without further training is called:
   a. discrimination
   b. habituation
   c. adaptation
   d. spontaneous recovery

6. Response strength over training trials is graphically displayed by:
   a. the interstimulus interval
   b. the learning curve
   c. sensory preconditioning
   d. reinforcement

7. Responding differently in the presence of stimuli similar to the original CS is referred to as:
   a. discrimination
   b. habituation
   c. adaptation
   d. spontaneous recovery

8. The person who pioneered studies of a form of extinction called systematic desensitization is:
   a. Pavlov
   b. Watson
   c. Wolpe
   d. Lurn

9. The main function of the orienting reflex seems to be to:
   a. ward off danger
   b. increase information flow
   c. cut down on arousal
   d. make life more interesting

10. Criticisms of the classical conditioning model have suggested that it is too:
    a. simple and cognitive
    b. cognitive and complex
    c. complex and automatic
    d. automatic and simple

d. Short-answer Items

Answer the following questions with short, concise statements. Reference pages for the material are given at the end of the unit.

1. Outline the basic paradigm of classical conditioning, defining its four components.

2. Why do you think that backward conditioning would be a difficult form of learning?

3. What are the important differences between extinction and counter-conditioning?

4. Outline two of the common criticisms of the classical conditioning model.

ANSWER KEY FOR UNIT 9

Unit Review

1. orienting reflex
2. classical conditioning
3. unconditioned
4. unconditioned
5. conditioned
6. unconditioned stimulus
7. conditioned response
8. precedes
9. ½ or 0.5
10. interstimulus
11. simultaneous conditioning
12. backward conditioning

13. higher-order
14. behaviorism
15. reinforcement
16. learning curve
17. extinction
18. spontaneous recovery
19. counter-conditioning
20. stimulus generalization
21. discrimination
22. different
23. sensory preconditioning
24. cognitive

Evaluation (Self-tests)

a. Fill-in-the-blanks Items

1. information flow (p. 211)
2. elicits (p. 212)
3. neutral (p. 212)
4. backward conditioning (p. 214)
5. CS, UCS (p. 217)
6. behaviorism (p. 215)
7. extinction (p. 218)
8. stimulus generalization (pp. 218–219)
9. discrimination (pp. 219–220)
10. mechanistic (pp. 220–222)

b. Matching Items: Correct order and page references are:

8 (p. 211); 9 (p. 211); 7 (p. 211); 3 (p. 213); 6 (p. 214);
2 (p. 214); 4 (p. 215); 5 (p. 217); 1 (p. 219); 10 (p. 219–220).

c. Multiple-choice Items: Correct answers and page references are:

1—b (pp. 214–215); 2—a (p. 214); 3—d (p. 214); 4—c (p. 218); 5—d (p. 218);
6—b (p. 217); 7—a (pp. 219–220); 8—c (p. 219); 9—b (p. 211); 10—d (pp. 220–222).

d. Short-answer Items: Page references for answer material are:

1. pp. 211–214; 2. p. 214; 3. pp. 218–219; 4. pp. 220–222.

Unit 10

INSTRUMENTAL OR OPERANT CONDITIONING

1. INTRODUCTION TO STUDY OF THIS UNIT

For quite some time a controversy has raged concerning whether one model of learning (e.g., classical conditioning) is sufficient to account for all learning or whether additional models are necessary. The approaches to learning taken by the two sides of the controversy are called the Uniprocess and the Multiprocess approaches. For our purposes here, this dispute is reflected by the distinction between classical conditioning and a second type of learning called instrumental, or operant, conditioning. Unit 9 reviewed the characteristics of classical conditioning.

In contrast with this fixed-stimulus procedure, it has long been recognized that organisms will act as if to obtain some goal (e.g., food) or to avoid some consequence (e.g., pain). The format of the learner in such situations would appear to be oriented toward response and consequence. Long ago, Edward Thorndike taught cats to lick themselves in order to be released from a cage. Some of Pavlov's students, in *his* laboratory, taught children to press a bulb in order to receive food. Thorndike explained his observations in terms of rather blind trial-and-error behavior, and Pavlov's colleagues explained theirs in terms of the classical conditioning paradigm. In more recent years, it has been convenient to refer to this seemingly different kind of learning as instrumental conditioning. B. F. Skinner and others have generalized the model to account for all learning, including very complex human emotional and social behaviors.

Two areas of contention regarding instrumental conditioning remain to the present time. The first is whether the instrumental model is really distinctive from the classical conditioning model or whether the differences represent only convention, emphasis, or a reference to somewhat different experimental procedures. Is it possible that all instrumentally conditioned behaviors contain important classically conditioned elements? The second area of disagreement concerns the extent to which this second relatively simple model can serve as an adequate explanation of behavior and as a central tool for social design. Skinner has suggested that it is quite adequate and has proposed that continued human existence may actually depend on our use of basic operant conditioning principles to achieve needed social engineering. Such notions have inspired quite a lot of criticism by persons both inside and outside psychology.

2. ISSUES AND CONCEPTS

The most important theme for you to understand in this unit is the response and consequence orientation of instrumental conditioning versus the stimulus orientation of classical conditioning. This is brought out initially by the presentation of Thorndike's law of effect, which states simply that pleasure and pain (consequences) stamp in or out (cause learning) what the organism is doing (responses). What the organism does is instrumental in modifying the environment (instrumental conditioning), or, as Skinner puts it, the organism's behavior operates on the environment to change it (operant conditioning).

An essential component of instrumental learning is reinforcement. You should know the definitions of both positive and negative reinforcement and understand what secondary reinforcement is, since much human behavior appears to be guided by secondary reinforcers. The definition of punishment should be studied as well as the different views concerning the efficacy of punishment in getting rid of behaviors. Do aversive consequences only suppress behavior, so that it appears later when punishment is not provided, or do they set the stage for effective learning if alternative and acceptable behaviors are positively reinforced at the same time? Keep in mind the important distinction between learning and performance since it suggests that reinforcement may be more necessary for the latter than the former. If that is true, then some cognitive processes may indeed be operating in much learning.

The principle of shaping, which follows the method of successive approximations, is important because on it rests the explanation of how very complex behaviors may be learned according to this model. You should recognize that there are schedules of reinforcement, some of which reinforce each appropriate behavior and others of which follow some other pattern. You should also learn the distinction between the fixed-ratio (in Box 10.4) and the variable-ratio schedule. Resistance to extinction is typically greater following partial reinforcement rather than continuous reinforcement. Why do you think this is?

Again review the important distinction between learning and performance and the role of motivation in learning. What does latent learning tell us about these relationships?

You should study as well the various similarities and differences between the two conditioning models, classical and instrumental. Is it possible that both types of conditioning are involved in much learning? Finally, think through the various criticisms and the limitations of this learning approach, as suggested in recent years.

3. UNIT REVIEW

Correct answers are given at the end of the unit.

In classical conditioning the UCS follows the CS on (1)_____ training trial, while in instrumental conditioning, reinforcement is (2)_____ upon the specific behavior of the learner. Instrumental conditioning appears to be related to the kind of learning described years ago by Edward Thorndike. His formulation of the (3)_____ states that "pleasure stamps in, pain stamps out." Instrumental conditioning is also called (4)_____ conditioning by B. F. Skinner and others. Both labels are based on the fact that the organism, through its behavior, (5)_____ the environment.

A crucial aspect of instrumental conditioning is the role of (6)_____, since this is the consequence that guides such learning. While there is some question about whether reinforcement must be related to the satisfaction of basic biological needs, it appears clear that learned reinforcement exists, money being a common example of such (7)_____.

Skinner and others speak about positive reinforcement as consisting of any stimulus that

(8)_____ the probability of the response that preceded it; they also

speak about negative reinforcement as consisting of any stimulus whose removal or reduction

(9)_____ the probability of a response preceding such reduction.

Skinnerians reserve the term punishment for a stimulus that (10)_____ the

probability of the response that has preceded it. While skepticism exists about the efficacy of punishment

for effective learning, it appears that it may work best when used in conjunction with the

(11)_____ of alternative behaviors.

Evidence has been presented suggesting that reinforcement may not be necessary for learning to take

place but rather has its main effect on (12)_____. This important distinc-

tion is based largely on experiments showing that latent learning may be occurring while the organism

is forming a (13)_____ of the learning situation.

Complex behaviors can be learned on the basis of instrumental conditioning through the use of

the method of successive approximations, or (14)_____. The method

involves revising at just the right times the successive standards of behavior that the trainee must meet in

order to be reinforced.

In this form of learning, reinforcement may be provided continuously — that is, after each appropriate

behavior — or according to some other pattern. All of these other patterns are referred to as

(15)_____. One such pattern reinforces behavior only every fifth or tenth or

nth time and this is called a (16)_____ schedule. Another reinforces behavior

the fifth or tenth or nth time *on average*, and this is called a (17)_____ schedule.

Whatever the schedule, behavior conditioned by partial reinforcement is more resistant to

(18)_____ than that conditioned under continuous reinforcement.

While it appears that reinforcement is more important for performance than for learning, motivation

may have some (19)_____ in learning situations by maintaining the

interest of the trainee and keeping the learner in the learning arena.

For both classical and instrumental conditioning, reinforcement is important, although for classical

conditioning it is defined as the contiguous presentation of the (20)_____, while

for instrumental it involves the presence or (21)_____ of a reinforcing stimulus.

In addition, both forms of conditioning follow the general rules of (22)_____,

(23)_____, and (24)_____. Although

it is clear that visceral responses, (e.g., heartbeat) can be classically conditioned, it is not clear

that such responses can also be instrumentally conditioned; recent evidence

involving (25)_____, however, suggests an increase in the instrumental control

of such responses.

Question has been raised about the relative independence of classical and instrumental conditioning and the possibility that both may be involved in much learning. For example, the phenomena of

(26)_____, in which learners classically condition their own behavior while

in an instrumental learning situation, and of (27)_____, in which

classically conditioned fear may be used as the reinforcement for instrumental conditioning, suggest

that both forms of learning may occur in the same learning situation.

Although classical and instrumental conditioning paradigms appear clearly to be relevant to much

everyday learning, critics have suggested that these models cannot explain all learning and have proposed

that other models of a more (28)_____ nature are required.

4. THOUGHT QUESTIONS

a. How could you use the method of successive approximations, or shaping, to train your pet dog to learn a
complex task, such as going to fetch your morning newspaper?

b. Why do slot machine gamblers continue playing for long periods of time even though they do not win very
often? Why do you suppose they do not quit after making a win, especially if they are "ahead" at the
time?

c. How might biofeedback training be used to aid the patient with high blood pressure?

d. We all know of persons who are fearful of high places or closed-in spaces or snakes. In many cases these
behaviors are called phobias because the fear involved is not based on reality. Why are such phobias so
persistent? How might you set up a conditioning program to extinguish such a fear?

5. EVALUATION (SELF-TESTS)

Correct answers and text page references are given at the end of the unit.

a. Fill-in-the-blanks Items

Write the word(s) that best complete(s) the sentence in the space provided.

1. In instrumental conditioning, reinforcement is _____*dependent*_____ upon the
behavior of the learner.

2. In instrumental conditioning, learning cannot take place without _____*reinforcement*_____.

3. A stimulus that increases the probability of the response that preceded it is called
_____*positive reinforcement*_____.

4. A stimulus that reduces the probability of the response that preceded it is called
_____*punishment*_____.

5. It appears that reinforcement has its main effect on _____*performance*_____ rather than
on learning itself.

6. The acquisition of complex behaviors in this instrumental model is explained on the basis of
_____*shaping*_____.

7. Responses learned instrumentally with _____*partial reinforcement*_____ appear to be more resistant to extinction than those learned under conditions of continuous reinforcement.

8. Reinforcing every *n*th response is an example of a _____*fixed ratio*_____ schedule of reinforcement.

9. Reinforcing every *n*th response *on average* is an example of a _____*variable ratio*_____ schedule of reinforcement.

10. In general, the rules of extinction, generalization, and discrimination seem to operate _____*equally well*_____ for classical and instrumental conditioning.

b. Matching Items

Write the number of the correct item from the right column in front of the matching item in the left column.

_3_ Thorndike	1. pairing of one stimulus with another
_7_ Skinner	2. reduces negative reinforcement
_6_ negative reinforcement	3. law of effect
_2_ escape training	4. learning occurring without obvious reinforcement
_5_ punishment	5. stimulus that reduces the probability of a response
_9_ Tolman	6. stimulus whose reduction increases the probability
_1_ contiguity	of a response
_10_ shaping	7. operant conditioning
_8_ variable-ratio schedule	8. reinforcing every *n*th response *on average*
_4_ latent learning	9. cognitive map
	10. method of successive approximations

c. Multiple-choice Items

Circle the letter in front of the answer that best completes the stem.

1. In instrumental conditioning, reinforcement is contingent upon:
   a. the pairing of the CS and the UCS
   b. the pairing of an S with an R
   c. what the learner does
   d. what the experimenter does

2. The law of effect states that:
   a. pleasure stamps in, pain stamps out
   b. pleasure stamps out, pain stamps in
   c. pleasure and pain both stamp in
   d. pleasure and pain both stamp out

3. A stimulus that increases the probability of the response preceding it is called:
   a. negative reinforcement
   b. positive reinforcement
   c. secondary reinforcement
   d. punishment

4. A stimulus whose reduction increases the probability of the response preceding it is called:
   a. negative reinforcement
   b. positive reinforcement
   c. secondary reinforcement
   d. punishment

5. A stimulus that reduces the probability of a response preceding it is called:
    a. negative reinforcement
    b. positive reinforcement
    c. secondary reinforcement
    d. punishment

6. Reinforcement has its greatest effect on:
    a. learning
    b. performance
    c. both learning and performance equally
    d. neither learning nor performance

7. Shaping is making use of the:
    a. method of limits
    b. method of simultaneous approximations
    c. method of successive approximations
    d. method of height approximations

8. The reinforcement schedule that reinforces every *n*th response *on average* is called:
    a. fixed-interval
    b. fixed-ratio
    c. variable-interval
    d. variable-ratio

9. The partial reinforcement effect is associated with:
    a. greater susceptibility to extinction
    b. greater resistance to extinction
    c. easier acquisition
    d. greater generalization

10. Continuous reinforcement, in contrast to partial reinforcement, is associated with:
    a. less rapid acquisition
    b. more rapid extinction
    c. less generalization
    d. more generalization

d. Short-answer Items

Answer the following questions with short, concise statements. Reference pages for the material are given at the end of the unit.

1. Contrast the views of Thorndike, Hull, and Skinner with respect to the nature of reinforcement.

2. What influences does motivation have on learning and on performance?

3. In what two ways are classical and instrumental conditioning similar and in what two ways seemingly different?

4. Discuss briefly the possibility that classical conditioning may be involved in many examples of instrumental conditioning.

ANSWER KEY FOR UNIT 10

Unit Review

1. every
2. contingent/dependent
3. law of effect
4. operant
5. changes
6. reinforcement
7. secondary reinforcement
8. increases
9. increases
10. reduces
11. positive reinforcement
12. performance
13. cognitive map
14. shaping
15. partial reinforcement
16. fixed-ratio
17. variable-ratio
18. extinction
19. incentive value
20. CS and UCS
21. reduction
22. extinction
23. generalization
24. discrimination
25. biofeedback techniques
26. autoshaping
27. avoidance learning
28. cognitive

Evaluation (Self-tests)

a. **Fill-in-the-blanks Items**

  1. contingent/dependent (p. 226)
  2. reinforcement (p. 230)
  3. positive reinforcement (p. 228)
  4. punishment (p. 230)
  5. performance (p. 230)
  6. shaping (p. 231)
  7. partial reinforcement (p. 232)
  8. fixed-ratio (pp. 232–233)
  9. variable-ratio (p. 233)
  10. equally well (p. 235)

b. **Matching Items: Correct order and page references are:**

  3 (p. 226); 7 (p. 226); 6 (p. 229); 2 (p. 229); 5 (p. 230);
  9 (p. 230); 1 (p. 230); 10 (p. 231); 8 (p. 233); 4 (p. 234).

c. **Multiple-choice Items: Correct answers and page references are:**

  1—c (p. 226); 2—a (p. 226); 3—b (p.228); 4—a (p. 229); 5—d (p. 230);
  6—b (p. 230); 7—c (p. 231); 8—d (p. 233); 9—b (p. 236); 10—b (pp. 232–233).

d. **Short-answer Items: Page references for answer material are:**

  1. pp. 226–233; 2. pp. 233–235; 3. pp. 235–237; 4. pp. 235–237.

Unit 11

MEMORY AND VERBAL LEARNING

1. INTRODUCTION TO STUDY OF THIS UNIT

As we mentioned previously, the study of verbal learning has about as long a history as modern experimental psychology. Hermann Ebbinghaus published several years of research in the area in 1885. Ebbinghaus, you may recall, "invented" the nonsense syllable and used it as a control for the effects of differential past experience on more meaningful verbal materials. On the basis of his studies, he laid down the basic principles of verbal learning, memory, and forgetting. Studies employing similar procedures continue to the present time.

More recent studies in this area have been concerned with the learning and memory of more complex and meaningful verbal materials, such as stories or narratives. While we may be able to generalize results of studies employing nonsense syllables to some aspects of complex human verbal learning and memory, to gain more complete knowledge we must study directly the more complex and meaningful materials. The results of recent studies reveal that human verbal learning and memory consists of several systems, levels, or methods for processing information for retention and retrieval. Whether these methods reflect only a single basic scheme or more than one is controversial.

Another controversy in this area pertains to the relationship of verbal learning to other models of learning that we have already studied: classical and instrumental conditioning. Some psychologists feel that the conditioning models are relevant as explanations only for rather simple human learning and for much of the learning of lower animals. Verbal learning seems to them to represent a different quality of learning, one that is more cognitive and meaningful. Other psychologists feel that the basic conditioning paradigms are adequate to account for *all* learning, including complex human learning, and the retention, or memory, of that material. Here, again, perhaps the controversy continues as a reflection of different subjects, procedures, and data collected.

Contemporary experimental procedures dealing with verbal learning and memory differ from those of conditioning studies in many important respects and, therefore, can be studied as though they represent a new model of learning, as indeed they might.

2. ISSUES AND CONCEPTS

Your initial learning task in the sutdy of this unit is to formulate a good idea of the kind of experimental procedures used in verbal learning research from the time of Ebbinghaus to the present. Know what nonsense syllables (CVCs or trigrams) are and why they were developed. Be able to differentiate the various methods used in the experimental study of verbal learning and memory, including serial learning, memory span, probe tasks, free recall, and paired-associate learning. Know also the three methods for measuring learning and retention: recall, recognition, and relearning. Be aware of the serial-position effect described in Box 11.1.

Your next task is to learn the characteristics of the three "types" of memory: sensory, short-term, and long-term. With sensory memory, be aware of the backward-masking phenomenon since this effect tells us something about what is going on during the brief period that sensory memory operates. For both short-term and long-term memory, acquire basic information concerning the encoding, storage, and retrieval processes. Know that imagery can be involved in the encoding and retrieving of long-term memories, as illustrated in the locus and pegwood methods described in Box 11.2. Forgetting appears to be largely an active process since there is little direct evidence for the decay or disuse explanation. Interference seems to account for most of forgetting. You must be able to differentiate between the two kinds of interference, proactive and retroactive inhibition, and how these processes are studied.

You should compare short-term and long-term memory in terms of the kinds of codes each uses predominantly, as well as the capacities and retrieval methods of each. Are these two memories really different or do they reflect different levels of processing or simply different stages of a single process, with the important intervention of rehearsal and the use of different codes?

Finally, you should be able to describe creative forgetting (constructive memory) and understand that this process is based on past experiences and reactions. Know that structure and meaning is important for the learning and memory of narratives. Be able to define repression. You should also learn the difference between episodic memory and semantic or generic memory, as described in Box 11.3.

3. UNIT REVIEW

Correct answers are given at the end of the unit.

The study of verbal learning dates back to Hermann Ebbinghaus, who first used (1)_____

in studies in an attempt to control for the effects of differential past (2)_____

with meaningful material. The most common measures of learning and retention involve "pulling out"

of memory the material one has been exposed to, termed (3)_____, or being

able to select the original material from a larger set of material containing it, termed (4)_____.

A third measure compares the efficiency of a second learning of material with that of the original learning,

a technique appropriately called (5)_____. Experimental methods used

in verbal learning and memory studies include the learning of items in a specific order, called

(6)_____; the memory-span test, in which the experimenter presents a

set of items in order once and the learner tries to (7)_____; a technique in

which the learner of a list presented once is asked to name the next item after having been give a

certain item from the list, called the (8)_____; free recall, in which the

learner reports as many items in a list as possible after each presentation without reference to

(9)_____; and paired-associate learning, in which the learner of a list of

pairs of items is given the first item of each pair and tries to produce the (10)_____.

In serial learning it has been found that items near the beginning and the end of the list are remembered

better, a phenomenon called (11)_____.

   Memory can be talked about in terms of three processes: sensory, short-term, and long-term memory.

The first refers to the fact that the sensory input into the eyes or ears lasts for about

(12)_____. It appears that the image must be processed during the first part

of that period, because of the results of (13)_____ studies. In short-term

memory, changing the input into a different form for remembering, or (14)_____,

is done by means of an (15)_____ code even for material presented visually.

Retaining this information, called (16)_____, must be accomplished

quickly, and the capacity of short-term memory is about (17)_____ items.

However, the capacity can be extended by grouping the items in a method called

(18)_____. Digging up these memories, or (19)_____,

probably is done on the basis of serial scanning and is aided by grouping items into subsets or by

providing (20)_____ . In long-term memory, while acoustic or articulatory

coding may be involved, encoding seems to be largely a matter of (21)_____

coding, based on meaning. Imagery may aid this process, as illustrated by the effectiveness of such

mnemonic techniques as the (22)_____ and (23)_____

methods. Storage capacity is large in long-term memory, and the amount stored can be increased through the active process of organizing the material into (24)_____. Retrieval is guided by processing cues probably present at the time of original (25)_____. This is nicely illustrated when retrieval works slowly or incompletely, as in the (26)_____ phenomenon.

Most forgetting, especially of simple materials, seems to be largely a function of (27)_____, and this is, at least in part, related to the effect of previous learning on later learning, called (28)_____. Interference produced by learning that preceded the original learning is referred to as (29)_____, while that resulting from other learning coming between original learning and the retention test is called (30)_____. There is not much evidence to support the notion that forgetting is largely the gradual fading of memory through disuse, or (31)_____.

To review, a comparison of short-term and long-term memory reveals that short-term memory makes use of an (32)_____ code, has a (33)_____ capacity, and retrieval occurs rather (34)_____, while long-term memory makes use of a (35)_____ code, has a (36)_____ capacity, and retrieval occurs through retrieval (37)_____, if interference has not occurred. As an alternative to a multiple-stores explanation of memory, the level-of-processing theory suggests that processing stages differ not only in time course, but also in (38)_____. How do short-term and long-term memory interact? Short-term memory is the first to deal with the sensory input, and if such input is to get into long-term memory, it must be held in short-term memory through the process of (39)_____, or through forming images or relating the input meaningfully.

Studies of memory for connected discourse (e.g., narratives), reveal distortions, or what Bartlett called (40)_____, based on the influence of our past experiences and reactions. The ''grammar'' of a story refers to the basic (41)_____ of the story, which is important for learning and memory.

Psychoanalytic theory suggests another active process of forgetting called (42)_____, in which extremely painful and/or threatening events are forgotten.

According to recent analysis there are two general kinds of memory. The first involves the tracing of an event to a particular time, and it is called (43)_____. The second involves more general memories, such as the definitions of words, called (44)_____.

4. THOUGHT QUESTIONS

a. Why was it necessary for Hermann Ebbinghaus to invent nonsense syllables in order to study verbal learning and memory? What alternative procedures might he have employed?

b. If you are planning to study for four different courses on the same evening, how would you order your studying based on what you know about interference in learning and memory?

c. What kinds of experimental evidence would you have to collect in order to demonstrate directly that decay or disuse may account for some amount of forgetting?

d. What kinds of design information would you need to have in order to program a computer to process narrative material and index its components as a human does in terms of meaningful relationships rather than on simpler bases, such as word counts?

5. EVALUATION (SELF-TESTS)

Correct answers and text page references are given at the end of the unit.

a. Fill-in-the-blanks Items

Write the word(s) that best complete(s) the sentence in the space provided.

1. Ebbinghaus invented nonsense syllables in order to control for the likely influence of differential past ___experience___ with meaningful material.

2. The three measures of learning and retention are ___recall___, recognition, and relearning.

3. Serial learning refers to the learning of a list of items in a ___specific order___.

4. The serial-position effect refers to the finding that items ___in the beginning & end___ of a list are remembered better.

5. Encoding in short-term memory makes use mainly of an ___auditory___ code.

6. Encoding in long-term memory depends predominantly on a ___semantay___ code.

7. Storage capacity for either short- or long-term memory can be increased significantly by ___chunking / clustering___ items.

8. Forgetting appears to be a function of ___interference___.

9. Proactive inhibition refers to interference produced by learning that ___precedes___ the original learning.

10. Remembering what you were doing last Saturday night at 8:00 P.M. is an example of ___episodic___ memory.

b. Matching Items

Write the number of the correct item from the right column in front of the matching item in the left column.

7	decay	1. grouping material for better retention
6	seven items	2. mnemonic technique
4	transfer	3. method for study of verbal learning
8	retrieval	4. effect of previous learning on later learning
10	recall	5. learning without an intention to learn
9	sensory memory	6. capacity of short-term memory
1	chunking	7. gradual fading of memory through disuse
2	method of loci	8. information brought out of storage
5	incidental learning	9. passive storage system
3	paired-associate learning	10. pull out of memory

c. Multiple-choice Items

Circle the letter in front of the answer that best completes the stem.

1. Which of the following is *not* one of the principal methods for measuring verbal learning and retention?
   a. recall
   b. retrieval
   c. recognition
   d. relearning

2. Which of the following is *not* one of the principal methods for studying verbal learning?
   a. serial learning
   b. paired-associate learning
   c. grope-task
   d. free recall

3. The type of memory or memory process that provides a copy of the stimulus for a brief period is called:
   a. sensory memory
   b. short-term memory
   c. long-term memory
   d. fond memory

4. Retrieval in short-term memory probably involves:
   a. retinal scanning
   b. memory scanning
   c. parallel scanning
   d. serial scanning

5. Encoding for long-term memory is predominantly:
   a. auditory
   b. acoustic
   c. semantic
   d. articulation

6. Retroactive inhibition refers to interference caused by material learned:
   a. between original learning and retention testing
   b. between sleep and original learning
   c. before original learning
   d. after retention testing

7. The capacity of long-term memory storage is:
   a. one second
   b. seven items
   c. up to 20 items
   d. huge

8. Retrieval in long-term memory is based on:
   a. a rather direct process
   b. auditory coding
   c. level of processing
   d. retrieval cues and meaning

9. The process of distorting narrative memory based on past experiences and reactions is termed:
   a. unconstructive remembering
   b. creative forgetting
   c. schematic remembering
   d. imagination

10. Our general memory of word definitions or well-known facts is called:
    a. generative memory
    b. semantic memory
    c. episodic memory
    d. factual memory

d. Short-answer Items

Answer the following questions with short, concise statements. Reference pages for the material are given at the end of the unit.

1. Of the three basic measures of verbal learning and retention, which one is usually associated with higher memory scores than the others? What is a possible explanation of this effect?

2. Cite evidence for the efficacy of using imagery in an attempt to improve memory.

3. What does the tip-of-the-tongue phenomenon tell us about the retrieval process in long-term memory?

4. In what two ways are short-term memory and long-term memory similar and in what two ways dissimilar?

ANSWER KEY FOR UNIT 11

Unit Review

1. nonsense syllables
2. experience
3. recall
4. recognition
5. relearning
6. serial learning
7. repeat them in order
8. probe task
9. fixed order
10. second item
11. serial-position effect
12. one second
13. backward-masking
14. encoding
15. auditory/acoustic
16. storage
17. seven
18. chunking
19. retrieval
20. cues
21. semantic
22. locus
23. pegwood

24. clusters/groups/chunks
25. encoding
26. tip-of-the-tongue
27. interference
28. transfer
29. proactive inhibition
30. retroactive inhibition
31. decay
32. auditory/acoustic
33. small
34. directly
35. semantic
36. very large
37. cues
38. depth
39. rehearsal
40. creative forgetting
41. structure
42. repression
43. episodic memory
44. semantic/generic memory

Evaluation (Self-tests)

a. Fill-in-the-blanks Items

1. experience (p. 246)
2. recall (p. 246)
3. specific order (p. 247)
4. near the beginning and end (p. 249)
5. auditory/acoustic (p. 249)
6. semantic (p. 252)
7. grouping/chunking/clustering (pp. 251, 255)
8. interference (p. 256)
9. preceded (p. 256)
10. episodic (p. 262)

b. Matching Items: Correct order and page references are:

7 (p. 257); 6 (p. 250); 4 (p. 256); 8 (p. 251); 10 (p. 246);
9 (p. 247); 1 (p. 251); 2 (p. 253); 5 (p. 254); 3 (p. 247).

c. Multiple-choice Items: Correct answers and page references are:

1—b (p. 246); 2—c (p. 247); 3—a (p. 247); 4—d (p. 251); 5—c (p. 252);
6—a (p. 256); 7—d (p. 254); 8—d (p. 255); 9—b (p. 260); 10—b (p. 262).

d. Short-answer Items: Page references for answer material are:

1. p. 246; 2. p. 253; 3. p. 255; 4. pp. 258–259.

Unit 12

PHYSIOLOGICAL BASES OF LEARNING AND MEMORY

1. INTRODUCTION TO STUDY OF THIS UNIT

For almost as long as systematic study of learning and memory has existed, scientists and others have speculated about, and more recently done research on, the biological or physiological processes that underlie or are at least associated with these phenomena. For hundreds of years, the notion that the brain and other parts of the body were somehow involved has persisted. It should be relatively easy, therefore, to track down more complete information about such relationships. Such has not been the case, however, and this may be due to the great complexity of the systems involved, the lack of sophistication of the experimental procedures employed in relevant research, or the need to build up more general knowledge of the physiological systems possibly involved before raising behavioral questions about how learning and memory are related to such systems. We have certainly come a long distance from F. J. Gall, G. S. Spurzheim, and Pierre Flourens in our knowledge of the mind-body relationship, but it is clear that we have a long way to go before precise information will be available.

This unit approaches the issues in this area in two ways. First, it reviews available information on the various mechanisms involved, or potentially involved, in those nervous system changes that may be associated with learning and those longer-lasting ones that may be associated with memory. Both the general mechanisms and the more specific cellular and chemical changes are examined. Second, the unit looks at evidence concerning the locus of learning or memory, or the part or parts of the nervous system in which learning takes place and information is stored. Keep in mind that these two approaches to the material are not independent; mechanism and locus may, indeed, be quite interdependent. Keep in mind as well that while we have accumulated much important information on these topics over the years, our knowledge of the physiological bases of learning and memory is sketchy and incomplete. This appraisal is brought out clearly in the last section of the unit in which the need for postulating a neural system to account for learning and memory is suggested and one is offered that may not be correct in most of its detail.

2. ISSUES AND CONCEPTS

In the first section of this unit, on mechanisms of learning and memory, you should strive to understand the concepts of habituation and sensitization. Habituation, or the decrease in strength of a response with repeated stimulation, is a very simple form of learning and may reflect the modified application of transmitter substances, as in the case of the Aplysia. The mechanism of sensitization, you will learn, may also reflect transmitter substance increase or may be a general priming or "toning." Be aware of the reverberating circuit, a concept that was originally presented nearly 40 years ago, and how it is related to the consolidation hypothesis, which explains how short-term memory runs its course, thus allowing for long-term memory to occur. Be familiar with the step-down procedure and how it has been coupled with ECS and anesthesia to test the consolidation hypothesis, as well as the difficulties suggested by the free-foot-shock study. Know what retrograde amnesia is and how these effects appear to support consolidation. Learn what research on consolidation supports the notion that there is something about learning and memory that is time-dependent.

You should also familiarize yourself with the two ways in which synaptic changes — (1) changes in axon terminals, dendritic branches, or cleft size and other anatomical changes, and (2) biochemical changes at the synapse, including the action of ACh and AChE — can be associated with learning and memory. Intraneural changes may occur with learning as well, and you should study the research on RNA and protein synthesis that may support that hypothesis.

In the second section of this unit, on the locus of learning and memory, become familiar with early studies that involved the "discipline" of phrenology and how they led to later, more widely approved research, such as the lesion studies of Flourens. Another important topic is how classical conditioning in lower animals and humans can occur through the spinal cord without brain involvement, even though such involvement may typically occur. You should learn, too, the possible role of the reticular formation in mediating the simple form of learning called habituation. The interesting case of H.M., illustrating anterograde amnesia and the possible involvement of the hippocampus and amygdala structures in the limbic system in this phenomenon should also be studied. Finally, you should learn the possible role of the thalamus and the hypothalamus in memory functioning. As indicated above, evidence indicates that conditioning can take place without cortical involvement, but such learning may be slower and retention loss may occur as compared with similar learning accomplished with the cortex functioning.

To fully understand the physiological bases of learning, we must be able to describe the neural system involved. Be aware of the system explained inthe text.

3. UNIT REVIEW

Correct answers are given at the end of the unit.

The basic mechanisms of learning are suggested by such phenomena as habituation and sensitization.

Habituation had been defined earlier as a (1)_____ in response strength

associated with repeated stimulus presentation. This is clearly illustrated in the siphon response of the

(2)_____, which is probably a function of change in

(3)_____ substance. Habituation may also occur in a spinal animal,

not because of sensory and motor neurons but rather because of (4)_____,

and also because of changes in (5)_____ substances. Sensitization refers

to the increase in response to certain stimuli as a result of the prior stimulation of (6)_____

sensory neurons. Sensitization effects in Aplysia may be due to changes in (7)_____,

while in higher organisms they reflect a (8)_____ effect.

It is difficult to generalize findings concerning habituation and sensitization to more complicated

learning, such as conditioning, because there is little evidence that simple organisms, such as Aplysia, are

(9)_____ of more complicated kinds of learning, and because we don't know

what happens during learning in (10)_____ animals.

To account for neural activity lasting for any appreciable length of time, researchers have proposed

the (11)_____, in which a closed loop will fire into itself to maintain the

activity. Such circuits could be the neural basis of (12)_____, except that some

conditions such as sleep, anesthesia, and convulsions disturb neural activity greatly but do not disturb

long-term memory. However, it is still possible that reverberating circuits are involved in

(13)_____. Firing in the loop may maintain the short-term memory

sufficiently to allow (14)_____ to occur in order to produce

(15)_____. This theory is a form of the consolidation hypothesis,

which has often been investigated with lower animals using a method called (16)_____.

In this procedure, if the animal is shocked for stepping down from a platform, it will on the next

occasion remain on the platform for a longer time. In conjunction with this procedure, if ECS, or

(17)_____, or a drug treatment, such as anesthesia, is provided right after

the step-down/foot-shock sequence, the animal may show no evidence of (18)_____

the incident. Such data suggest that consolidation of the (19)_____ has

not occurred. On the other hand, injection of stimulants at the same time in a different learning sequence

may actually (20)_____ learning. One problem with the consolidation

hypothesis is the finding that an unrelated ''sensitization-type'' shock may lead only to

(21)_____ on the platform the next day, which argues against a ''pure''

(strong) version of the hypothesis. The fact remains that the effects produced by ECS and drugs are

(22)_____, with the effect being greatest when the treatment is given

(23)_____ after the trial, and small or nonexistent when the treatment is

(24)_____. At the human level, head injury may result in selective forgetting

of more recent events than longer-term memories, a phenomenon called (25)_____.

The (26)_____ hypothesis would suggest such an effect.

Several explanations of learning and memory in terms of changes at the level of the synapse have been

proposed. For example, it has been suggested that learning may consist of the development of more and

larger (27)_____ arriving at a synapse, or a (28)_____

of the relevant synaptic clefts. Another possibility is that certain cells that are not fully developed at

birth do develop because of (29)_____. It has been found that certain

experiences, such as (30)_____ in rats, help to develop such cells. Con-

sistent with this finding are the facts that (31)_____ has been found to change

the size and weight of the cerebral cortex in rats and that such enriched rats also have more complicated

patterns of branches in their (32)_____. However, as indicated in Box 12.1,

it is possible that experience can also be associated with (33)_____ but

more appropriate synapses.

Biochemical effects in the form of transmitter substance changes have also been implicated in learning and memory at the level of the synapse. For example, it has been found that absolute and relative amounts of one of the neurotransmitters, called (34)_____, and an enzyme that breaks it down, called (35)_____, in the brain are related to effective learning. Rats with enriched experiences have been shown to have higher (36)_____ activity in the cortex. In humans, administration of drugs that decrease ACh activity has been associated with poorer (37)_____.

Changes within neurons have been proposed to account for some aspects of learning and memory. Specifically, since RNA controls (38)_____, learning and its attendant neural activity may change the structure of RNA within relevant neural cells, perhaps through (39)_____ release. Experiments support the contribution of RNA and of (40)_____ to effective learning and memory, but it isn't clear whether this is a direct action or an indirect one through a (41)_____ system, or whether it is only a by-product of the system. This unit also examines the possible locus of learning and memory in the organism. Early investigations undertaken by Gall and Spurzheim (see Box 12.2) studied relationships between bumps on the heads of subjects and important human characteristics; the discipline they founded was called (42)_____. Their investigation probably influenced Flourens to employ the (43)_____ method to study locus issues. At the level of the spinal cord (44)_____ is possible in lower animals and humans. Involvement of the (45)_____ does not appear necessary although it is usual in such learning, of course. The reticular formation appears to display physiological habituation; thus, this locus may underlie more general (46)_____, a simple form of learning. Damage to the hippocampus and amygdala areas of the limbic system in humans may produce (47)_____, as in the case of H. M., suggesting that while the short-term and long-term memory systems are intact, such damage may disturb (48)_____ between the two memory systems. Lower-animal research reinforces this notion. Korsakoff's syndrome, associated with (49)_____ and (50)_____ as well as damage to the (51)_____ and (52)_____, is often displayed as a sweeping (53)_____ and is probably due to poor processing of available stimulus information. While classical and instrumental conditioning may take place in the decorticate animal, cortical lesions may still be associated with learning and memory (54)_____.

To fully understand the physiological bases of learning and memory we will ultimately have to be able to describe the neural (55)_____ involved.

4. THOUGHT QUESTIONS

a. Why is it so difficult (and perhaps foolhardy?) to generalize the results of experiments on simple organisms so that they apply to organisms higher on the phyletic scale, especially humans?

b. What kinds of applications to human problems, such as those associated with aging, might be made of knowledge concerning the influence of the neurotransmitter acetylcholine (ACh) on memory?

c. What kinds of experiments would have to be done to test the possible direct contribution of RNA and protein synthesis to learning and memory?

d. Assume that you are the leader of Brave New World II or Walden III. How would you make use of various biochemical products, including ACh, AChE, DNA, and RNA, to improve the lot of your citizens, especially those who are very young and those who are quite old?

5. EVALUATION (SELF-TESTS)

Correct answers and text page references are given at the end of the unit.

a. Fill-in-the-blanks Items

Write the word(s) that best complete(s) the sentence in the space provided.

1. To account for neural activity persistence, a closed neural loop, or ___reverberating circuits___ has been proposed.

2. Such circuits are probably involved only in ___short___-term memory.

3. The theory that a memory must be preserved until it gets into long-term memory is called the ___consolidation hypothesis___.

4. Providing ECS or anesthesia to an animal immediately after an event may result in a weakening of the ___memory___ of that event.

5. Synaptic changes associated with learning and memory may include more and larger ___axon terminal___ arriving at a synapse.

6. Enriched environmental experience has been shown to change the ___size___ and ___wt___ of the cerebral cortex in rats.

7. Acetylcholine is a ___transmitter substance___ that has been found to be associated with the learning process.

8. Protein ___synthesis___ may also be associated with learning and memory improvement.

9. Classical and instrumental conditioning is possible in lower animals without ___brain___ involvement.

10. Anterograde amnesia may be caused by damage to the ___limbic system___.

b. Matching Items

Write the number of the correct item from the right column in front of the matching item in the left column.

5	Korsakoff's syndrome	1. forgetting going backward in time
3	flexion reflex	2. lesion method for studying locus
6	interneurons	3. withdrawal of a limb in response to pain
7	presynaptic excitation	4. forgetting going forward in time
9	step-down procedure	5. associated with alcoholism and malnutrition
1	retrograde amnesia	6. located completely within the spinal cord
8	infantile amnesia	7. sensitization
2	Flourens	8. inability of adults to recall much of their early life
10	Gall	9. used to test the consolidation hypothesis
4	anterograde amnesia	10. phrenology

c. Multiple-choice Items

Circle the letter in front of the answer that best completes the stem.

1. A decrease in response strength associated with repeated stimulus presentation is called:
   a. habituation
   b. sensitization
   c. retrograde amnesia
   d. anterograde amnesia

2. An increase in response strength associated with prior stimulation of another sensory system is called:
   a. habituation
   b. sensitization
   c. retrograde amnesia
   d. anterograde amnesia

3. Forgetting going backward in time is called:
   a. habituation
   b. sensitization
   c. retrograde amnesia
   d. anterograde amnesia

4. Forgetting going forward in time is called:
   a. habituation
   b. sensitization
   c. retrograde amnesia
   d. anterograde amnesia

5. The theory that short-term memory must run its course without disruption if long-term memory is to occur is called:
   a. reverberating circuits
   b. presynaptic excitation
   c. step-down integration
   d. consolidation hypothesis

6. Which of the following has been used to account for persistence in neural activity?
   a. reverberating circuits
   b. presynaptic excitation
   c. step-down integration
   d. consolidation hypothesis

7. A transmitter substance important in learning and memory is:
   a. ACh
   b. AChE
   c. DNA
   d. RNA

8. An enzyme that helps to remove a transmitter substance after activation is:
   a. ACh
   b. AChE
   c. DNA
   d. RNA

9. RNA has been implicated in learning and memory because of its function in producing:
   a. disturbance
   b. DNA
   c. protein
   d. head bumps

10. In lower animals, classical and instrumental conditioning can occur without:
    a. reverberating circuits
    b. reticular system involvement
    c. spinal cord involvement
    d. brain involvement

d. Short-answer Items

Answer the following questions with short, concise statements. Reference pages for the material are given at the end of the unit.

1. What do examples of retrograde amnesia in humans tell us about memory processes, especially those related to the consolidation hypothesis?

2. What kinds of evidence can you provide to support the notion that something about learning and memory is time-dependent?

3. Specify four synaptic changes that may be associated with learning and memory changes.

4. What are the implications of the finding that classical and instrumental conditioning may take place in lower animals without brain involvement?

ANSWER KEY FOR UNIT 12

Unit Review

1. decrease
2. Aplysia/snail/sea hare
3. transmitter
4. interneurons
5. transmitter
6. different
7. transmitter substances
8. "toning"/priming
9. capable
10. more complex
11. reverberating circuit
12. memory
13. short-term memory
14. consolidation
15. long-term memory
16. step-down procedure
17. electroconvulsive shock
18. remembering
19. short-term memory
20. facilitate
21. hesitation
22. time-dependent
23. immediately
24. delayed
25. retrograde amnesia
26. consolidation
27. axon terminals

28. narrowing
29. learning and memory
30. handling
31. environmental stimulation
32. dendrites
33. fewer
34. ACh (acetylcholine)
35. AChE (acetylcholinesterase)
36. AChE (acetylcholinesterase)
37. memory
38. protein production
39. transmitter substance
40. protein synthesis
41. better functioning
42. phrenology
43. lesion
44. classical conditioning
45. brain
46. habituation
47. anterograde amnesia
48. transfer
49. alcoholism
50. malnutrition
51. thalamus
52. hypothalamus
53. memory disturbance/amnesia
54. disturbance
55. system

Evaluation (Self-tests)

a. Fill-in-the-blanks Items

1. reverberating circuit (p. 272)
2. short (p. 272)
3. consolidation hypothesis
   (pp. 272-273)
4. memory (p. 273)
5. axon terminals (p. 274)

6. size, weight (pp. 244-275)
7. (neuro)transmitter/
   biochemical (p. 276)
8. synthesis (pp. 277-279)
9. brain (p. 283)
10. limbic system/hippocampus and
    amygdala (p. 282)

b. Matching Items: Correct order and page references are:

5 (p. 282); 3 (p. 269); 6 (p. 269); 7 (p. 271); 9 (p. 273);
1 (p. 274); 8 (p. 275); 2 (p. 279); 10 (p. 280); 4 (p. 282).

c. Multiple-choice Items: Correct answers and page references are:

1—a (p. 267); 2—b (pp. 270-271); 3—c (p. 274); 4—d (p. 282); 5—d (pp. 272-273);
6—a (p. 272); 7—a (p. 276); 8—b (p. 276); 9—c (pp. 276-277); 10—d (p. 283).

d. Short-answer Items: Page references for answer material are:

1. p. 274; 2. pp. 272-274; 3. pp. 274-275; 4. p. 283.

Unit 13

DEVELOPMENT OF THINKING AND LANGUAGE

1. INTRODUCTION TO STUDY OF THIS UNIT

Thinking was one of the topics regularly studied by early psychologists. The study of the mind was one of the principal objectives of these investigators, and introspection was the method they typically used. All sorts of studies, some quite exotic, were done, including analyses of problem solving, creativity, and the role of images in thinking. Needless to say, these efforts, based as they were on subjective methodology, were not warmly received by John Watson and his fellow behaviorists. Watson himself began to study thinking, attempting to test the hypothesis that thinking can occur only through behavior of the organism. The most likely site for such behavior is in the speech apparatus. Such studies were frustrating, and the results did not dissuade the subjectivists from the notion that ''pure'' thinking, with or without images, could occur. Watson gave up investigations of thinking, and this topic became the focus of relatively few researchers over the years, largely because it did not fit easily into the overwhelmingly behavioristic tradition that developed in psychology in the United States.

The more subjective tradition persisted in Europe, however, and studies on thinking continued there. Certainly one of the best known of those doing such research was Jean Piaget, a Swiss developmental psychologist at the University of Geneva for many years. Piaget's earliest publications in the 1920s were translated and began to have important influence in this country some years later, even though his studies did not meet the more rigorous methodological demands of most psychologists here. In them, Piaget outlined his theory of cognitive development, which was based on his meticulous observation of a small number of children, including his own. The basic aspects of his model are presented in the first part of this unit. It should be said that studies of thinking and cognitive development have flourished in this country in the past three decades, both because of Piaget's influence and because of the development of new methods that make more objective study possible.

The second part of this unit, which discusses some issues concerning the structure and development of language, reflects the fact that thinking and language have always been felt to be interrelated. Explanations of language development have typically stressed either an innate predispositional model or an experiential, learning one — the familiar nature-nurture controversy again. As in other instances of this controversy, many of them unproductively argumentative, there is evidence for both sides. The appropriate conclusion seems to be that both biological and experiential factors make essential contributions to the development of language.

2. ISSUES AND CONCEPTS

The most important concepts for you to learn in the first part of this unit are those relating to Piaget's theory of cognitive development. Know the definitions of the general developmental principles of organization, equilibration, and adaptation, and how these processes allow for assimilation and accommodation. Learn the four stages of cognitive development, roughly when they occur, what takes place in each, and how they are related to each other. Recent attempts to apply Piagetian theory to adults, including speculation about further development stages and about stage regression in older persons, should also be studied.

Remember that the age and stage proposals in Piaget's theory appear to generalize reasonably well to other cultures, though there are some cultural variations apparently associated with differential experiences. The role of training in developmental acceleration, or at least avoidance of developmental deficit, should be learned.

The basic principles of Bruner's theory of cognitive development, including the three modes of representing experience of the world — enactive, iconic, and symbolic — also should be learned. Be able to state several similarities between Piaget's and Bruner's models of cognitive development, as well as several differences.

The structure and development of language is treated in the second part of this unit. With respect to language structure, know what is meant by productive knowledge of language and the rules of phonology, morphology, syntax, and semantics, as well as how redundancy influences communication. With respect to language development, become familiar with the field of developmental psycholinguistics, how studies in this area, including studies of grammatical structure and context, are done, and what they mean. Be able to explain grammar development, including first words, word combinations, sentence-length limitation, and the construction of sentences phrase by phrase.

Be aware, as well, of the nature-nurture controversy regarding language development and at least two kinds of observations used to support each of these extreme positions. The attempts to teach various lower animals a form of language and of the successes and limitations of such studies should also be studied. At the conclusion of this part of the unit, you should appreciate the truth of the statement that both biological and experiential factors are essential contributors to language development.

3. UNIT REVIEW

Correct answers are given at the end of the unit.

Basic to Piaget's theory is the notion that mental growth depends on the interaction of the infant or child with the (1)_____. His theory encompasses three general developmental principles of organization. The first is the notion that mental elements, or (2)_____, become integrated into (3)_____ systems. The second principle, equilibration, states that structures are intrinsically motivated to function at a (4)_____ level. The third principle holds that (5)_____ results in the complex growth of mental structures. This latter process occurs through (6)_____, which accounts for the selective taking-in of information, and (7)_____, wherein new schemata are formed or old ones modified to create more complex new organizations.

According to Piaget, the stages of cognitive development are (8)_____ and hierarchical and are four in number. The first is the sensorimotor stage, which occurs from birth to about (9)_____ years of age. In it the infant develops the concept of an (10)_____, which at first is transient but later on becomes

(11)_____. By 18 months of age, the child appears to be able to think about things even when they are not (12)_____. The second stage is called the (13)_____ stage. In it, the child of from two to (14)_____ years of age is developing language rapidly. His or her view of reality is highly (15)_____. This is illustrated by the failure of the child to grasp the principle of invariance, or (16)_____—the notion that an object remains constant even though it goes through irrelevant but visible changes. Research reported in Box 13.1 suggests that some aspects of conservation may be grasped earlier than Piaget has suggested, at least under some circumstances. The third stage is called the (17)_____ stage and takes place from about seven years of age to (18)_____ or beyond. In it, conservation is mastered in a variety of contexts, usually with (19)_____ first, (20)_____ next, and (21)_____ last. The person begins to think as an adult but can only apply these cognitive abilities to (22)_____ objects and not to (23)_____ concepts. In the fourth stage, called the stage of (24)_____, which begins in (25)_____ and is completed in the late teens or later (or never), concrete operations are abandoned and abstract concepts, characteristic of (26)_____ thought, are developed.

In attempting to apply Piagetian theory to the adult, there is little evidence that additional stages, beyond the stage of (27)_____, are necessary to account for advanced types of thought, or that there is a stage of (28)_____ in the elderly.

The age and stage aspects of Piaget's model appear to apply rather well to cultures that have been studied. However, there is sufficient cultural variation — for example, in the Mexican children cited in Box 13.3 — to suggest that aspects of conservation are subject to (29)_____ modification. Recent attempts to accelerate development of cognition through training have produced important effects, but it is not known how (30)_____ the changes may be.

In a second cognitive developmental model, that of Jerome Bruner, mental life progresses from actions and percepts through images to symbolic manipulations. In the first stage of development, experience of the world is represented through an (31)_____ mode, which reflects an internal organization of (32)_____. The second way of representing knowledge is through an (33)_____ mode, which makes use of (34)_____. Both of these modes are used throughout life, but the first is more characteristic of the (35)_____ and the second of the child of (36)_____ years of age. In a third mode, called the (37)_____ mode, elements like (38)_____ are used to represent knowledge. In contrast to Piaget, Bruner emphasizes the (39)_____ values of different modes of representing experience and also the role of specific (40)_____. In addition, Bruner sees cognitive growth as determined

by the active use of (41)_____ while Piaget feels that the child's use of

language is determined by his or her level of (42)_____.

The fact that each of us uses oral language so readily implies that we are able to decode and encode

speech and that we use the basic rules of language. Such linguistic knowledge is (43)_____

for most of us. Since there is no limit to the number of new sentences that can be spoken and understood,

we must credit each person with (44)_____ of language, involving command

of the rules of phonology (or (45)_____), of (46)_____

(or word structure), of (47)_____ (or the order of words), and of semantics (or

the (48)_____); each person must also know something about the

(49)_____ pattern of his or her language. "Inefficiency" of language,

called (50)_____, may actually aid in communication since we do not have

to be aware of all elements in order to reach a reasonable understanding. (51)_____

are concerned with the learning and use of the structures and characteristics of adult language by children.

Early study of the development of language centered on the (52)_____

structure, but later study focused on what the child was doing and looked at language in

(53)_____. Findings about grammar include the fact that first words,

usually (54)_____, tend to occur between one and (55)_____

years of age. Word combinations are then discovered with the production of (56)_____-word

utterances. In the early days of language acquisition, there are sentence-length limitations, probably

based on limits associated with (57)_____. Later increases in length are

accomplished by constructing sentences (58)_____. The discovery of linguistic

universals has led to the suggestion that all children follow the same basic procedures in discovering the

structure of (59)_____ language.

Explanations of language development have emphasized the two extreme approaches, reflecting

the (60)_____ controversy. Proponents of innate theories stress evidence

based on (61)_____, while proponents of experience stress the likely involve-

ment of (62)_____, and the fact that even (63)_____ can

be taught the rudiments of language. Perhaps the best appraisal of this controversy at this time is that

both (64)_____ and (65)_____ factors

make essential contributions to the development of language.

4. THOUGHT QUESTIONS

a. To what extent is Piaget's theory of cognitive development limited in its generalizability since it is based on limited observations of a small number of children?

b. Assume that you are the teacher of a second grade class. Why would it be important for you to determine the stage of cognitive development of each of your pupils before you developed an appropriate curriculum of study? What would be the likely nature of the curriculum you finally develop?

c. Linguistic nativists feel that language structure and development are innate because several linguistic universals have been found. Knowing that human language is concerned with expressing things and action, is it surprising that such universals have been found? Does it necessarily imply the innateness of language systems? Explain.

d. Sarah, the chimpanzee at the University of Pennsylvania, is able to display a conservation ability level equal to that of a seven-year-old human but only a preoperational language level. What does this finding tell us about Piagetian developmental levels in the chimpanzee? In the human?

5. EVALUATION (SELF-TESTS)

Correct answers and text page references are given at the end of the unit.

a. Fill-in-the-blanks Items

Write the word(s) that best complete(s) the sentence in the space provided.

1. According to Piaget, new schemata are formed or old ones modified through a process called

   _____.

2. Object permanence first occurs in the _____ stage of the Piagetian

   model.

3. For Piaget, abstract thought first occurs in the _____ stage.

4. Bruner's theory differs from Piaget's largely in his emphasis on the _____

   value of cognitive development.

5. For Bruner, the most important mode of knowledge representation is

   _____.

6. Productive knowledge of language includes command of the rules of sound structure, or

   _____.

7. Productive knowledge of language also includes command of the rules of word meanings, or

   _____.

8. Language inefficiency that may aid the communication process is called _____.

9. For a young child, limitation in short-term memory probably is reflected in limitation of

   sentence _____.

10. Information about language universals has been used as the principal evidence in support of the

    _____ explanation of language development.

b. Matching Items

Write the number of the correct item from the right column in front of the matching item in the left column.

_____ Locke	1.	ordering of words
_____ Plato	2.	ability to think abstractly
_____ equilibration	3.	backs innate explanations
_____ preoperational stage	4.	tabula rasa
_____ formal operations	5.	age two to seven years
_____ enactive mode	6.	Piaget's theory of motivation
_____ decode speech	7.	sound structure
_____ syntax	8.	ideas are universally given
_____ phonology	9.	convert sounds into meanings
_____ nativist	10.	internal organization of motor acts

c. Multiple-choice Items

Circle the letter in front of the answer that best completes the stem.

1. In Piaget's theory, the selective taking-in of information is called:
   a. organization
   b. equilibration
   c. assimilation
   d. accommodation

2. In Piaget's theory, the formation of new schemata or the modification of old ones is done through:
   a. organization
   b. equilibration
   c. assimilation
   d. accommodation

3. In Piaget's theory, the stage at which one's view of reality is highly egocentric is the:
   a. sensorimotor stage
   b. preoperational stage
   c. concrete operations stage
   d. formal operations stage

4. In Piaget's theory, the stage at which conservation is mastered in most areas is the:
   a. sensorimotor stage
   b. preoperational stage
   c. concrete operations stage
   d. formal operations stage

5. In Bruner's theory, the mode of knowledge representation that makes use of images or pictures is the:
   a. enactive mode
   b. iconic mode
   c. symbolic mode
   d. adaptive mode

6. In Bruner's theory, the mode of knowledge representation that emphasizes motor acts is the:
   a. enactive mode
   b. iconic mode
   c. symbolic mode
   d. adaptive mode

7. For most of us, linguistic knowledge of the structure of our language is:
   a. implicit
   b. conscious
   c. written down
   d. impossible

8. The rule of language that refers to the structure of words is:
   a. phonology
   b. morphology
   c. syntax
   d. semantics

9. The branch of psychology concerned with the acquisition, structuring, storage, and use of knowledge is called:
   a. linguistics
   b. neurolinguistics
   c. experimental psychology
   d. cognitive psychology

10. The field of science concerned with the relationships between the brain and language development and use is called:
    a. linguistics
    b. neurolinguistics
    c. experimental psychology
    d. cognitive psychology

d. Short-answer Items

Answer the following questions with short, concise statements. Reference pages for the material are given at the end of the unit.

1. Contrast Piaget's theory of cognitive development with that of Bruner, specifying at least two similarities and two differences.

2. How can the data obtained from the case of Genie, the isolated child in Los Angeles, be used to refute, at least in part, those who propose that language development is innate?

3. What are the principal arguments that the nativists use to support their approach to language development?

4. Outline briefly one important criticism of the various studies attempting to teach chimpanzees a form of language.

ANSWER KEY FOR UNIT 13

Unit Review

1. physical world
2. schemata
3. larger
4. higher
5. adaptation
6. assimilation
7. accommodation
8. discrete
9. two
10. object
11. permanent
12. present
13. preoperational
14. (about) seven
15. egocentric/self-centered
16. conservation
17. concrete operations
18. adolescence
19. matter
20. weight
21. volume
22. concrete
23. abstract
24. formal operations
25. adolescence
26. adult
27. formal operations
28. regression
29. experiential
30. permanent
31. enactive
32. motor acts
33. iconic

34. images/pictures
35. infant
36. six/seven
37. symbolic
38. words
39. adaptive
40. training/teaching
41. language
42. cognitive growth
43. implicit/unconscious
44. productive knowledge
45. sound structure
46. morphology
47. syntax
48. meaning of words
49. intonation
50. redundancy
51. Psycholinguists
52. grammatical
53. context
54. nouns
55. two
56. two
57. short-term memory
58. phrase by phrase
59. any
60. nature-nurture
61. linguistic universals
62. learning
63. lower animals
64. biological
65. experiential

Evaluation (Self-tests)

a. Fill-in-the-blanks Items

1. accommodation (p. 293)
2. sensorimotor (p. 293)
3. formal operations (pp. 295–297)
4. adaptive (p. 300)
5. symbolic (p. 300)
6. phonology (p. 302)
7. semantics (p. 302)
8. redundancy (pp. 302–303)
9. length (p. 307)
10. innate (p. 308)

b. Matching Items: Correct order and page references are:

4 (p. 291); 8 (p. 291); 6 (p. 291); 5 (p. 294); 2 (pp 295–297);
10 (p. 300); 9 (p. 301); 1 (p. 304); 7 (p. 302); 3 (p. 308).

c. Multiple-choice Items: Correct answers and page references are:

1—c (p. 292); 2—d (p. 293); 3—b (p. 294); 4—c (p. 294); 5—b (p. 300);
6—a (p. 300); 7—a (p. 301); 8—b (p. 302); 9—d (p. 304); 10—b (p. 304).

d. Short-answer Items: Page references for answer material are:

1. pp. 291–301; 2. p. 311; 3. pp. 308–309; 4. pp. 313–314.

Unit 14

THE MEASUREMENT OF MENTAL ABILITIES

1. INTRODUCTION TO STUDY OF THIS UNIT

The study of individual behavioral differences, now called differential psychology, began systematically with the work of Sir Francis Galton in England. Galton was a gentleman scientist in the sense that he had no university appointment and was independently well-to-do. Throughout his life he collected a great deal of information on human differences in physical and sensorimotor dimensions. On one occasion he arranged for an anthropometric laboratory at an international exhibition, which allowed over 9,000 persons the privilege of paying a small amount to be measured in a variety of ways — certainly an interesting way to collect data! Galton felt that many important human characteristics, including intelligence, were inherited, and he wrote several treatises on the inheritance of genius. He gave us the twin-study method of investigating nature-nurture issues, and he also founded the human eugenics movement, which advocated restricted and selective breeding.

While Galton promoted intelligence theory and the use of statistical methods to assemble and process collected data, it was Alfred Binet in France who produced the first workable intelligence measuring device. An education commission in Paris had been given the task by the minister of public instruction to look into the special education problems of defective children. Could all children profit from the same educational system or should special courses of instruction be provided? First, one had to be able to differentiate those who could from those who could not so profit. The commission hired Binet to investigate the matter since he had already been studying higher mental functions in children. Binet and a colleague devised a test of general intelligence to aid the commission in differentiating the two groups. The test was the first successful measure of intelligence and became the prototype for most intelligence tests which followed. In this unit, you will learn generally about intelligence and its measurement, and how these measures relate to important aspects of human behavior, such as school success or occupational selection and success. Since the test movement in general, and especially intelligence measurement, has been criticized so vigorously of late, knowing just what is being measured and how well it is being accomplished is important. It should always be kept in mind throughout your reading that while you and many others for hundreds of years may have thought that intelligence referred to genetically determined adaptive characteristics, there is little evidence to suggest that this is what the modern IQ test measures.

2. ISSUES AND CONCEPTS

Focus early in this unit on why intelligence tests were developed, since this information reveals the applied nature of such measurement. Be aware of Binet's contribution and of the difficulty of defining intelligence, leading to the operational definition of intelligence as "what the intelligence test measures." Learn to distinguish the different kinds of mental tests (e.g., individual versus group) and the kinds of items included, along with the criteria for their selection. A test is usually standardized on the basis of large samples of relevant persons; learn how intelligence tests have been scored, from the mental-age approach of early Binet through the intelligence quotient of later Stanford-Binet to the more contemporary approach of comparing the performance of an individual with that of the standardization group (but still expressed usually as an IQ). Be able to contrast the Wechsler adult and children scales with the Binet type of scales. In assessing the advantages and disadvantages of group testing, learn the definitions of reliability and validity and know how they are measured, and be able to evaluate the validity of studies relating IQ to school and occupational performance.

Know why the Scholastic Aptitude Test was developed, how it was standardized, how it is scored, and how it relates to later educational performance. Is test or cultural bias involved in this test?

With respect to the development of intelligence, learn how age and intelligence are related, so that you can speak to the issue of how stable mental ability is across age and the general population, at least as measured typically by the IQ scale. Keep in mind that the IQ is not necessarily constant across time for any specific individual and that growing old does not necessarily bring on massive intellectual decline.

With respect to the stability and predictability of intelligence, it is important to recognize that the average smooth curve of development does not necessarily hold for any particular individual; that measures obtained early in life may not predict later performance well; that measures obtained for not-too-distant periods, especially after adolescence, are better predictors; and that some items may be better predictors across age than others. This latter point suggests that intelligence may not be a unitary trait.

Know the three points of view concerning the structure of intelligence and how intercorrelation of test scores and factor analysis helps to sort out the patterns involved and contributes to knowledge about intelligence structure. Be able to contrast the two-factor and the group-factor theories. Since overall intelligence may really reflect cognitive processing abilities, be able to relate this fact to what the IQ test measures. On the basis of your reading, you may well conclude, with the authors, that while mental tests can be criticized, they are useful predictors of some performance, and therefore should be used.

3. UNIT REVIEW

Correct answers are given at the end of the unit.

Intelligence tests have been developed and refined, among other reasons, to help separate intellectual from (1)_____ factors in assessing students and to avoid the mixed messages conveyed by school grades, which are assigned by schools having different (2)_____.
These tests were first developed in France by (3)_____ and were used to identify (4)_____ students.

Experts in psychological mental measurement, or (5)_____, have tried to define intelligence, without much general success. Many psychologists prefer the operational definition of intelligence as what the (6)_____ measures.

There are many different kinds of mental tests. They can be classified as individual versus (7)_____, (8)_____ versus power, or verbal versus (9)_____. These classifications are not (10)_____.

In developing an IQ test, the items selected should have something to do with (11)_____ and should satisfy several other criteria, including being in the (12)_____ of the person being tested, being interesting, not favoring or disfavoring any societal groups (a criterion called (13)_____), reflecting increasing ability with increasing (14)_____, and showing a positive relation to the (15)_____ mental-test score. To apply these criteria, the test developer collects relevant information from a large representative sample of persons (a process termed (16)_____) to ascertain if the test is (17)_____—that is, whether or not it measures what it is supposed to.

In scoring his intelligence test, Binet introduced the concept of the average age of those children who pass the same items, or (18)_____. Later he developed the notion of Intelligence Quotient (IQ), which is the ratio of mental age to (19)_____. This quotient must be 1.0 for the children of any particular age group in the standardization sample, and therefore average IQ must be (20)_____, since the quotient is multiplied by 100. Today test IQ is determined by comparing the test performance of the child with that of other children of the same (21)_____.

The Wechsler Intelligence Scales were initially developed as a test of intelligence for (22)_____, but they later added a test to measure intelligence in (23)_____. In these tests there are two broad subscales, (24)_____ and (25)_____, each represented by several subtests. A separate (26)_____ can be obtained for each subscale.

Group intelligence tests have been developed because they are less (27)_____ to administer than individual tests. They are good for screening large numbers of persons but provide less specific information than does (28)_____ testing.

The reliability of a test refers to the (29)_____ with which an individual repeats the same test performance, and it is very (30)_____ for the Stanford-Binet and Wechsler tests. Validity refers to the fact that the test measures (31)_____. It is usually measured by relating test scores to other measures of "intellectual" performance. These correlations turn out to be quite (32)_____. For example, IQ correlations with measures of school success and grades are positive and around 0.50, but they tend to get lower as educational level (33)_____. In addition, test scores of general intelligence correlate with most kinds of work proficiency, but such scores seem only to relate (34)_____ to occupational selection.

Another type of test of mental ability is the Scholastic Aptitude Test (SAT). While not designed as an IQ test, it has a similar format. In theory, this test measures (35)_____ rather than achievement and is based on the assumption that students taking it have had

(36)_____ past exposure. The mean score on this test is

(37)_____. SAT scores predict success in specific college courses

quite well but are less successful in predicting college (39)_____. A better

predictor of the latter is SAT score combined with (40)_____. The SAT has

been accused of being culturally biased and discriminating against some groups. An investigating

committee concluded that there was (41)_____ evidence for this kind of

unfairness, since SAT scores predict college grades (42)_____ for both

black and white students. However, high school GPA (43)_____ the college

performance of disadvantaged students, probably because of (44)_____ in

their high schools.

　　Investigations of the development of intelligence have related age and IQ. From early age to adolescence

IQ tends to (45)_____. To see what changes may occur in adult years, cross-

sectional studies have been done, but these tend to confound age with changing (46)_____.

Longitudinal studies, in which the (47)_____ are tested across time, reveal

that for some test items performance is maintained or may (48)_____ over

the years. This seems to be true for items that are highly (49)_____. Items

that measure performance, and especially speed of responding, tend to show (50)_____

with age. IQ score pattern has even been used to predict (51)_____ for older

persons who are in good health when tested. The conclusion to be reached about mental ability and aging is

that growing old does not necessarily bring on (52)_____.

　　Longitudinal studies have been made of the stability and predictability of intelligence. Test scores

over (53)_____ periods of time are fairly stable. Test scores derived

very early in life have (54)_____ predictive utility for most later periods.

Some items may predict better over longer periods than others, indicating that intelligence may not be

a (55)_____.

　　How many separate and distinguishable aspects of intelligence are there? There are three possible

answers to this question. The first is that intelligence is a (56)_____ trait;

the second that it is compounded of broad and relatively (57)_____ factors;

and the third, that it consists of many (58)_____ abilities. We use test

intercorrelations and a statistical reducing technique called (59)_____ to see

which of these different answers makes the most sense. Theories such as those of Charles Spearman,

called (60)_____ theories, and L. L. Thurstone, called

(61)_____ theories, emphasize either the unitary approach or the

specific-abilities approach, but in each both kinds of factors seem to be involved.

　　Cognitive processing abilities appear to be involved in effective mental functioning, and it may well

be these skills that determine (62)_____ intelligence, as measured by

IQ tests or the SAT.

Perhaps it is remarkable that we can predict other performances at all from test scores, at least for groups if not for (63)_____. Even though tests have been criticized, they are the most (64)_____ instruments available to contemporary psychology. As such, they should be used, but their limitations should be understood.

4. THOUGHT QUESTIONS

a. If you set out to develop a new IQ test, what would you do to make certain that your test was fair — that is, that it had no cultural, societal, age, or sex biases?

b. On what bases do you think that tests given to infants of six months of age can be referred to as "intelligence" tests? How can such labeling be defended?

c. How is the validity of a measure, such as an IQ test, ultimately determined? What is the typical procedure used, and who has the final say-so?

d. L. M. Terman found that high IQ children tended as adults to be stronger, healthier, more socially mature, less mentally ill, and so on, than adults whose IQs had been measured to be considerably lower as children. Are you surprised at such findings? Why should Terman really have expected these findings if he had had a better appreciation of cultural and societal differences and influences?

5. EVALUATION (SELF-TESTS)

Correct answers and text page references are given at the end of the unit.

a. Fill-in-the-blanks Items

Write the word(s) that best complete(s) the sentence in the space provided.

1. The definition of intelligence as what the intelligence test measures is an example of an _____ definition.

2. A mental test that has a time limit or on which time of response is measured is called a _____ test.

3. Items are selected for a mental test initially because they are _____ to the area to be measured.

4. For Binet, the intelligence quotient was MA/CA multiplied by _____.

5. If a test consistently gives the same, or nearly the same, score with several administrations to the same persons, we say that the test is _____.

6. If the test score correlates highly with other measures of the same general area, we say that the test is _____.

7. The SAT, at least in theory, is an aptitude test and not an _____ test.

8. The average score on the SAT is 500 while that on the Stanford-Binet is _____.

9. SAT scores predict college GPA more poorly than success in _____.

10. The best conclusion to be made about age and IQ is that mental decline _____ in old age.

b. Matching Items

Write the number of the correct item from the right column in front of the matching item in the left column.

_____ psychometrics	1. what you are trying to predict
_____ test fairness	2. predicts occupational success
_____ mental age	3. reduces the number of intercorrelations
_____ 100	4. mental measurement
_____ Wechsler	5. not biased in terms of group differences
_____ Bayley	6. average age of children who pass the same items
_____ Terman	7. test of infant development
_____ aptitude test	8. adult intelligence test pioneer
_____ criterion	9. study of the mentally gifted
_____ factor analysis	10. average performance on an IQ scale

c. Multiple-choice Items

Circle the letter in front of the answer that best completes the stem.

1. The type of mental test in which the difficulty of the tasks successfully completed determines the score is called a:
   a. speed test
   b. power test
   c. performance test
   d. group test

2. Which of the following is typically *not* a criterion for selecting a test item?
   a. younger children do as well with it as older children
   b. it is in the repertoire of the people taking the test
   c. it correlates positively with total test score
   d. it should be interesting

3. For Binet, the average age of those children who pass the same test items is called the:
   a. standardization age
   b. chronological age
   c. mental age
   d. ice age

4. The Wechsler scales contain two broad subscales:
   a. performance and power
   b. power and speed
   c. speed and verbal
   d. verbal and performance

5. The reliability of a test refers to its:
   a. measuring what it is supposed to
   b. measuring systematically
   c. consistency of measurement
   d. meaningfulness

6. The validity of a test refers to its:
   a. measuring what it is supposed to
   b. measuring systematically
   c. consistency of measurement
   d. meaningfulness

7. The IQ test is really an example of:
   a. a motor ability test
   b. an aptitude test
   c. an achievement test
   d. hereditary transmission

8. The SAT is supposed to be an example of:
   a. a motor-ability test
   b. an aptitude test
   c. an achievement test
   d. hereditary transmission

9. There is some tendency for elderly persons to do more poorly than younger persons on:
   a. power tests
   b. group tests
   c. verbal tests
   d. performance tests

10. Cross-sectional studies of age and IQ have tended to confound age with:
    a. changing moral values
    b. changing educational opportunities
    c. different motivation patterns
    d. different language standards

d. Short-answer Items

Answer the following questions with short, concise statements. Reference pages for the material are given at the end of the unit.

1. Why is it that holders of Ph.D. degrees have higher IQs than college graduates, who, in turn, have higher IQs than persons that stop their education after high school, and so on?

2. Why is it that correlation does *not* imply causation?

3. What does the fact that national SAT scores have dropped 50 points in recent years tell us about what kind of test it is?

4. Why does high school GPA *overpredict* the college performance of disadvantaged students?

ANSWER KEY FOR UNIT 14

Unit Review

1. motivational
2. standards
3. Binet
4. mentally deficient
5. psychometrics
6. intelligence test
7. group
8. speed
9. performance
10. independent
11. intellect
12. repertoire
13. test fairness
14. age
15. total
16. standardization
17. valid
18. mental age (MA)
19. chronological age (CA)
20. 100
21. age
22. adults
23. children
24. verbal
25. performance
26. IQ score
27. expensive
28. individual
29. consistency
30. high
31. what it is supposed to
32. high

33. increases
34. partly
35. aptitude
36. equal
37. 500
38. 100
39. GPA
40. high school GPA
41. no
42. equally well
43. overpredicts
44. lower standards
45. increase
46. educational opportunities
47. same persons
48. increase
49. verbal
50. decline
51. time of death
52. intellectual decline
53. short
54. little
55. unitary trait
56. general/unitary
57. independent
58. separate/discrete
59. factor analysis
60. two-factor
61. group-factor
62. verbal
63. individuals
64. valid

Evaluation (Self-tests)

a. Fill-in-the-blanks Items

1. operational (pp. 318–319)
2. speed (p. 320)
3. relevant (pp. 320–321)
4. 100 (pp. 322–323)
5. reliable (p. 324)
6. valid (p. 324)
7. achievement (pp. 326–327)
8. 100 (p. 323)
9. specific college courses (p. 328)
10. does not necessarily occur (pp. 330–331)

b. Matching Items: Correct order and page references are:

4 (p. 318); 5 (p. 320); 6 (pp. 321–322); 10 (p. 323); 8 (pp. 323–324); 7 (p. 324); 9 (p. 326); 2 (p. 327); 1 (p. 327); 3 (p. 333).

c. Multiple-choice Items: Correct answers and page references are:

1—b (p. 320); 2—a (pp. 320–321); 3—c (p. 321); 4—d (p. 323); 5—c (p. 324); 6—a (p. 324); 7—c (p. 325); 8—b (p. 327); 9—d (p. 331); 10—b (p. 330).

d. Short-answer Items: Page references for answer material are:

1. pp. 326–332; 2. p. 326; 3. pp. 328–329; 4. pp. 328–329.

Unit 15

VARIATIONS IN MENTAL ABILITIES

1. INTRODUCTION TO STUDY OF THIS UNIT

This unit is concerned with the assessment of the roles of heredity and environment in intellectual performance and with an examination of factors involved in maximizing the development of potential abilities. The first issue treated is another visit with our old acquaintance, the nature-nurture controversy. With respect to intellectual ability, the nativist would emphasize the role of inheritance, while the empiricist would emphasize the role of experience. The European tradition was largely nativistic. Thus, it is no surprise that the British researcher Sir Francis Galton, the originator of twin study for assessment of intellectual development, felt that intelligence was largely a matter of inheritance. The genius was born, not made. More recently, and also in England, Sir Cyril Burt has said much the same thing, supporting the claim with a great deal of data over many studies and years. As you will read, there is reason to question the validity of at least some of Burt's work. Indeed, some believe that much of his data came more from his mind than from his subjects.

While there are doubtless many believers in the importance of heredity in this country, the prevailing view here is that experience plays a far more important part in intellectual development than the nativistic position would suggest. The empiricist approach is a far more hopeful one since it allows for change and promotes social action. Much relevant social action has taken place in this country and elsewhere, and you will read about some of it in the latter part of the unit.

The nature-nurture controversy about intellectual development will probably continue, and for good reason. Most of the data used to forward one position or the other are correlational in nature or based on comparisons of groups assembled by other than random assignment. That is, the data are not experimentally derived. To do experiments on these issues, one would have to control carefully either the genetic or the experiential variable and vary the other systematically. This has not been done, nor is it likely to be done in the foreseeable future. Consequently, subjectivity, appeal to authority, and the weight of the evidence have largely determined the position of many on the issue. Until better, experimentally based evidence is available, perhaps it is wise to maintain a position that is open and that permits individual and group change. This is possible even if you feel, deep-down, that heredity is more important than environment in the determination of intellectual development.

2. ISSUES AND CONCEPTS

The first part of this unit is concerned with theoretical issues about the roles of heredity and environment in intellectual performance. Note the differences in IQ within groups, based largely on data derived from identical twins reared apart and comparisons of the IQs of biological and adopted children with those of their biological and adoptive parents. Be aware of selective placement as a possible explanation of findings. The definition of heritability is important, and you should learn how regression toward the mean occurs in IQ scores over generations. Evaluate the position of R. Herrnstein that if the environment is truly equal for all, then heredity will largely determine an individual's place in society.

With respect to differences in IQ between groups, it is important to realize that even if high heritability of IQ within groups does exist, this does not imply that any differences between or among groups are also due to heredity. The measured black-white difference in IQ is about 15 points, but heredity and environment are hopelessly confounded in this comparison, and you should understand why. Analyze the evidence based on transracial adoption and evaluate the generalization that differences within groups are greater than differences between groups. Socioeconomic differences are also related to IQ generally, but the text will acquaint you with the fact that children may be brighter or duller than their parents in any social, economic, or occupational grouping. There are sexual differences in intellectual test performance as well that you should become familiar with though interpretation of those data is highly speculative.

The second part of this unit is concerned with practical issues of changing academic performance. Study findings about the school desegregation program and its potential benefits are presented for your consideration, as are findings about compensatory education programs, especially Headstart, and their relationship to the regular school programs. The decline of SAT scores over the last dozen or so years, and over the entire distribution of scores, but especially verbal parts of the test, should be looked at and analyzed. You should also consider the influence of grade inflation on the use of tests, the recent decline in the writing ability of students, and the effectiveness of programs attempting to remedy educational deficits.

The text also touches on the importance of measured intellectual differences. After reading it, you should know the relationship between high IQ and SAT scores and academic success as well as employment opportunities.

Since studies of individual and group differences in intellectual ability are not typically accomplished in a laboratory or with tight experimental controls, you should realize at the end of this unit that alternative explanations of virtually all of the reported results are possible.

3. UNIT REVIEW

Correct answers are given at the end of the unit.

Concern with individual differences and group differences in intellectual performance is directed toward understanding the interacting roles of (1)_____ and (2)_____ and toward providing practical opportunities for individuals to maximize their own (3)_____ .

Identical twins reared apart show more similarity of IQ than fraternal twins reared (4)_____ , but not as high a similarity as (5)_____ reared together. The correlation between a child's IQ and that of either parent is about (6)_____ . The IQs of adopted children are more similar to the IQs of their adoptive parents than the IQs of unrelated children. This could reflect environmental influence or be the result of selective (7)_____ . The IQs of adopted children are more highly correlated with the educational level of their (8)_____ mother than with that of the adoptive mother. This finding supports a (9)_____ interpretation. However, the IQs of these children were considerably higher than those of their biological mothers, and this finding supports an

(10)_____ interpretation. Heritability refers to that portion of IQ due

to (11)_____ differences. Extreme variations in environmental conditions

can produce (12)_____ differences in IQ. Heredity and environment

interact so that children with a slight genetic advantage may be provided with more

(13)_____ opportunities. The IQs of children are usually closer to 100 than the

IQs of their parents, a phenomenon called (14)_____.

 If there is high heritability of IQ within groups, this does not imply that group differences are also due to

(15)_____. The IQ of the average white person is about

(16)_____ points higher than the average black in this country. The

school performance of black children is also very poor, but the factors of heredity and environment

are (17)_____. Studies of black children raised by white parents with high

IQs show the children to have (18)_____ IQs and to score

(19)_____ on tests of school achievement. Intellectual differences between

groups are less than such differences (20)_____ groups.

 There are large differences in IQ associated with social class. Higher IQs generally are found among

families of (21)_____ socioeconomic levels. Even if all had equal opportunity,

we would expect in each occupational group to find children who are (22)_____

than their parents and children who are (23)_____. Human equality of

opportunity best exploits the large potential of (24)_____ (see Box 15.8).

 The average IQ for males is 100 and for females (25)_____. However,

males do better than females on visual-spatial tasks, verbal reasoning, and (26)_____.

Females do better than males on spelling and (27)_____. On the SAT,

(28)_____ score about 50 points higher on mathematics and

(29)_____ on verbal tests. However, any interpretation of sexual differences

in intellectual performance is (30)_____.

 With respect to racial, socioeconomic, and sex differences in mental abilities, heredity and environ-

ment factors are (31)_____ in most studies.

 School desegregation was instituted largely because it was felt that schools for poor children were not

(32)_____ oriented. It had already been found that black children born in the

South but schooled in the North displayed higher (33)_____ than black

children educated in the South, and that these measures display higher values over a

(34)_____ in the North. The potential benefits of desegregation include

cultural understanding and also improved (35)_____ on the part of the

disadvantaged. Most studies indicate that performance after school desegregation

(36)_____.

Compensatory education programs represent attempts to provide additional or special instruction for groups not (37)_____ in the regular curriculum. A well-known example of this type of program is the (38)_____ Project. This program provided enriched preschool experiences to (39)_____ children. Immediate intellectual gains were reported, but they appeared to disappear after (40)_____ years of regular schooling. In this area it seems to be true that compensatory education gains are eradicated soon if not followed up by intensive enrichment programs in the regular (41)_____.

SAT scores have been used to compare the intellectual levels of students over a number of years. They have (42)_____ over the past dozen years or so. The decline has occurred over the (43)_____ of scores, and not just in the low-score area. It appears that all segments of society are placing less emphasis than formerly on (44)_____. The decline has been greater for (45)_____ than for (46)_____ parts of the SAT. At the same time, grade inflation has resulted in a greater (47)_____ on standardized tests for selection purposes. Along with the decline in SAT scores has been the decline in writing ability. Remedial programs at the college level seem to work for students who are only (48)_____ lacking in preparation.

Measured intellectual differences are important, even though high IQ or SAT scores do not guarantee cultural success, because employment potential, for example, seems to be related to (49)_____. The cultural answer to the problems of the disadvantaged seems to be (50)_____, but changes in programs meant to aid the disadvantaged will be complex.

It is important to keep in mind that most studies conducted on differences in intellectual ability have not been done in the (51)_____, nor have they had tight experimental (52)_____.

4. THOUGHT QUESTIONS

a. Herrnstein and others have said that if environment were really equal for all people, then heredity would determine a person's place in society. Do you think it is possible to equalize environment for everyone? Why or why not?

b. Are the differences observed between the mental abilities of males and females the result of genetic differences, as the sociobiologists and others think, or of environmental differences, as the women's liberation movement and others believe?

c. Within the school desegregation program, how can the problem of having great discrepancies in academic ability in the same class be avoided?

d. What practical suggestions can you assemble to counteract the decline in SAT scores among college applicants in this country?

5. EVALUATION (SELF-TESTS)

Correct answers and text page references are given at the end of the unit.

a. Fill-in-the-blanks Items

Write the word(s) that best complete(s) the sentence in the space provided.

1. Twins showing the greatest similarity of IQ are _____ and reared together.

2. The typical correlation of IQs among siblings is about _____.

3. That portion of IQ that is due to inherited differences is referred to as _____.

4. The children of genius parents are likely to have IQs that are _____.

5. In assessing the poor performance of blacks on IQ and school performance tests, heredity and environment factors are _____.

6. Those who do better on most verbal IQ tasks tend to belong to the _____ sex.

7. Those who do better on mathematics tests tend to belong to the _____ sex.

8. The expectation that the school performance of blacks after school desegregation would be improved generally has been _____.

9. The Headstart Project is an example of _____ programs.

10. Recent decreases in SAT scores have occurred for low scorers and also for _____ scorers.

b. Matching Items

Write the number of the correct item from the right column in front of the matching item in the left column.

_____ heritability	1. compensatory education program
_____ 0.5	2. average female IQ
_____ regression toward the mean	3. portion of IQ due to heredity
_____ 100	4. medical aptitude test
_____ sociobiologists	5. correlation of a child's IQ with that of the parents
_____ males	6. school desegregation ruling
_____ females	7. favor genetic explanations
_____ separate cannot be equal	8. do better on mathematics tests
_____ Headstart	9. children have lower or higher IQs than parents
_____ MCAT	10. do better on most verbal tests

c. Multiple-choice Items

Circle the letter in front of the answer that best completes the stem.

1. Which of the following show the lowest correlation of IQ scores?
   a. identical twins reared together
   b. identical twins reared apart
   c. fraternal twins reared together
   d. all of the above are about the same

2. The IQs of adopted children correlate most highly with the:
   a. educational level of the adoptive mother
   b. educational level of the biological mother
   c. occupational level of the adoptive father
   d. occupational level of the biological father

3. Heritability refers to that portion of intellectual ability due to:
   a. body structure
   b. early experience
   c. all experiences prior to maturity
   d. genetic factors

4. Regression toward the mean is always reflected by children having:
   a. higher IQs than their parents
   b. lower IQs than their parents
   c. higher or lower IQs than their parents
   d. IQs which are unrelated to those of their parents

5. The IQ of the average black person relative to the average white person in this country is:
   a. 15 points lower
   b. 15 points higher
   c. about the same
   d. not measurable

6. Virtually all studies attempting to assess hereditary and environmental contributions to the black-white IQ differences are:
   a. in agreement that the differences are due to heredity
   b. in agreement that the differences are due to environment
   c. in agreement that the differences are real
   d. confounded

7. Females do better than males on tests of:
   a. verbal reasoning and spelling
   b. spelling and vocabulary
   c. vocabulary and visual-spatial performance
   d. visual-spatial performance and verbal reasoning

8. Males do better than females on tests of:
   a. verbal reasoning and spelling
   b. spelling and vocabulary
   c. vocabulary and visual-spatial performance
   d. visual-spatial performance and verbal reasoning

9. Black children born in the South but educated in the North display _____ IQs relative to black children born and educated in the South.
   a. higher
   b. lower
   c. about the same
   d. a different pattern of

10. The Headstart Project is an attempt to provide enriched experiences to:
    a. infants
    b. preschool children
    c. elementary school children
    d. secondary school children

d. Short-answer Items

Answer the following questions with short, concise statements. Reference pages for the material are given at the end of the unit.

1. Define heritability and indicate how it is measured typically.

2. Provide an environmental explanation of why identical twins should have IQs that are very much alike.

3. How can selective placement of adopted children influence attempts to use these persons to assess the relative contribution of heredity and environment to intellectual ability?

4. What is the most likely explanation of the reported recent decline in SAT scores?

ANSWER KEY FOR UNIT 15

Unit Review

1. heredity
2. environment
3. potential
4. together
5. identical twins
6. 0.5
7. placement
8. biological
9. genetic
10. environmental
11. genetic
12. large
13. environmental
14. regression toward the mean
15. heredity
16. 15
17. confounded
18. above average
19. well
20. within
21. upper
22. brighter
23. duller
24. genetic diversity
25. 100
26. mathematics
27. vocabulary
28. males
29. slightly lower
30. highly speculative
31. confounded
32. academically
33. IQs
34. longer time
35. school performance
36. improves
37. doing well
38. Headstart
39. disadvantaged
40. one to two
41. school system
42. declined
43. entire distribution
44. intellectual achievement
45. verbal
46. mathematical
47. reliance
48. minimally
49. measured abilities
50. education
51. laboratory
52. controls

Evaluation (Self-tests)

a. Fill-in-the-blanks Items

1. identical (p. 343)
2. 0.5 (p. 343)
3. heritability (p. 347)
4. lower (p. 347)
5. confounded (pp. 349–351)
6. female (p. 354)
7. male (p. 354)
8. confirmed (pp. 356–358)
9. compensatory education (p. 358)
10. high (p. 359)

b. Matching Items: Correct order and page references are:

3 (p. 347); 5 (p. 343); 9 (p. 347); 2 (p. 354); 7 (p. 354);
8 (p. 354); 10 (p. 354); 6 (p. 357); 1 (p. 358); 4 (p. 362).

c. Multiple-choice Items: Correct answers and page references are:

1—c (p. 343); 2—b (p. 344); 3—d (p. 347); 4—c (p. 347); 5—a (p. 349);
6—d (p. 355); 7—b (p. 354); 8—d (p. 354); 9—a (pp. 356–357); 10—b (p. 358).

d. Short-answer Items: Page references for answer material are:

1. pp. 341–347; 2. pp. 341–343; 3. pp. 343–346; 4. pp. 359–362.

Unit 16

THINKING, PROBLEM SOLVING, AND DECISION MAKING

1. INTRODUCTION TO STUDY OF THIS UNIT

Analysis of the thought process began formally with the early Greeks. While Plato felt that ideas, and therefore manipulation of them, or thinking, existed at least somewhat independently of the direct experience of the organism, Aristotle proposed that thinking involved the association of ideas, which in itself was dependent on the experience of the organism. You will recall that the most fundamental statement that René Descartes, nearly 2,000 years after the early Greeks, could make about his existence was that he was able to think, and as such, there must be an organism to do the thinking.

For many years, aspects of the thought process have been used to differentiate the level of functioning of the human from that of lower animals. Needless to say, the human has made out rather well in these comparisons, perhaps only partly because the human was making the comparisons. Not too long ago, it was felt that lower animals, even other primates, were not able to think at all, and that examples of horses being able to solve mathematical problems were only training tricks. During this century, however, much information has been collected to demonstrate that lower animals, at least throughout the mammalian species, are able to combine information internally — that is, to think. They are also able to solve some problems, demonstrating "insight," and to make decisions by choosing from alternatives. These abilities appear to be limited when compared with the same abilities in the human, but keep in mind that the problems involved were structured by humans, and in human terms. That is, their solutions could be aided greatly by internal image manipulation, especially of words. Perhaps the imagery of lower animals is much more kinetic and available for the manipulation of ideas more relevant to the animal form. It has been said that a lower animal can think pretty well all the way to the mountain but not beyond it. Perhaps predicting what is on the other side of the mountain is expressly a human characteristic, but we do not know this to be so.

It is curious that for all the centrality of the issues of thinking for us, we know so little of the process. Part of our ignorance is due to the difficulty of the subject matter, and much of it is due to the subjective nature of most of the relevant inquiries. J. B. Watson had good reason to do battle with subjective analysis. Unfortunately his own "objective" analyses of thinking led him nowhere, and the topic was not pursued as vigorously as it should have been. It might be more fruitful to take the information derived from the subjective analyses — for example, the suggested problem-solving stages of preparation, incubation, illumination, and verification — as hypotheses to be tested by scientific procedures. Computers may aid us in processing the data of such investigations, but it is not likely that they will tell us how we think.

2. ISSUES AND CONCEPTS

First of all in this unit you should learn the definitions of, and be able to differentiate clearly, thinking, problem solving and decision making. You should also recognize that thinking is sometimes directed, sometimes uncontrolled, and sometimes autistic, and that any of these forms may be adaptive. Study the different ways that have been used to study the thought process. Be able to differentiate percept and image, but be able to describe also how they are alike. Language contributes to human silent thought and to communicative thought, but be aware that it seems not to be necessary for thinking and that our thought processes sometimes follow simple algebraic rules we have no awareness of following.

After reading the chapter, you should be able to differentiate between reproductive and productive thinking. One type of the latter kind of thinking is problem solving, and you should learn the three kinds of problems that have been studied in problem-solving research. Learn, too, the four stages that have been proposed for problem solving and the notions of funneling, functional fixedness, and *Einstellung*, or set. Be able to contrast the motivational and the behavioristic approaches to problem solving. You should also be able to describe the information-processing approach to problem solving, its relationship to computer processing of information, and the notion of artificial intelligence. The six practical suggestions provided to help you improve your problem-solving ability may indeed help you to do so if you learn them well.

Finally, after reading the chapter, you should be able to describe decision making. Learn the distinction between the normative and descriptive approaches to decision-making analysis and the definition of the concept of subjective expected utility. Most of us make use of a variety of heuristics, or shortcut strategies, in decision making rather than the utility model, and you should understand why this may be so after your reading. The three practical suggestions made for the improvement of your decision making at the end of the unit should also be studied.

3. UNIT REVIEW

Correct answers are given at the end of the unit.

Thinking is the internal manipulation of (1)_____ elements, such as images, concepts, and (2)_____, to represent aspects of reality. Thinking is the final stage in human cognitive development for Bruner and (3)_____. Thinking is sometimes controlled, sometimes uncontrolled, and sometimes (4)_____, or dominated by one's wants and feelings. It is possible that any of these thought forms can be (5)_____.

There are several ways to study thinking. Like Aristotle, we can look at our own (6)_____. In more contemporary times this might involve using Wilhelm Wundt's technique of (7)_____ in examining such images. However, if (8)_____ can occur, introspection would not be a very complete method. In addition, perhaps the introspectionist approach is too analytical, as the followers of (9)_____ psychology have claimed. Watson, of course, argued against any appeal to (10)_____ mental experience. Today it is possible to employ more (11)_____ methods in analyzing thought, and we can also make use of computer (12)_____.

Two kinds of mental elements make up a person's experience. The first are of objects that exist here and now in the physical world, called (13)_____, and the second of objects that are not immediately present, called (14)_____. The latter may focus on what we remember of an object, or our (15)_____, or it may focus on an object that never existed in the real world, so-called (16)_____. People differ greatly in the (17)_____ of their thinking; some experience highly detailed images, a phenomenon called (18)_____. People may also vary in the (19)_____ of their images or the degree to which the images are visual, auditory, and so on. In many respects percepts and images are (20)_____ and therefore may be confused. When a person thinks his or her images are percepts, we speak of (21)_____.

The elements used most frequently in thinking are (22)_____. While language appears to be helpful in thought, it does not appear to be (23)_____. Language in silent thought is abrupt, incomplete and relatively independent of the (24)_____; language in communicative thought, on the other hand, is more precise with attention paid to (25)_____. If the latter were not the case, there might be great difficulty in (26)_____. Sometimes our thought processes follow simple algebraic rules that we are (27)_____.

When thinking is directed toward reaching a solution, we refer to the process as (28)_____. Thinking that is highly imbued with memory is called (29)_____, while that which requires new and original solutions is called (30)_____. Problem solving is created when whatever is novel in it is so for the (31)_____ and not for all persons. Three types of problems have been examined in research on problem solving. The first, called problems of inducing structure, involves finding a (32)_____ that relates different elements. The second, called problems of transformation, involves the manipulation of objects to achieve a given end-state under certain restrictive (33)_____. The third, problems of arrangement, require the problem solver to rearrange elements, as in an (34)_____.

In his analysis of problem solving, Max Wertheimer emphasized the difference between rote memory and (35)_____ in productive thinking. Wolfgang Köhler, in studying problem solving in the chimpanzee, concluded that insight was a function of (36)_____. Four stages have been suggested for the problem-solving process, the first being (37)_____, the fourth being (38)_____, and the two in between being (39)_____ and (40)_____. Problem solving, it has been suggested, involves (41)_____, or narrowing from general to functional to specific solutions. Sometimes problem solving becomes difficult when an individual is inhibited in finding a new use of an object, a phenomenon called (42)_____. Difficulty may also arise because of *Einstellung*, or (43)_____ effects.

The contribution of motivation to problem solving can include the influence of actual or perceived (44)_____ on a decrease in intellectual performance. In addition, motivation may be so strong that it induces (45)_____, which may lead to a decrease in problem-solving ability. The relationship between motivation and problem-solving efficiency appears to be an (46)_____ U curve. As motivation increases, so does efficiency to an (47)_____, and then it decreases.

The behavioristic approach to problem solving emphasizes the stimuli, responses, and habits involved. One example is Harlow's (48)_____ observations.

The information-processing approach to problem solving emphasizes the flow of information through a (49)_____. Detailed computer programs are used to create (50)_____. A (51)_____ indicates the kinds of operations to be done and the sequence of them. It should not be thought that computers solve a problem in the same manner as do (52)_____. There may be important differences, for example, between the exhaustive search of the computer and the (53)_____ that humans use. In a sense, computer simulation may be a better example of (54)_____ than productive thinking. After all, the problem is also identified by a (55)_____.

Practical suggestions for improving problem-solving ability include trying out different (56)_____ arrangements of objects and events, taking a (57)_____, working on a (58)_____ problem, trying a different (59)_____ of the parts of the problem, not becoming too attached to (60)_____ method of attack, and thinking of different (61)_____ of objects.

In decision making we make a choice from (62)_____ or more alternatives and should anticipate the (63)_____ of each selection. The normative approach to the study of decision making is an attempt to find out how to make (64)_____ decisions. Its goal is to choose an alternative that (65)_____ an individual's values. The descriptive approach is designed to study how people actually (66)_____ decisions. One illustration of the normative approach is based on rationality and consistency. In it personal and subjective values are referred to as (67)_____, and the basic idea is that the rational person will make a decision that (68)_____ the subjective expected value, thus yielding the greatest (69)_____. Do people actually follow the SEU, or (70)_____, model? The results of studies appear to be mixed. A good deal of evidence suggests that many people instead use simple, shortcut methods, called (71)_____, in order to ease the strain of making (72)_____ decisions.

We should try to reach better decisions without so complicating the task that it becomes (73)_____ to reach any decision at all. Ways to do this include sketching out the (74)_____, placing emphasis on the (75)_____ effects of important choices, and trying to take into account the relativity of (76)_____.

4. THOUGHT QUESTIONS

a. Do you think that the role of images in thought may be related to what someone is thinking about? Perhaps some thinking involves few images because few images exist for the relationship thought about, while other thinking involves many images because the object, event, or relationship is more common to experience. Evaluate this notion.

b. A mental set, or *Einstellung*, may cause us at times to use indirect solutions to some problems. Is it possible that sets may contribute to very efficient problem solving as well? Why or why not?

c. What kinds of instructions would you provide your subjects if you wished to reduce the amount of functional fixedness in their problem-solving efforts?

d. Do you think it will ever be possible to produce computers that can engage in productive as well as reproductive thinking? Why or why not?

5. EVALUATION (SELF-TESTS)

Correct answers and text page references are given at the end of the unit.

a. Fill-in-the-blanks Items

Write the word(s) that best complete(s) the sentence in the space provided.

1. Autistic thinking refers to thinking that is dominated by _____ wants _____ and _____ feeling _____ .

2. The two kinds of mental elements involved in thinking are _____ percepts _____ and images.

3. Those who have highly detailed images are referred to as having _____ eidetic _____ imagery.

4. Communicative thought involves _____ precise _____ language.

5. Reproductive thought is thought based largely on _____ memory _____ .

6. The third stage of the four proposed for problem solving is _____ illumination _____ .

7. Functional fixedness refers to the inhibitions a subject experiences in finding a _____ new use _____ for an object.

8. *Einstellung* means the same as mental _____ set _____ .

9. The "thinking" of computers might best be described as _____ reproductive _____ thinking.

10. Rather than follow utility models of decision making, humans tend to employ _____ short cut _____ models.

b. Matching Items

Write the number of the correct item from the right column in front of the matching item in the left column.

2	hallucination	1. rote memory
5	silent thought	2. thinking an image is a percept
6	communicative thought	3. personal or subjective value
8	productive thinking	4. behavioristic approach to thinking
1	reproductive thinking	5. language deficient in grammar
9	GPS	6. grammatical language
10	incubation	7. narrowing of solutions to problem
7	funneling	8. creative problem solving
4	learning how to learn	9. artificial intelligence computer program
3	utility	10. second stage of problem solving

c. Multiple-choice Items

Circle the letter in front of the answer that best completes the stem.

1. Realistic thinking is illustrated by:
   a. controlled thinking
   b. uncontrolled thinking
   c. autistic thinking
   d. good thinking

2. Images representing an object that never existed in the real world are called:
   a. memory images
   b. eidetic images
   c. vivid images
   d. created images

3. The images people create differ greatly in:
   a. naturalness and vividness
   b. vividness and quality
   c. quality and subjectiveness
   d. subjectiveness and naturalness

4. Which word describes the relationship of language to thinking?
   a. necessary
   b. helpful
   c. hindrance
   d. independent

5. Language in silent thought is:
   a. precise and grammatical
   b. grammatical and incomplete
   c. incomplete and abrupt
   d. abrupt and precise

6. Manipulating objects following restrictive rules is an example of:
   a. problems of inducing structures
   b. problems of arrangement
   c. problems of transformation
   d. problems of simulation

7. Narrowing possible solutions to problems from general to functional to specific is called:
   a. simulation
   b. *Einstellung*
   c. functional fixedness
   d. funneling

8. Computer simulations of the thought process may be examples of:
   a. learning how to learn
   b. incubation
   c. productive thought
   d. reproductive thought

9. Figuring out how to make good decisions illustrates the:
   a. normative approach
   b. descriptive approach
   c. motivational approach
   d. behavioristic approach

10. The shortcut, intuitive decision-making methods humans use are called:
    a. decision trees
    b. heuristics
    c. SEU approaches
    d. anagrams

d. Short-answer Items

Answer the following questions with short, concise statements. Reference pages for the material are given at the end of the unit.

1. Define and contrast percepts and images.

2. Describe the relationship between language and thought.

3. Contrast the motivational and behavioristic approaches to problem solving.

4. Describe the subjective expected-utility approach to decision making.

ANSWER KEY FOR UNIT 16

Unit Review

1. symbolic
2. words
3. Piaget
4. autistic
5. adaptive
6. private experience
7. introspection
8. imageless thought
9. Gestalt
10. subjective
11. objective
12. simulation
13. percepts
14. images
15. memory image
16. created images
17. vividness
18. eidetic imagery
19. quality
20. alike
21. hallucinations
22. words
23. necessary
24. rules of grammar
25. grammar
26. communication
27. unaware of
28. problem solving
29. reproductive
30. productive
31. individual
32. pattern
33. rules
34. anagram
35. structural understanding
36. perceptual reorganization
37. preparation
38. verification
39. incubation
40. illumination
41. funneling
42. functional fixedness
43. set
44. failure
45. stress
46. inverted
47. optimal point
48. learning-how-to-learn
49. system
50. artificial intelligence
51. flow chart
52. humans
53. shortcuts
54. reproductive
55. human
56. spatial
57. break
58. related
59. sequence
60. one
61. uses
62. two
63. consequences
64. good
65. optimizes
66. make
67. utility
68. maximizes
69. utility
70. subjective expected utility
71. heuristics
72. complex
73. impossible
74. problem
75. long-range
76. value experiences

Evaluation (Self-tests)

a. Fill-in-the-blanks Items

1. wants, feelings (p. 367)
2. percepts (pp. 368-369)
3. eidetic (p. 369)
4. precise (p. 373-374)
5. memory (p. 375)

6. illumination (p. 378)
7. new use (p. 380)
8. set (p. 381)
9. reproductive (p. 385)
10. heuristic/shortcut (p. 388)

b. Matching Items: Correct order and page references are:

2 (p. 369); 5 (pp. 373-374); 6 (pp. 373-374); 8 (p. 375); 1 (p. 375);
9 (p. 375); 10 (p. 377); 7 (p. 379); 4 (p. 382); 3 (p. 387).

c. Multiple-choice Items: Correct answers and page references are:

1—a (p. 366); 2—d (p. 369); 3—b (p. 369); 4—b (pp. 369-374); 5—c (pp. 373-374);
6—c (p. 375); 7—d (p. 379); 8—d (p. 385); 9—a (p. 386); 10—b (p. 388).

d. Short-answer Items: Page references for answer material are:

1. pp. 368-369; 2. pp. 369-374; 3. pp. 381-382; 4. pp. 387-388.

Unit 17

PHYSIOLOGICAL BASES OF THE HIGHER MENTAL PROCESSES

1. INTRODUCTION TO STUDY OF THIS UNIT

The goal of this unit is to describe bodily structures and processes involved in experience and behavior. For a good many years it has been assumed that higher mental functioning in the human was mediated by the central nervous system. This assumption appeared to derive support from a comparison of the brains of humans with those of lower animals. For example, the rat brain seemed to be entirely devoted to sensory and motor functioning, while that of the monkey had some "silent" tissue left over. The human had a large amount of tissue that was not mediating sensory and motor functions. Thus, it became common to identify the intellectual superiority of the human with the total amount of silent tissue (or association areas, in the terminology of information processing) in the brain or with a ratio of the silent tissue to the amount of sensory or motor tissue. Again, humans selected a feature for comparison that would favor humans over the lower animals, although we face stiff competition from some of the aquatic mammals in this case.

Much of the information we have about the role of neural tissue in important behavioral functions comes from cortical localization studies, which have been conducted for well over 100 years and are closely identified with the histories of physiology and medicine. The earlier crude methods of Gall and Spurtzheim of associating behavioral functioning with brain development based on cranial bumps (remember phrenology?) were replaced by direct intervention methods with lower animals and more precise observations in humans. Findings seemed to depend to a large extent on the level of animal used in the specific study. Karl Lashley used the rat as the subject of his important studies and found that the specific locus of damage was much less crucial than the amount of damage. This led to his specification of the principle of equipotentiality, which simply says that one part of the brain is interchangeable with any other part for some functions. But since the rat brain he studied is almost entirely sensory and motor in function, and most learning tasks are sensory and motor in nature for the rat, Lashley's observation is not at all surprising. However, this principle does not hold for the human brain, where a good deal of localization of function has been demonstrated.

You should keep two things in mind while reading this unit. First, much of the data in the first half of the unit is based on lower animal research, and we do not know to what extent we can generalize this information to the human level. Second, although we have learned much about sensory and motor functioning in the human brain we still know woefully little about the mediation of higher mental functions and the role of association cortex in them.

2. ISSUES AND CONCEPTS

We assume that the cerebral cortex is the center of human intellectual functioning, and the text presents the historical argument that pitted localized mediation against nonlocalized mediation of such functioning, which you should study. (Learn the definition of potentiality while studying that.) Learn as well why we call some cortex association cortex, the location and function of the primary and secondary visual cortex, the effects of damage to the inferotemporal area, and the connections of this area to limbic structures and back to sensory cortex (in addition to the possible functions of these connections). Be able to differentiate the sensory-perceptual and the perceptual-memory views of the functioning of this tissue. The two major similarities and differences between the visual system and the auditory and somatosensory systems should also be mastered. In addition, you should study the interesting multimodal area in the posterior parietal lobe.

Become familiar with how damage to the frontal association area affects delayed responses in lower animals and how such damage may be related to memory, perseveration, and emotionality.

Keep in mind, as you are reading, where most of the information on human brain functioning was derived and some of the problems with those sources. When you are finished, be able to define each of the aphasias and describe how the two hemispheres of the brain relate to language functioning. Remember that dyslexia and minimal brain dysfunctioning have not been associated with any brain abnormality. Learn about the phenomenon of neglect and the two types of agnosia. Study the three functions for which there is evidence of frontal lobe involvement, but keep in mind that there have been many more functions "localized" there for which there is little supporting evidence. The involvement of the left hemisphere in verbal functions and the right in spatial functions should also be noted.

Learn a definition of mental retardation, and appreciate that this disturbance may be due to genetic factors or to environmental factors. Be able to point to specific examples of the two types of mental retardation. Be aware that in many cases of retardation the causes are unknown and that there is no clear indication of neurological changes. Remember, finally that there is no known anatomical or biochemical factor that is known to correlate with intelligence.

3. UNIT REVIEW

Correct answers are given at the end of the unit.

Neuroscientists assume that the (1)_____ is the center of human intellectual

functions. Lashley's notion of (2)_____ suggests that localization of function

in the brain is nonspecific as to area and functioning related only to the (3)_____

of cortex. More recent explanations have emphasized greater (4)_____,

especially for the human brain. Cortex that is not primarily involved in sensory or motor functioning is called

(5)_____.

Within the posterior cortex of the monkey are areas that are (6)_____ for

vision, audition, and so on. In the visual cortex are the primary sensory area and secondary sensory area,

which also has input from the subcortical (7)_____. This secondary area

appears to mediate visual-perceptual functions such as color, movement, and (8)_____.

Lesions to the inferotemporal area may lead to profound disturbance on learning tasks involving

(9)_____ information, although monkeys with such lesions perform

normally on (10)_____ or (11)_____ learning

tasks. Two hypotheses have been offered to account for the normal functioning of this region. The first

suggests that the area is involved in putting together visual information to form a perception of an object (called the (12)_____ view), while the second suggests that this is an area where stimulation converges from many different parts of the field (called the (13)_____ view). The inferotemporal region may send information to (14)_____ structures for motivation associations and does feed back to sensory cortex, thereby influencing sensory responses to an (15)_____.

The auditory and the somatosensory systems are similar to the visual system in that they each have a primary sensory area that receives input from the receptor and also a (16)_____ that receives input from the primary area and from (17)_____. On the other hand, damage to the primary auditory area has (18)_____ effect than damage to the primary visual area, and the somatosensory system has (19)_____ different sensation modalities at the primary cortical level rather than (20)_____. A multimodal area in the posterior parietal region appears to provide a possible (21)_____ among visual, tactual, and motor activity.

Lesions of the frontal association cortex in primates do not affect learning of individual discrimination problems but do produce disturbances on (22)_____ tasks. This has been explained in terms of a loss in (23)_____ memory and also a loss of flexibility in behavior, called (24)_____. Frontal cortex receives impulses from (25)_____ of the sensory systems and also has rich connections to the limbic system, which may be involved in (26)_____.

Information on human brain function usually comes from persons who suffer lesions because of disease or the attempt to control disease or who experience brain damage accidentally. Such damage can produce a disturbance of language ability, called (27)_____. The damage is usually in the (28)_____ hemisphere, especially in (29)_____ -handed persons. Recent research also indicates a higher cortical/subcortical tissue ratio in the (30)_____ hemisphere. In Broca's aphasia there is a disturbance in (31)_____ speech while there remains fairly good (32)_____. The basic loss may be in grammatical structure, and the disturbance has been called (33)_____ aphasia. The lesion here is usually in the (34)_____ lobe. In Wernicke's aphasia there is much disturbance in speech (35)_____; analysis indicates that the trouble is with the meaning of words, and this has been called (36)_____ aphasia. The lesion here is found frequently in the (37)_____ lobe.

Experiments with split-brain subjects and observations with children indicate that both hemispheres are involved in language until about (38)_____ years of age in normal development, and after this the (39)_____ hemisphere loses most of this function.

Certain brain injuries can produce an inability to read, called (40)_____, or an inability to write, called (41)_____. No brain abnormality has been established for (42)_____, in which a person does not learn to read at a normal rate. The term (43)_____ has been used to describe this condition, even though no (44)_____ has been discovered to exist.

Brain damage can produce unilateral (45)_____, in which the person is unresponsive to stimuli presented to the side opposite that on which a (46)_____ exists. Cerebral damage may also lead to an inability to recognize formerly familiar objects, a condition called (47)_____. A special form of this condition involves an inability to recognize persons formerly familiar to one, called (48)_____.

Humans with frontal lobe damage do not share with monkeys the difficulty of (49)_____. With such damage in humans there seems to be an enhanced tendency to (50)_____; the affected individuals do less well on tests involving dependence on proper orientation and (51)_____, and on preparing for (52)_____ responses.

The left hemisphere seems to be more important for (53)_____ functions and the right for (54)_____ functions. We do not yet know if other functions can be ascribed to the two hemispheres.

Mental retardation refers to a performance in intellectual functioning that is (55)_____. Some conditions, such as Down's syndrome, are attributable to (56)_____ etiology. Other conditions, including malnutrition, oxygen deficiency, and the like, result from (57)_____ factors that can cause retardation. The causes of most cases of diagnosed retardation are unknown; where there is no clear indication of neurological changes associated with the condition, the retardation is referred to as (58)_____.

Summing up, there is no known anatomical or biochemical factor that is known to correlate with (59)_____.

4. THOUGHT QUESTIONS

a. Why do you think that the term minimal brain dysfunction has been coined to describe a group of disorders, including dyslexia, for which no brain abnormality has been established?

b. Do you believe that the development of some forms of psychosurgery on humans on the basis of reports of reduced emotional reactivity in apes after frontal lobe damage represents a rather large jump from laboratory knowledge to field application? Why or why not?

c. Much of our knowledge of human brain functioning is derived from subjects whose brains had been diseased for years before surgical lesioning occurred. How can this fact influence the findings of such research? How can better human information be obtained ethically?

d. It is an entertaining notion that one side of the brain is rational and the other side is intuitive. What kinds of evidence would we need to support these opinions?

5. EVALUATION (SELF-TESTS)

Correct answers and text page references are given at the end of the unit.

a. Fill-in-the-blanks Items

Write the word(s) that best complete(s) the sentence in the space provided.

1. Association cortex is not primarily involved in _____*sensory*_____ or motor functioning.

2. Visual-perceptual functions, including the perception of color and movement, are mediated by the _____*secondary*_____ visual cortex.

3. Ability on learning tasks involving visual information is profoundly disturbed in monkeys by lesions in the _____*inferotemporal*_____ area.

4. An area that may provide for a linkage among visual, tactual, and motor activities exists in the _____*parietal*_____ lobe.

5. Delayed-response ability has been greatly disturbed in monkeys by lesions in the _*frontal*_ lobe.

6. Language disturbances in the human typically are produced by damage in the _____*left*_____ hemisphere.

7. Broca's aphasia usually is produced by damage to the _____*frontal*_____ lobe.

8. Wernicke's aphasia is usually produced by damage to the _____*temporal*_____ lobe.

9. Neglect is defined as a difficulty in _____*attention*_____ .

10. Genetic involvement in Down's syndrome is indicated clearly since persons suffering from it have an extra _____*chromosome*_____ .

b. Matching Items

Write the number of the correct item from the right column in front of the matching item in the left column.

_10_ multimodal area	1.	inability to recognize familiar objects
_3_ cross-modal transfer	2.	inability to be flexible
_2_ perseveration	3.	disrupted by a frontal cortex lesion
_9_ aphasia	4.	inattention
_8_ alexia	5.	language functions
_1_ agnosia	6.	IQ well below average
_4_ neglect	7.	spatial functions
_5_ left hemisphere	8.	inability to read
_7_ right hemisphere	9.	language disturbance due to brain damage
_6_ mental retardation	10.	posterior parietal region

c. Multiple-choice Items

Circle the letter in front of the answer that best completes the stem.

1. The secondary visual cortex receives input from:
   a. the retina and the primary visual cortex
   b. the primary visual cortex and the superior colliculus
   c. the superior colliculus and the frontal lobe
   d. the frontal lobe and the retina

2. Which of the following is *not* true if one compares the auditory system and the visual system?
   a. Damage to the primary cortex has much less effect on one.
   b. Each receives input from the thalamus.
   c. Each has a secondary area.
   d. There is a primary sensory area in the cortex for each.

3. The results of the delayed-response studies suggest that frontal association cortex may mediate:
   a. sensory memory
   b. short-term memory
   c. long-term memory
   d. permanent memory

4. The frontal cortex receives impulses from all of the:
   a. spinal nuclei
   b. thalamic nuclei
   c. sensory systems
   d. perceptual systems

5. In left-handed persons, aphasia results from lesions in the left hemisphere:
   a. in all cases
   b. in about 25 percent of the cases
   c. in about 50 percent of the cases
   d. in about 75 percent of the cases

6. Inability to read due to brain damage is called:
   a. alexia
   b. agraphia
   c. dyslexia
   d. neglect

7. Brain damage may lead to inattention, also called:
   a. alexia
   b. agraphia
   c. dyslexia
   d. neglect

8. No brain abnormality has been found for which of the following?
   a. alexia
   b. agraphia
   c. dyslexia
   d. neglect

9. Which of the following conditions has *not* been associated with frontal lobe disturbance?
   a. Wernicke's aphasia
   b. perseveration
   c. organization of voluntary responses
   d. emotionality

10. The right hemisphere has *definitely* been shown to be involved in the mediation of:
    a. verbal functions
    b. rational functions
    c. intuitive functions
    d. spatial functions

d. Short-answer Items

Answer the following questions with short, concise statements. Reference pages for the material are given at the end of the unit.

1. What are two difficulties of generalizing the observations made from lesion experiments on lower animals to human brain functioning?

2. Contrast the sensory-perceptual view with the perceptual-memory view of the functioning of the posterior association cortex.

3. Specify two similarities between the functioning of the visual system and that of the auditory and somatosensory systems.

4. Compare the functioning of the monkey and the human on delayed-response tasks after frontal lobe damage.

ANSWER KEY FOR UNIT 17

Unit Review

1. cerebral cortex
2. equipotentiality
3. amount
4. specificity/localization
5. association cortex
6. modality specific
7. superior colliculus
8. distance
9. visual
10. tactual
11. auditory
12. sensory-perceptual
13. perceptual-memory
14. limbic
15. incoming stimulus
16. secondary sensory area
17. subcortical nuclei/areas
18. less
19. three
20. one
21. linkage
22. delayed-response
23. short-term
24. perseveration
25. all
26. emotionality
27. aphasia
28. left
29. right
30. left
31. spontaneous
32. understanding
33. syntactic
34. frontal
35. comprehension
36. semantic
37. temporal
38. ten
39. right
40. alexia
41. agraphia
42. dyslexia
43. minimal brain dysfunction
44. brain damage
45. neglect
46. lesion
47. agnosia
48. prosopagnosia
49. delayed response
50. perseverate
51. motor control
52. voluntary
53. verbal
54. spatial
55. well below normal
56. genetic
57. environmental
58. spontaneous
59. intelligence

Evaluation (Self-tests)

a. Fill-in-the-blanks Items

1. sensory (p. 396)
2. secondary (p. 396)
3. inferotemporal (pp. 398–399)
4. parietal (p. 400)
5. frontal (pp. 400–402)
6. left (p. 403)
7. frontal (p. 403)
8. temporal (p. 403)
9. attention (p. 407)
10. chromosome (p. 412)

b. Matching Items: Correct order and page references are:

10 (p. 400); 3 (p. 401); 2 (p. 402); 9 (p. 403); 8 (p. 406);
1 (p. 407); 4 (p. 407); 5 (pp. 405–411); 7 (p. 411); 6 (p. 412).

c. Multiple-choice Items: Correct answers and page references are:

1—b (p. 396); 2—a (pp. 399–400); 3—b (p. 402); 4—c (p. 402); 5—d (p. 403);
6—a (p. 406); 7—d (p. 407); 8—c (p. 406); 9—a (pp. 402–404); 10—d (p. 411).

d. Short-answer Items: Page references for answer material are:

1. pp. 395–396; 2. pp. 398–399; 3. pp. 399–400; 4. pp. 407–410.

Unit 18

HUMAN MOTIVATION

1. INTRODUCTION TO STUDY OF THIS UNIT

Conceptions of human motivation have varied greatly over the years, and you will read of several possible approaches that have been suggested. One of the earliest is allied somewhat to the view of fatalism presented in the text. There was a tendency in early times, perhaps dating back even to prehistoric days, for humans to attribute their own experience and behavior — and much more likely, that of fellow humans — to forces outside of their own experience, that is, to supernatural forces. This kind of causal attribution probably was especially invoked to explain more extreme behaviors, such as those associated with emotional disturbance today. Why did *X* attack his former companions without warning? Why did *Y* not share his hunt with others? The answer probably was stated, at least sometimes, in terms of magical and foreign forces that had invaded *X* and *Y* and taken control of their experience (mental processes) and behavior. Here was a neat, complete, and irrefutable explanation of motivated behavior. Prehistoric skills have been found with evidence of trephine holes in them, suggesting that attempts to exorcise such "evil" forces may have taken place long before lobotomy was ever contemplated.

Obviously, this kind of attempt to explain motivated behavior was prescientific, because it occurred so many years ago. It is also antiscientific, and it continues to occur today. When we concoct "scientific" explanations of motivated behavior in terms of untestable hypotheses and undefined constructs, and offer irrefutable theories, we are being every bit as unscientific as our early predecessors. There appears to be a greater tendency to do just this in certain areas of the field of psychology than in others, and motivation is one of them.

This unit presents theoretical approaches that appear to be attractive because they seem to make sense, and some that appear so, not just for this reason, but because they have led to the collection of considerable data, most of it consistent with the model. Thus, the tension-decrease and tension-increase models have much evidence to support aspects of each, while Abraham Maslow's need-hierarchy approach has not led to a great deal of data collection itself, and its merits therefore are based on the merits of other models for which data are available or else on the wish of many that such a schema were "true." In motivation, as in all other areas of psychology, we must be more attracted to those concepts and theories that are supported by the greatest amount of objectively collected data.

2. ISSUES AND CONCEPTS

In reading this chapter, you should learn, first of all, acceptable definitions of motive and motivation, and how motivation and all of the other areas of the field of psychology are related. Five broad theoretical approaches to the explanation of human motivation are presented. Be able to describe each one in brief detail and to list their similarities and differences.

Motivation as a biological deficiency has been researched a great deal over the years. Tissue needs, drives, and the principle of homeostasis are key concepts of this approach that you should know. In addition, be able to offer at least two criticisms of this approach.

Regarding the abundancy approach to motivation, which stresses tension increase and the apparent need for stimulation, be able to explain how arousal is elicited and its possible relationship to uncertainty.

Be aware that Maslow's need-hierarchy theory is an attempt, at least in part, to integrate aspects of the tension-increase and tension-decrease models of motivated behavior. You should also learn the basic structure of the model and the relationships among the different levels.

The unit deals next with how the phenomenon of learned helplessness has been produced in the laboratory and how it has been related to attribution theories of motivation. Study this approach, and learn the three basic dimensions of perceived causality, an important part of a recent attribution model.

You should then consider how conflicting motives may relate to motivated behavior, the notion of valence, and how conflicting notions may be positively valenced (attractive) or negatively valenced (repelling). Learn the characteristics of the three conflict paradigms presented: approach-avoidance, approach-approach, and avoidance-avoidance.

Frustration is another important topic. Learn the two meanings of frustration and have a clear notion of the frustration-aggression hypothesis. Be able to cite at least two effects of frustration.

Finally, we evaluate incentives in accordance with certain relational characteristics of our perceptions of them, and you should learn what these appear to be. Be able to describe how social reinforcers typically operate as incentives for human behavior.

3. UNIT REVIEW

Correct answers are given at the end of the unit.

The concept of motivation is used to explain how behavior is (1)_____,
energized, and directed toward some (2)_____.

Five broad conceptions of human nature take different approaches to understanding human motivation. One approach suggests that all living organisms are basically (3)_____,
to be understood as automatic mechanisms. This assumes that events are predictable on the basis of knowledge of their antecedents, a position known as (4)_____. Opposed to this assumption is the notion of (5)_____, which emphasizes volition in human thinking and behavior. A third related assumption suggests that supernatural forces determine our behavior; it is called (6)_____.

A second broad approach to motivation has been most influential in experimental psychology; it emphasizes the (7)_____ basis of motivation. For many, this is a special form of the (8)_____ approach, and it calls attention to the shared characteristics of humans and (9)_____. According to this view, the most basic motives that instigate behavior are (10)_____, which are themselves based on (11)_____, including requirements for food and other necessities.

Both are presumably built into the organism, or (12)_____. Sometimes there

can be a need but no (13)_____, and vice versa. The quantity or quality of a

goal constitutes a kind of pulling force, or (14)_____. The term

(15)_____ refers to innate patterns of behavior; many psychologists have

rejected this concept as lacking sufficient (16)_____ power. Since all behavior

cannot be traced to the direct operation of a tissue need and corresponding drive, the concept of second-order,

or (17)_____, drives has been added to explain the motivation of other

behaviors.

A third approach to motivation suggests that human beings are masters of their own fate, and it is called

the (18)_____ view. The main ingredient of this approach is

(19)_____, which says that we act to obtain (20)_____

and to avoid (21)_____. This model has been criticized in terms of the vague-

ness of the notion of pleasure and the model's lack of (22)_____ power. An

updated version of the approach is modern decision theory, which emphasizes the notion of subjective

value, or (23)_____. As we have read earlier, we are not always rational

about the decisions we make but rather frequently adopt shortcut strategies called (24)_____.

Opposed to the rational view is a fourth approach, that of Sigmund Freud, who suggested that humans

are often (25)_____ of the real reasons for some highly motivated behavior.

This model emphasizes (26)_____ motivation. Freud's viewpoint is opposed

especially by the (27)_____, who dislike the appeal to hidden instincts.

The last of the five broad approaches to motivation emphasizes the role of society in the determination

of behavior, and it is called the (28)_____ view. It holds that society sometimes

suffers (29)_____, or slowness in establishing a new social order; moreover, we

can understand individual behavior only in terms of the dominant motives of the person's culture

because of (30)_____. Our behaviors are really determined

(31)_____ because the laws of society transcend individual human nature.

Such a position suggests that we as individuals are (32)_____, but the fact is

that some environmental changes may lead to changes in social (33)_____.

The animal approach to motivation emphasizes biological (34)_____,

suggesting that action results from a lack of something important, and also from the self-regulating

equilibrium of conditions necessary for survival, or (35)_____. However, not

every need is associated with a corresponding (36)_____, as was indicated

above. This is partly due to the effect of stimuli in the external environment that operate as

(37)_____, as is demonstrated by obese persons who respond more to

(38)_____ cues and less to (39)_____ cues than

persons of (40)_____ weight (see Box 18.5 A and B). The broader homeostatic

theory says that motivation occurs with tension arousal, whether by (41)_____, external stimulus, or an (42)_____ idea, and motivation ceases with

(43)_____. The deficiency-homeostatic model faces difficulty in explaining

such behaviors as (44)_____ in the young and (45)_____ of

novel objects. To say that these behaviors are (46)_____ drives would appear

to be an overstatement of the tissue-need approach.

Abundancy motivation presents an alternative conception by proposing that some behaviors seem to

occur in order to produce a tension (47)_____, based on a need for

(48)_____. Research on sensory (49)_____

has supported this notion. Other supporting evidence has resulted from study of arousal elicited by a

(50)_____ in the stimulus field, which itself may be a function of

(51)_____ of what is happening. The general finding in this area that a person

needs greater than (52)_____ stimulation but not (53)_____

stimulation would seem to support a combination of the (54)_____ and

(55)_____ views of motivation.

Maslow's need-hierarchy theory may be viewed as an attempt to integrate deficiency and abundancy

motives into a single framework, in which the lowest motives are (56)_____

and the highest is a need for (57)_____. In between are needs for safety,

love, and (58)_____. Each lower need has to be satisfied to some extent

before a (59)_____ need can come into action.

Causal attribution theory is illustrated in the example of giving-up behavior called

(60)_____, in which the organism attributes its own

(61)_____ to a relatively permanent condition that cannot be

(62)_____. Another attribution theory emphasizes information seeking as the

basic (63)_____. Here, consequences of perceived

(64)_____ in motivation are stressed. The basic dimensions of this process

are locus, stability, and (65)_____.

Conflicts arise when different motives are (66)_____ to one another.

Objectives may have different subjective value, or (67)_____ either attracting

(68)(_____), or repelling (69)(_____). In one

system based on these notions, the attraction of a goal (70)_____ with distance,

either physical or (71)_____, from the goal. Three different types of conflict

—approach-approach, avoidance-avoidance, and (72)_____— are character-

ized by different resolutions.

Frustration refers to an (73)_____ in the path to a goal or to the effect

on the individual of being (74)_____ from a goal. Frustration can have

good or bad effects. On the one hand, it may be an aid in problem solving; on the other, it may lead to

(75)_____ or (76)_____. The frustration-aggression hypothesis states that (77)_____ is always preceded by

(78)_____.

   We evaluate incentives on the basis of how they compare with what we (79)_____

to get, what we have received in the past, or what (80)_____ are getting.

Resentment at not having something that others have is called (81)_____,

and it is an example of the (82)_____ character of incentive motivation. In

human motivation (83)_____ reinforcers such as verbal praise are more

common than primary reinforcers. These incentives also follow the pattern of (84)_____

effectiveness described above.

4. THOUGHT QUESTIONS

a. Think of all the similarities and differences that appear to exist between human behavior and the operation of a complicated machine, such as a computer. Then, attempt to assemble several specific arguments against the proposal that the human being is simply a very complicated machine.

b. Why do you think that stimulus-reduced environments might be effective in reducing unwanted behaviors, such as cigarette smoking?

c. How might you set up training situations for your children in their early life so that learned helplessness will never take place?

d. Many of us go to hot Athens in the summer and to cold Stowe in the winter. What are the possible satisfactions for us in placing ourselves in uncomfortable environments and even risking our lives (e.g., skiing) in some of them?

5. EVALUATION (SELF-TESTS)

Correct answers and text page references are given at the end of the unit.

a. Fill-in-the-blanks Items

Write the word(s) that best complete(s) the sentence in the space provided.

1. Determinism suggests that all events are ___predictable___.

2. The importance of biological needs and drives is emphasized in the ___animal/biological___ approach to motivation.

3. Hedonism proposes that the goal of all behavior is the seeking of ___pleasure___.

4. The possibility that humans are unaware of the motives underlying their behavior is basic to the ___unconscious motivation / Freudian___ theory.

5. According to the social-product view, our behavior is a function of ___society___.

6. Homeostasis is a system of self-regulating ___equilibrium___.

7. In the determination of their behavior, obese persons appear to respond most to ___external___ cues.

8. Abundancy motivation emphasizes the importance of tension ___increase___.

9. Of the three conflict situations described, the easiest one to resolve is ___approach___.

10. Frustration may sometimes lead to aggression and sometimes to ___regression___.

b. Matching Items

Write the number of the correct item from the right column in front of the matching item in the left column.

_5_	fatalism	1. tissue needs
_6_	incentive	2. we are pawns of social values
_10_	instinct	3. verbal praise
_2_	social determinism	4. causal attribution theory
_8_	effectance	5. supernatural forces determine behavior
_1_	deficiency motivation	6. amount or quality of the goal
_7_	abundancy motivation	7. need for stimulation
_9_	self-actualization	8. tendency to explore the environment
_4_	learned helplessness	9. highest need for Maslow
_3_	social reinforcer	10. innate pattern of behavior

c. Multiple-choice Items

Circle the letter in front of the answer that best completes the stem.

1. In motivation studies, tissue needs are the focus of the theoretical perspective that views humans as:
   a. machines
   b. animals
   c. rational masters
   d. social products

2. In motivation studies, determinism is the focus of the theoretical perspective that views humans as:
   a. machines
   b. animals
   c. rational masters
   d. social products

3. In motivation studies, cultural values are the focus of the theoretical perspective that views humans as:
   a. machines
   b. animals
   c. rational masters
   d. social products

4. In motivation studies, hedonism is the focus of the theoretical perspective that views humans as:
   a. machines
   b. animals
   c. rational masters
   d. social products

5. The law of effect could be called a hedonism of the:
   a. past
   b. present
   c. future
   d. spirit

6. Freud's reality principle could be called a hedonism of the:
   a. past
   b. present
   c. future
   d. spirit

7. The deficiency-homeostatic model in motivation has difficulty in explaining:
   a. tension reduction
   b. playful behavior
   c. biological drives
   d. hedonism

8. Research on sensory deprivation effects is most closely associated with which of the following views?
   a. fatalism
   b. utilitarianism
   c. deficiency motivation
   d. abundancy motivation

9. Learned helplessness is most closely associated with which of the following theories?
   a. deficiency motivation
   b. abundancy motivation
   c. attribution theory
   d. conflict theory

10. Which of the following is the most difficult conflict situation to resolve?
    a. approach-approach
    b. approach-avoidance
    c. avoidance-avoidance
    d. triple approach-avoidance

d. Short-answer Items

Answer the following questions with short, concise statements. Reference pages for the material are given at the end of the unit.

1. Contrast the biological view of motivation with the view that characterizes human beings as the rational masters of their own fate.

2. Contrast the deficiency approach with the abundancy approach to motivation.

3. List the lowest and the highest needs within Maslow's hierarchical motivational system and indicate their relationship.

4. Briefly describe the frustration-aggression hypothesis.

ANSWER KEY FOR UNIT 18

Unit Review

1. instigated
2. goal/incentive
3. machines
4. determinism
5. free will
6. fatalism
7. animal/biological
8. mechanistic/machine
9. lower animals
10. biological drives
11. biological needs
12. innate
13. drive
14. incentive
15. instinct
16. explanatory
17. acquired
18. rational master
19. hedonism
20. pleasure
21. pain
22. explanatory
23. utility
24. heuristics
25. unaware
26. unconscious
27. mechanists
28. social product
29. cultural lag
30. cultural relativism
31. socially
32. powerless
33. values
34. deficiency
35. homeostasis
36. drive
37. drive instigators
38. external
39. internal
40. normal
41. tissue need
42. internally elicited
43. tension reduction
44. playfulness
45. exploration
46. biological
47. increase
48. stimulation
49. deprivation
50. change
51. uncertainty
52. zero
53. too much
54. deficiency
55. abundancy
56. biological
57. self-actualization
58. esteem
59. higher
60. learned helplessness
61. failures
62. changed
63. motive
64. causality
65. controllability
66. opposed

67. valence
68. positive
69. negative
70. diminishes
71. psychological
72. approach-avoidance
73. obstacle
74. blocked
75. aggression

76. regression
77. aggression
78. frustration
79. expect
80. others
81. relative deprivation
82. relational
83. social
84. relational

Evaluation (Self-tests)

a. Fill-in-the-blanks Items

1. predictable (p. 421)
2. animal (p. 424)
3. pleasure (p. 426)
4. Freudian (p. 427)
5. society (p. 428)

6. equilibrium (p. 430)
7. external (p. 434)
8. increase (pp. 434–436)
9. approach-approach (p. 443)
10. regression (p. 444)

b. Matching Items: Correct order and page references are:

5 (p. 423); 6 (p. 425); 10 (p. 425); 2 (p. 429); 8 (p. 433);
1 (p. 430); 7 (pp. 434–435); 9 (p. 437); 4 (pp. 438–439); 3 (p. 448).

c. Multiple-choice Items: Correct answers and page references are:

1—b (pp. 423–424); 2—a (p. 421); 3—d (p. 428); 4—c (p. 426); 5—a (p. 426);
6—c (p. 426); 7—b (p. 433); 8—d (pp. 434–435); 9—c (pp. 438–439); 10—c (p. 443).

d. Short-answer Items: Page references for answer material are:

1. pp. 423–427; 2. pp. 430–437; 3. pp. 437–438; 4. pp. 443-444.

Unit 19

HUMAN EMOTION

---

1. INTRODUCTION TO STUDY OF THIS UNIT

Humans have been concerned about emotions for thousands of years. Love, fear, and other emotional states have been written about and analyzed from the time of the early Greeks by poets, philosophers, and scientists. In many respects, William Shakespeare may have been one of the keener analysts of emotion in his descriptions of persons suffering certain emotions, which include much detail of facial and bodily expression, and in his reports of physiological change. It is curious that with all this concern, the general area of human emotion has not been as greatly researched as many other areas of psychology. The lack of research may be due to the complexity of the area and the methodological pitfalls encountered in early studies, or it may be due to our intuitive feeling that emotion is an irrational, disorganizing state that cannot be studied objectively.

One of the earliest systematic theories of emotion was proposed independently by William James and by Carl Lange shortly before the turn of the present century. Each suggested that our *awareness* of our bodily responses to an emotion-provoking situation *is* the emotion. That is, we see a frightful-looking snake before us and we turn and run away immediately, as we express dread, experience an increased heartbeat, and suffer other symptoms. The emotion is our awareness of the running and the physiological changes. Later W. B. Cannon proposed a thalamic theory of emotion, which stressed that the stimulus situation leads to great changes in the body, usually mediated by the sympathetic nervous system but orchestrated by the thalamus. The thalamic firing and organization of these "emergency" reactions is the emotion. While the Cannon theory seems to be opposed to the James-Lange model, this evaluation is largely due to a misunderstanding of the latter model. A Cannonite might ask how one could differentiate emotions since the bodily processes that accompany them are so alike. But, according to the James-Lange theory, the bodily responses of running away, staying, or even attacking are quite different, and these aid in the determination of what emotion is being experienced. During this century other theories of emotion have been offered that are explored in the unit.

The nature-nurture issue has been raised for emotion just as it has for most of the other areas of psychology. Charles Darwin thought, largely based on his observations of lower animals, that many of the emotions were innate. He felt that at the human level cross-cultural universals in emotional expression existed, indicating the likely innate nature of some human emotions. Even the behaviorist Watson found evidence that the emotions of fear, rage, and love were present in the human infant and that through conditioning these emotions became attached to many stimuli and were elaborated. There is still controversy over whether each of the separate emotions is innately determined or whether they evolve out of a single general excitement. There is also little agreement on the extent to which learning is involved in all aspects of emotional expression.

2. ISSUES AND CONCEPTS

The unit begins by presenting the important aspects of the James-Lange theory of emotion and the criticisms of it by Cannon and others, which you should learn. Be able to distinguish the James-Lange model from the Schachter-Singer approach, and know some of the drug research employed to support the latter theory. Study, too, the cognitive appraisal theory, its two stages, and how they interact.

Darwin felt that some emotions were innate and suggested the existence of cross-cultural universals in emotional expression. Evaluate the evidence that tends to support this contention. You should also analyze the evidence favoring and opposing the Tomkins theory, which treats emotions as innate motives. The Plutchik approach also views emotion as innate and proposes eight basic functional sequences. Study those sequences and how learning influences them.

The structure of emotions has been studied and two structural schemes proposed — that of Schlosberg and that of Plutchik. Determine how these approaches are similar and how they differ.

Studies of the different kinds of love and of how couples come together, stay together, or break up are the next topic for your consideration. Focus on what has been found out about love, especially the sex differences cited. Be able to discuss how emotion can intensify love feelings, even if the emotions are irrelevant to love.

Concentrate next on the effects of stress in our lives, and specifically, the stages of the General Adaptation Syndrome of Hans Selye. Be able to describe the evidence that supports this model in terms of the distinction between Type A and Type B persons and life-styles and to discuss how different people cope with stress.

The unit next takes us to the different procedures for detecting and measuring emotions, which do not necessarily lead to the same conclusions. Focus on the reliability and validity problems of the self-report method, and be aware that studies of bodily processes in emotion have not led to the identification of isolated somatic cues to emotional state and only to some extent have they identified patterns of such cues as indicators. Be able to describe the use of the physiological polygraph in lie detection and the analysis of voice tremors in emotional detection and evaluate the accuracy of these methods.

The development of emotions is the final topic. Be aware that the infant expresses a very limited range of emotions and that this repertoire increases greatly up to the age of two. Learn the two theoretical views of this developmental process. Finally, be able to describe the influence of caretaker-child interaction on emotional development.

3. UNIT REVIEW

Correct answers are given at the end of the unit.

Emotion appears to be the stuff of human existence, but it has not been studied extensively by psychologists, probably because of the (1)_____ in this area.

One of the first important theories of emotion was formulated independently by Carl Lange and (2)_____. This theory holds that the emotion-provoking stimulus situation provokes a bodily response and that our (3)_____ of this response pattern is the emotion. W. B. Cannon criticized this approach as unable to differentiate emotions since the bodily pattern is so (4)_____ for many emotional experiences; he also held that bodily changes occur too slowly to be the (5)_____ of emotional feelings. More recent research indicates that with some emotions the bodily patterns are (6)_____ and that learning may be associated with a more (7)_____ feeling state.

The Schachter-Singer theory states that physiological, social, and (8)_____ factors combine to produce felt emotions. Specifically, responses that are not understood by a person to be due to some physical cause (e.g., a drug) lead to the perception of some form of emotional

(9)_____, the form being determined by the (10)_____.

The cognitive appraisal theory (Lazarus) states that emotion first involves assessment of the (11)_____; then a secondary appraisal is made of a possible (12)_____ strategy. The interaction of these two appraisals determines the quality and the (13)_____ of the emotional response. The psychological responses that occur are not the causes of emotional experience but only the (14)_____ of the process.

Darwin felt that some emotions were (15)_____ and that, at the human level, there was evidence for this in terms of cross-cultural universals in emotional (16)_____. Some recent evidence supports this contention and suggests that (17)_____ might be a very important cue to emotion.

Tomkins has presented another innately based theory that treats emotions as (18)_____. He feels that biological drives have motivational impact only when amplified by the (19)_____ system. Emotions are easily apprehended largely on the basis of (20)_____, and individuals themselves become aware of their continuing (21)_____. Further research (see Box 19.3) questions whether facial expression is a (22)_____ of emotional experience, even though it may function as a reliable (23)_____ of emotion to others. Tomkins' theory states that innately some (24)_____ are positive and some are negative. With maturation, the individual learns ways of (25)_____ positive states and (26)_____ negative ones. The innate positive and negative emotions derive from three basic emotions built into the organism by (27)_____: the innate fear response to a (28)_____, the feeling of (29)_____, and pleasurable excitement produced by (30)_____.

Plutchik's theory also emphasizes the (31)_____ nature of emotion. He suggests that there are (32)_____ basic functional sequences, each containing a stimulus event, a (33)_____, a feeling and a (34)_____. These sequences are innate in nature, but learning may determine which (35)_____ trigger which sequence.

The structure of emotions has been studied usually by having subjects report in several ways which emotions are (36)_____ or by having subjects report the emotions they perceive in pictures of (37)_____. Of the two schemes discussed, each reports differences in the intensity and (38)_____ of emotion. The studies also have found that emotions low in (39)_____ are difficult to differentiate. Schlosberg uses

(40)_____ dimensions to differentiate quality: pleasant-unpleasant and

(41)_____. Plutchik presents (42)_____

qualitatively different emotions and uses this scheme to describe (43)_____

structure.

In the study of love, the intermingling of cognition and (44)_____ is

evident. With couples, those who say they love each other more tend to (45)_____

less. Of the two sexes, (46)_____ are more accurate predictors of whether the

couple stays together. A breakup is more often initiated by (47)_____. It

appears that (48)_____ fall in love more easily and

(49)_____ fall out of love more easily. There are different kinds of love and love

may occur in a variety of styles. One distinction is that between passionate love and

(50)_____ love, which is based on devotion and (51)_____.

Emotions can (52)_____ feelings of love even if the emotions are

(53)_____ to love.

Too much stress can be unpleasant and (54)_____. Selye proposed a

sequence of events in response to stress that he termed the (55)_____. It

has three stages: the alarm stage, the (56)_____ stage, and the

(57)_____ stage. Intense and prolonged stress can contribute to various

kinds of (58)_____, and persons who report more life

(59)_____ report more stress. With respect to coping strategies, the Type A

person seemingly (60)_____ stress, while the Type B person

(61)_____it. Type A persons are twice as likely as Type B persons to have

(62)_____. Cognitive appraisal theory suggests that some persons respond to

stress by (63)_____ that the stress-provoking event exists and others by

(64)_____, or trying to learn all about the threatening situation.

There are various ways of measuring emotion, including finding out how a person feels, observing

how he or she is (65)_____, or measuring the (66)_____

at the time. These different measures do not necessarily lead to the same (67)_____.

Self-report measures are not very (68)_____; there is better behavioral con-

sensus when others (69)_____ an emotion. It seems clear that people have

learned to (70)_____ the expression of some emotions. The

(71)_____ side of the face seems to be more involved in emotional expression

(see Box 19.5). It appears also that smiling occurs as a social (72)_____.

There are many bodily changes associated with emotion but single, isolated somatic cues are not

(73)_____ indicators of specific emotional states. Rather,

(74)_____ of physiological cues have been more successful in identifying emotions. Such measures are made by the "lie detector," or (75)_____

A recent technique of human voice analysis measures absence of (76)_____

normally present in the unstressed voice. The (77)_____ of this measure

has been challenged.

    The infant expresses only a (78)_____ of emotions, and this increases up

to about the age of (79)_____ years. Two hypotheses about this developmental

process have been offered. In one, all of the more elaborate emotions develop out of

(80)_____. In the other, all of the emotions are separate,

(81)_____ systems that mature when each becomes

(82)_____ for the individual. It is likely that the interaction of the

infant with his or her primary (83)_____ is important in emotional

development.

4. THOUGHT QUESTIONS

    a. Think of peer love relationships that you may have experienced in recent years. How did each begin and how did each end? How were the two partners involved in the beginning and ending behaviors? Were the relationships passionate or companionate?

    b. Is there a chicken-and-egg problem in the finding that Type A persons are twice as likely as Type B persons to have heart disease? How would you tease out the various possibilities in further research?

    c. Why do you suppose that it has been so difficult to find common patterns of emotional expression in self-reports, body observations, and physiological responses? What does this difficulty indicate about possible genetic and environmental contributions to these important systems?

    d. Does the lie detector really detect lies? If not, what does it detect and how is this related to the discovery of criminal behavior? Why do you think that most courts do allow the presentation of such evidence?

5. EVALUATION (SELF-TESTS)

Correct answers and text page references are given at the end of the unit.

a. Fill-in-the-blanks Items

Write the word(s) that best complete(s) the sentence in the space provided.

1. The James-Lange theory of emotion emphasized the individual's _____ of bodily response to the situation.

2. The Schachter-Singer theory emphasizes the importance of the _____

3. It is not likely that facial expression is a _____ of emotion.

4. Structural schemes all report on differences in the quality and _____ of emotion.

5. In couples research, females tend to fall _____ love more easily than males.

6. _____ love is based on devotion and permanence.

7. The stage in Selye's theory that can lead to death is called _____.

8. Type B persons tend to _____ stress.

9. It seems clear that the one emotion the human infant has is _____.

10. Interaction of infant and primary caretaker appears to be important in emotional

_____.

b. Matching Items

Write the number of the correct item from the right column in front of the matching item in the left column.

_____ Tomkins' theory	1.	repair damage of emotional responding
_____ Plutchik	2.	invites stress
_____ males	3.	voice tremor analysis
_____ females	4.	emotions as primary motives
_____ GAS resistance stage	5.	fall in love more easily
_____ GAS exhaustion stage	6.	fall out of love more easily
_____ Type A	7.	eight basic emotions
_____ Type B	8.	lack of achievement of normal physical growth
_____ Psychological Stress Evaluator	9.	avoids stress
_____ failure to thrive	10.	slowing of bodily functions

c. Multiple-choice Items

Circle the letter in front of the answer that best completes the stem.

1. The name most closely identified with the theory of emotion that emphasizes consideration of possible coping strategies is:
   a. James-Lange
   b. Schachter-Singer
   c. Lazarus
   d. Tomkins

2. The name most closely identified with the theory of emotion that emphasizes social contributions to felt emotion is:
   a. James-Lange
   b. Schachter-Singer
   c. Lazarus
   d. Tomkins

3. The name most closely identified with the theory of emotion that emphasizes awareness of bodily change is:
   a. James-Lange
   b. Schachter-Singer
   c. Lazarus
   d. Tomkins

4. The name most closely identified with the theory of emotion that emphasizes that emotions are primary motives is:
   a. James-Lange
   b. Schachter-Singer
   c. Lazarus
   d. Tomkins

5. Structural analyses of emotion have all found differences in:
   a. innateness and quality
   b. quality and intensity
   c. intensity and duration
   d. duration and innateness

6. Which is the more accurate predictor of whether a couple will stay together?
   a. the parent of either member
   b. the best friend of either member
   c. the male member
   d. the female member

7. Which of the following couples tend to break up less?
   a. those who fight a lot
   b. those who do not fight at all
   c. those whose members say they love each other more
   d. those whose members say they like each other more

8. The stage in Selye's theory in which the body begins to repair damage due to stress is the:
   a. alarm stage
   b. resistance stage
   c. exhaustion stage
   d. southwest stage

9. Which is more true of Type B than Type A persons?
   a. more likely to report fatigue
   b. more aggressive when frustrated
   c. work at the maximum rate at all times
   d. work more attentively at the task at hand

10. Which of the following measures are the most reliable and valid in detecting and measuring an emotion?
   a. self-reports
   b. observations of body response
   c. measurements of physiological changes
   d. there are no great differences

d. Short-answer Items

Answer the following questions with short, concise statements. Reference pages for the material are given at the end of the unit.

1. Contrast the James-Lange theory with the Schachter-Singer theory of emotion.

2. Compare the structure of emotions as characterized by Schlosberg and by Plutchik.

3. Describe briefly Selye's General Adaptation Syndrome, identifying its three stages.

4. Distinguish clearly between Type A and Type B persons.

ANSWER KEY FOR UNIT 19

Unit Review

1. methodological difficulties
2. William James
3. awareness
4. similar
5. cause
6. different
7. rapid
8. cognitive
9. arousal
10. social situation
11. stimulus situation
12. coping
13. intensity
14. by-products
15. innate
16. expression
17. facial movement
18. primary motives
19. affective
20. facial muscles
21. emotional state
22. determiner
23. indicator
24. affects
25. maximizing
26. avoiding
27. natural selection
28. life threat
29. pleasure
30. novelty
31. innate
32. eight
33. cognition
34. behavior
35. stimuli
36. similar
37. faces
38. quality
39. intensity
40. two
41. attention-rejection
42. eight
43. personality
44. physiology
45. break up
46. females
47. females
48. males
49. females
50. companionate
51. permanence
52. intensify
53. irrelevant
54. unhealthy
55. General Adaptation Syndrome
56. resistance
57. exhaustion
58. illness
59. changes
60. invites
61. avoids
62. heart disease
63. denial
64. intellectualizing
65. behaving
66. physiological events
67. conclusion
68. accurate
69. judge
70. control
71. left
72. gesture/communication
73. reliable
74. patterns
75. polygraph
76. muscle tremor
77. accuracy/legality
78. limited range
79. two
80. general excitement
81. innate
82. adaptive
83. caretaker

Evaluation (Self-tests)

a. **Fill-in-the-blanks Items**

1. awareness (p. 453)
2. social situation (p. 453)
3. determiner (pp. 455–457)
4. intensity (p. 459)
5. out of (p. 461)

6. Companionate (p. 461)
7. exhaustion (p. 462)
8. avoid (p. 463)
9. general excitement (p. 468)
10. development (p. 470)

b. **Matching Items: Correct order and page references are:**

4 (p. 455); 7 (p. 460); 5 (p. 461); 6 (p. 461); 1 (p. 462);
10 (p. 462); 2 (p. 463); 9 (p. 463); 3 (p. 468); 8 (p. 470).

c. **Multiple-choice Items: Correct answers and page references are:**

1—c (p. 454); 2—b (p. 453); 3—a (pp. 452–453); 4—d (p. 455); 5—b (pp. 458–460);
6—d (p. 461); 7—c (p. 460); 8—b (p. 462); 9—a (p. 463); 10—d (pp. 465–468).

d. **Short-answer Items: Page references for answer material are:**

1. pp. 452–454; 2. pp. 458–460; 3. pp. 461–462; 4. pp. 462–463.

Unit 20

STATES OF CONSCIOUSNESS

1. INTRODUCTION TO STUDY OF THIS UNIT

As you have read earlier in the text, experimental psychology began in the nineteenth century as the study of mental contents or consciousness. Wundt and his colleagues and followers, who comprised the school of psychology called structuralism, used introspection to study the mind. This brand of psychology came to the United States around the turn of the century and was very popular for a time. In many psychology departments, there are still traces of this movement in storage rooms where "brass instrument" apparatus associated with this approach to the field can be found. The movement died out quickly for a number of reasons. First of all, the study of consciousness largely precluded an examination of young children, adults with emotional disorders, and, of course, animals. Second, John Watson made a good case for behavioral analysis and against the subjectivity of the study of conscious experience. Finally, Sigmund Freud was proposing at the same time that unconscious mechanisms were operative, and they were not available for study by the usual introspective means. It is also true that the esoteric nature of structuralism did not fit easily into an America that was growing rapidly in population, industry, and in problems that had to be solved. The methods and findings of structuralism could not be applied easily to these problems. So it was little wonder that functionalism and behaviorism came to be popular substitutes. The death knell sounded for structuralism in this country early in this century.

Along with structuralism went a deep interest in consciousness as a central topic in psychology. Watson's advice was to forget it completely, and this advice was largely taken. Why does it appear to be returning in recent years? One reason probably is that behaviorism, so fully ingrained in psychology in this country, is taking on characteristics of an old shoe: it is comfortable and serviceable, but it is getting to be too predictable and dull. Another reason may be that psychologists are getting to feel confident enough in their field and in their methodologies to return to the study of mind. In addition, many persons in this culture have turned to and have been turned on by alcohol, meditation, and drugs, or various combinations of these mind-altering stimuli. The manipulation of consciousness has become a favored pastime for many. It then becomes important to attempt to understand conscious phenomena, and psychologists, among others, have responded to this need. The ready availability of research funding probably encourages this kind of response as well.

2. ISSUES AND CONCEPTS

The unit begins with the distinction between NSC and ASC, which should be learned. You also should be able to identify the hypnogogic state and its three substates (intact, destructuralized, and restructuralized ego states). The topic of sleep has received a great deal of attention lately. From your reading here, you should be able to distinguish REM and NREM, especially in frequency and type of dreaming, and to explain the primary difference between dreaming and NSC. You should also be able to discuss the role of dreaming in Freud's theory, and the results of dream deprivation studies.

On the subject of hypnosis, note the great differences among people in their susceptibility to hypnosis, and learn the various phenomena which can be produced under hypnosis, including hyperesthesias, hypo-esthesias, hallucination, negative hallucination, and analgesia.

Another state of consciousness treated here is the peak experience. Be able to define it and describe its role in Maslow's theory. You should also be able to differentiate concentrative, opening-up, and transcenden-tal forms of meditation.

Regarding alcohol, learn the behavioral and experiential effects of different dosages of the substance, what the social lubricating effect of it derives from, and what influence cultural expectations have on its effect.

Other controlled substances that affect consciousness are investigated as well. Learn the name of the major active ingredient in marijuana, the physiological changes associated with the usual human dosages, and the possible impact of long-term use of the drug on sexual functioning. Be able to explain why the effects of the drug on observable behavior are not prominent and to describe what effects have been observed in car-driving simulation studies. Since nondrug factors can influence the effects of the drug, you should learn some of those nondrug factors as well. In addition, be able to discuss the kinds of behavior and experience that are associated with different levels of marijuana intoxication.

The text treats psychedelic drugs next, and you should learn what is meant by the label and the names of three such drugs. Be aware of the great variation among individuals in response to these drugs, and the non-drug factors important in the drug's effect. There is no definitive answer to the question of the potential harm of drugs like LSD, but familiarize yourself with the possible emotional and mental harm such drugs may cause under some conditions.

What constitutes use and abuse of a drug is largely determined by the values of a culture or subculture, but some drugs are considered dangerous. Learn the names of these drugs and why they are considered dangerous.

Finally, you should learn what the prevailing opinion of ASCs is in this country and in some of its professional groups, the cultural and subcultural pressures that determine the seeking out of ASCs, and the hazards faced by those experimenting with ASCs.

3. UNIT REVIEW

Correct answers are given at the end of the unit.

Psychology in its earliest experimental days was considered to be the study of (1)_____,
but the discipline changed its orientation and ignored this topic for a number of years, largely because
research results were (2)_____ and experimenter (3)_____
was not dealt with properly. Modern psychology is returning to this area.

While much variation occurs, there is sufficient regularity of pattern in day-to-day consciousness
to speak of NSC, or (4)_____. Other states, such as those occurring in
dreaming, are referred to as ASC, or (5)_____. The hypnagogic state
is the transitional ASC that occurs for a few minutes on the verge of (6)_____.
While there is enormous variation in experience in this state, research indicates a pattern of brain waves,
eye movement, and (7)_____. The first state of consciousness to occur

during the onset of sleep is called the (8)_____ state; in this state, EEG records show either a normal, awakened alpha rhythm of (9)_____ cycles per second and occasional REM (or (10)_____), or rolling SEM (or (11)_____), of the closed eyes. In addition, the subject can distinguish what is in his or her mind and what is (12)_____ to it. In the second state of consciousness during sleep onset, called the (13)_____, the physiological pattern is one of (14)_____ sleep with the EEG showing a slower, more irregular pattern and other instruments showing (15)_____ eye movements. Here, the subject loses contact with external stimuli and may report (16)_____ mental content. The third state is called the (17)_____ and is like (18)_____. In it, the EEG shows the (19)_____ sleep pattern with "spindles," which are bursts of (20)_____ cycles per second, in addition to random, slow activity and (21)_____ eye movements. The subject reports (22)_____ mental content. Correspondence between physiological pattern and the mental phenomena in these three states is not (23)_____.

Research indicates that there are rather distinct stages of sleep and that the ASC called dreaming primarily occurs during (24)_____ sleep. Either no mental content or mental activity without imagery occurs in (25)_____ sleep, along with sleep-walking, sleeptalking, and (26)_____. The dreamer loses almost all contact with the external world and usually ignores (27)_____, though occasionally they are integrated into the dream. Most of the elements of a dream are drawn from the ordinary world, but they may be reorganized into (28)_____ combinations. The primary cognitive difference between dreaming and our NSC is the greatly (29)_____ comparison of ongoing events with our internalized beliefs and knowledge of how things are and should be.

Some investigators argue that dream consciousness is understandable. Freud felt that dreams represented in symbolic form the dreamer's current (30)_____ and could be very useful in (31)_____. For him, dreams are the window to the (32)_____, and they serve the function of partially discharging sexual and (33)_____ drives. This theory is (34)_____. Dream deprivation studies in which stage-1-REM sleep is interrupted show an (35)_____ amount of this stage during later uninterrupted sleep but do not necessarily show psychological (36)_____. Dreaming in which people can think critically that "this is a dream" and can exercise a higher than usual degree of control over the content is called (37)_____. Out-of-the-body experiences in dreaming may be regarded as (38)_____ in which the apparent locus of perceptions is radically altered. Though rare, they often follow a close (39)_____.

People vary greatly in their susceptibility to hypnosis, the most widely (40)_____

ASC. Up to 10 percent are totally (41)_____, 10 to 20 percent can achieve

(42)_____ hypnotic states, and the rest are in between. Children generally

are (43)_____ susceptible than adults. In (44)_____

hypnosis, the subject is aware but shows little self-initiated mental activity. A feeling of being hypersensitive

to sensory stimuli, known as (45)_____, can be created in hypnosis, as can

the perception of something that is not physically present, or (46)_____.

Being less sensitive to specific kinds of sensory stimuli, or (47)_____, and not

being aware of something physically present, or (48)_____, can also be

produced, as can dissociation of action from awareness and the nonexperience of painful stimuli, called

(49)_____, and posthypnotic effects. To allow oneself to be hypnotized by

an untrained or professionally irresponsible person is a (50)_____ business.

Peak experiences refer to the (51)_____ of life that occur spontaneously

and infrequently and only in psychologically (52)_____ persons, according

to Maslow. In this unproven theory, the person finds the peak experiences intensely

(53)_____ and revealing, and such experiences may profoundly affect his or

her values and (54)_____.

Mediation is a set of (55)_____ for achieving various ASCs, some of

which result in ecstatic characteristics of peak experiences. One form develops a total focus by restricting

attention to a single object for long periods; it is called (56)_____. Another

form involves a nonfused, free-floating state of alertness in which there is more direct contact with reality;

it is called (57)_____. Probably the most widely practiced form of meditation

in the United States is (58)_____, which involves the repeating of certain

words or sounds, called (59)_____ (see Box 20.8). There is no evidence that

meditation is more beneficial than other forms of (60)_____, although one

study indicates that perceptual enhancement, through a decrease in (61)_____,

may result.

The behavioral and experiential effects of alcohol intoxication are a function of

(62)_____. Even though we do not know when NSC ends and ASC begins

with alcohol, the point of alcohol intoxication is reached when there is about (63)_____

percent alcohol in the blood. While there is great individual variability with respect to one's reaction to a

given dose of alcohol, generally at low levels of intoxication there are feelings of relaxation, bodily warmth,

somewhat intensified (64)_____, and lowering of (65)_____,

along with impaired (66)_____ functioning. At higher levels, there is more

serious motor dysfunction up to a total loss of (67)_____. At even higher levels,

stupor and ultimately (68)_____ result. The social lubricating effect of alcohol

does not result apparently from the reduction of (69)_____ but rather from

the induction of strong fantasies of (70)_____. Cultural expectations regarding the effects of alcohol are very influential in determining its (71)_____.

       Marijuana is prepared from the leaves and flowers of the (72)_____ plant

and is usually smoked but can be (73)_____. Its major active ingredient is

(74)_____. The usual human dosages result in a small

(75)_____ in heart rate and a dilation of the small blood vessels of the

(76)_____. After long use it may result in a reduction in

(77)_____ count and the level of (78)_____ in the

blood. Long-term excessive use may have (79)_____ effects, but there is no

definite conclusion available about moderate use. Some reports suggest that marijuana influences the

(80)_____ nervous system and neural (81)_____.

The effects of marijuana or THC intake on observable behavior are not (82)_____,

partly due to tolerance and experiential factors; however, tests of tracking ability and perceptual performance

in car-driving simulation studies present clear evidence of (83)_____ effects.

Nondrug factors, including cultural differences, individual needs, and personal (84)_____,

may affect the influence of the drug. As with alcohol, reaction is related to level of

(85)_____. Low levels may produce transitory restlessness and sensory

(86)_____, while very high levels may produce loss of sensory contact,

mystical experiences, and even (87)_____.

       The most widely used psychedelic, or (88)_____, drug is

(89)_____. Others include mescaline and (90)_____.

All three drugs seem to have similar effects, but variations among individuals are so great that it is

impossible to present a coherent picture of the (91)_____ produced by a

specific psychedelic. Nondrug factors are (92)_____. While it is not clear if

LSD use is harmless or can produce psychosis-like experiences, frequent use by individuals who suffer

generally poor mental health or are going through a period of great personal stress can probably lead to

emotional breakdown and to serious mental (93)_____. A person who is

considering achievement of an ASC by drug or nondrug means should be well informed of the psychological,

physical, and legal (94)_____, and their possible minimization.

       In spite of strong (95)_____ attitudes toward drugs, our society uses

them in enormous amounts. What constitutes use and abuse of a consciousness-altering drug is largely

determined by (96)_____. Almost all authorities agree that hard narcotics

(such as dexedrine sulfate, referred to as (98)_____), and strong sedatives

(such as (99)_____), are (100)_____, because

they are associated with (101)_____, unhappiness, and wrecked lives.

       America, as a whole, has disapproved of most deliberately induced ASCs. The majority psychiatric

and psychological view is that deliberate induction of an ASC is suggestive of already

(102)_____ mental health and that some ASCs may be dangerous to a person's mental health. Cultural and subcultural (103)_____ determine the seeking out of ASCs. There are real (104)_____ in experimenting with ASCs, and it is wise to realize that experimentation, and especially self-experimentation, must not be lightly considered.

4. THOUGHT QUESTIONS

a. The Senoi of Malaysia "train" their children to have more lucid dreams. If you wished your children to increase the amount of their lucid dreaming, what training program would you devise? What specific steps would be included in this program?

b. Why do you think that some persons can be readily hypnotized and others seem to be entirely resistant to this form of suggestion? What factors are more likely to be involved in such susceptibility differences?

c. In some states, alcoholic impairment for purposes of driving an automobile is legally set at 0.10 or 0.15 percent concentration of alcohol in the blood. In other states, it is set at 0.08. In some foreign countries, it is set at 0.05, and in one, any measurable amount may bring trouble. What level do you think is best to use? What would you recommend?

d. There are cultures today in which exotic drugs are used regularly but only in connection with religious ceremony. Why do you suppose this relationship came about and why does it continue?

5. EVALUATION (SELF-TESTS)

Correct answers and text page references are given at the end of the unit.

a. Fill-in-the-blanks Items

Write the word(s) that best complete(s) the sentence in the space provided.

1. The transitional ASC that occurs on the verge of falling asleep is called the ___hynagogic___ state.

2. The part of falling asleep in which the subject may report bizarre mental content is called the ___destructualised___ ego state.

3. A frequent ASC associated with stage-1-REM sleep is ___dreaming___.

4. Sleepwalking usually occurs in ___NEM___ sleep.

5. For Freud, the window to the unconscious is the ___dream___.

6. Hypoesthesia in hypnosis is the feeling of being ___+ insensitive___ to specific kinds of sensory stimuli.

7. In concentrative meditation, there is a total focus of ___attention___.

8. A level of 0.10 percent alcohol in the blood is commonly accepted as indicating ___intoxication___.

9. Car-driving simulation studies present clear evidence of the negative effects of ___marijuana___ on tracking ability.

10. Mind-expanding drugs are frequently called ___psychedelic___.

b. Matching Items

Write the number of the correct item from the right column in front of the matching item in the left column.

_3_	alpha activity	1. difficulty in staying awake
_4_	sleep spindles	2. follows a close brush with death
_8_	restructuralized ego state	3. 8 to 12 cycles per second
_1_	narcolepsy	4. 14 cycles per second
_9_	lucid dreaming	5. high point of life
_2_	OOBE	6. mind expanding
_10_	NDE	7. stupor and possible death
_5_	peak experience	8. third state during sleep onset
_7_	0.50 percent alcohol in blood	9. more control over dream content
_6_	psychedelic	10. can be compared to a drug state

c. Multiple-choice Items

Circle the letter in front of the answer that best completes the stem.

1. The third state that occurs when we are on the verge of falling asleep is called the:
   a. intact ego state
   b. restructuralized state
   c. isomorphic state
   d. the destructuralized state

2. The third state of falling asleep shows which of the following EEG and eye movement patterns?
   a. alpha rhythm and REM
   b. alpha rhythm and SEM
   c. stage-1 EEG and no eye movements
   d. stage-2 EEG and no eye movements

3. Dreaming primarily occurs during:
   a. stage-1-REM sleep
   b. stage-1-SEM sleep
   c. stage-2-REM sleep
   d. stage-2-SEM sleep

4. Sleeptalking seems to occur primarily in:
   a. stage-1-REM sleep
   b. stage-2-SEM sleep
   c. stage-1-SEM sleep
   d. NREM sleep

5. The number of people who can achieve deep hypnotic states is approximately what percent of the population?
   a. 1 to 10
   b. 10 to 20
   c. 20 to 50
   d. 50 to 80

6. According to Maslow, peak experiences occur:
   a. with effort and frequently
   b. frequently and spontaneously
   c. spontaneously and infrequently
   d. infrequently and with effort

7. Transcendental meditation is a form of meditation that employs:
   a. mantras
   b. focusing of attention on an object
   c. a free-floating state of alertness
   d. specific body positioning

8. The social lubricating effect of alcohol is apparently due to:
   a. loss of coordination
   b. loss of anxiety
   c. fantasies of powerfulness
   d. fantasies of sexual prowess

9. The major active ingredient in marijuana is:
   a. LSD
   b. THC
   c. NDE
   d. OOBE

10. The most widely used psychedelic drug is:
    a. mescaline
    b. psilocybin
    c. lysergic acid diethylamide
    d. aspirin

d. Short-answer Items

Answer the following questions with short, concise statements. Reference pages for the material are given at the end of the unit.

1. Specify and contrast the three ego states of the hypnagogic state.

2. Discuss briefly the statement that dreaming occurs only during stage-1-REM sleep.

3. Describe and contrast the two hypnotic states called hyperesthesia and hypoesthesia.

4. Contrast the behavioral effects of 0.1 percent and 0.5 percent alcohol concentration in the blood on a twenty-year-old college student.

ANSWER KEY FOR UNIT 20

Unit Review

1. consciousness
2. contradictory
3. bias
4. normal state of consciousness
5. altered states of consciousness
6. falling asleep
7. mental content
8. intact ego
9. 8 to 12
10. rapid eye movements
11. slow eye movements
12. external
13. destructuralized ego state
14. stage-1
15. no
16. bizarre
17. restructuralized ego state
18. NSC
19. stage-2
20. 14
21. no
22. plausible
23. perfect
24. stage-1-REM
25. NREM
26. nightmares
27. external stimuli
28. strange
29. reduced
30. personality
31. psychotherapy
32. unconscious
33. aggressive
34. unproven
35. increased
36. disturbance
37. lucid dreaming
38. ASCs
39. brush with death
40. investigated
41. unresponsive
42. deep
43. more
44. neutral
45. hyperesthesias
46. hallucination
47. hypoesthesias
48. negative hallucination
49. analgesia
50. risky
51. high points
52. mature
53. satisfying
54. future life
55. techniques
56. concentrative meditation
57. opening-up meditation
58. transcendental meditation
59. mantras
60. relaxation
61. habituation
62. dosage
63. 0.1
64. emotions
65. inhibitions
66. motor
67. coordination
68. death
69. anxiety
70. powerfulness
71. effects
72. hemp
73. eaten
74. THC (tetrahydrocannibinol)
75. increase
76. eyes
77. sperm
78. testosterone

79. adverse
80. sympathetic
81. transmitters
82. prominent
83. negative
84. expectations
85. intoxication
86. enhancement
87. nausea/vomiting
88. mind-expanding
89. LSD (lysergic acid diethylamide)
90. psilocybin
91. ASCs

92. important
93. deterioration
94. dangers
95. negative
96. cultural values
97. heroin
98. "speed"/"meth"
99. barbiturates
100. dangerous
101. addiction
102. imperfect
103. pressures
104. hazards

Evaluation (Self-tests)

a. Fill-in-the-blanks Items

1. hypnagogic (p. 473)
2. destructuralized (p. 474)
3. dreaming (p. 475)
4. NREM (p. 475)
5. dream (p. 477)

6. less sensitive (p. 480)
7. attention (p. 483)
8. intoxication (p. 485)
9. marijuana (p. 487)
10. psychedelic (p. 489)

b. Matching Items: Correct order and page references are:

3 (p. 473); 4 (p. 473); 8 (p. 474); 1 (p. 476); 9 (p. 477);
2 (p. 478); 10 (p. 479); 5 (p. 482); 7 (p. 485); 6 (p. 489).

c. Multiple-choice Items: Correct answers and page references are:

1—b (p. 474); 2—d (p. 474); 3—a (p. 475); 4—d (p. 475); 5—b (p. 479);
6—c (p. 482); 7—a (p. 484); 8—c (p. 486); 9—b (p. 486); 10—c (p. 489).

d. Short-answer Items: Page references for answer material are:

1. pp. 474–475; 2. p. 475; 3. p. 480; 4. pp. 485–486.

Unit 21

PHYSIOLOGICAL BASES OF MOTIVATION AND EMOTION

1. INTRODUCTION TO STUDY OF THIS UNIT

One of the areas reviewed in this unit is the topic of sleep cycles. Theories of sleep and of dreaming have been plentiful over the years, attesting to the importance of this inactive period for most of us. After all, an adult living to 75 years will have spent about 25 of those years sleeping, perhaps more time than he or she will spend in any other "state." Some of the theories concerning sleep have been exotic, such as the Freudian notion that sleep permits the release of pent-up unconscious processes through the dreaming mechanism. Others are more mundane, suggesting that the sleep period is necessary for processes that rebuild the body, such as protein synthesis in the brain cells. Other theories are delightfully speculative; for example, one proposes a correspondence between the sleep-waking cycle and periods of relative safety in moving about the environment. Presumably, humans retired to their safe caves during the dark period when they might be the victims of predators. In the cave, of course, they could dream of a successful hunt in the morning and also release a few unconscious impulses in the bargain.

The sleep-waking cycle is a circadian rhythm, that is, a cycle of about 24 hours. The sleep rhythm of about 90 minutes is called an ultradian rhythm because there are several of these within a 24-hour period. We have known about periodicities in functioning for about 200 years. Two centuries ago botanists placed plants in caves to see if they would open and close when they did not have light and temperature changes to guide them. The plants did, although they did not necessarily stay on a 24-hour timing. Humans also depart from 24-hour timing when they are deprived of light, temperature, and other time cues, as in a controlled sound-proofed chamber or in a cave. Whereas the plants varied by a few hours around the 24-hour value, however, humans typically go to a longer than 24-hour "day" when they are subjected to these constant environmental conditions. Studies put the value of this lengthened day at about 24.8 hours. This value corresponds to a moon rhythm in relation to the earth, which might indicate that by nature the human is less solar-tic and more lunar-tic.

2. ISSUES AND CONCEPTS

In this unit you will first learn the EEG characteristics of the four stages of the sleep cycle. Be able to differentiate NREM from REM sleep and state the physiological and dreaming differences between the two sub-REM stages The physiological structures mediating the waking state, and those involved in NREM and in REM sleep, are also presented for your study. Learn how these systems control waking and sleep, respectively. The sleep-waking cycle is a circadian rhythm, and you should attend to evidence supporting the notion of internal control of such rhythms. Become familiar with the fact that neural systems are always active and learn what the physical and psychological effects of sleep loss are, and what the survival explanation of the sleep-waking pattern is.

The unit also presents the sensory inputs to the autonomic nervous system and the division of this system into the sympathetic and the parasympathetic nervous systems. Learn the difference in the reactions of these two systems and the neural transmitters for each.

The endocrine system consists of a number of glands producing chemicals called hormones. For the posterior pituitary, the anterior pituitary, the adrenal cortex, the adrenal medulla, and the thyroid glands, become familiar with what controls the glands, what hormone(s) they secrete, and the effects on the body of these hormones.

The bodily responses accompanying emotional experience are under the control of the autonomic nervous system and the endocrine system. Learn the characteristics of the electrodermal response and its relationship to emotion. Learn also the other physiological responses that accompany emotion and the possible differences in hormonal production in the different emotional states. You should become familiar as well with the several theoretical approaches to emotion, including the James-Lange theory, the hypothalamic theory, the activation theory, and a model emphasizing the role of the limbic system. Be able to describe the evidence implicating various neural structures in emotion, including the hypothalamus, the reticular formation, and parts of the limbic system.

The catecholamine theory of depressive psychosis is presented next, and you should learn the two transmitters involved and the role of antidepressant drugs (such as MAO inhibitors and the transmitter serotonin) in modifying synaptic connections. Familiarize yourself with the action of lithium in modifying manic states, how dopamine may be involved in schizophrenia, and the effects that antipsychotic drugs have on ''normal'' people as well as patients. You should also recognize, after your reading, that the drug findings outlined do not constitute evidence against the environmental causation of psychosis.

For the hunger, thirst, and sex motives, learn the sensory conditions associated with each, the physiological changes accompanying these states, the hormones involved in them, and the neurological structures that probably mediate aspects of the motives. Specifically, for the hunger motive, learn the difference between the glucostatic and the lipostatic theories, and for the sex motive, be able to describe the role of hormones in the development of sex organs and normal sexual behavior and in the maintenance of such behavior.

3. UNIT REVIEW

Correct answers are given at the end of the unit.

The EEG of a relaxed subject who is not paying attention to any strong stimulus is characterized by a regular alpha rhythm of (1)_____ waves per second. If the person becomes involved in real or imagined perceptual activity or concentrated mental activity, these waves are replaced by more irregular ones that are (2)_____ in frequency and smaller in size. In the light sleep of stage 1, the EEG is less (3)_____ and smaller than in the waking alpha rhythm. In later stages 2 and 3, this rhythm is interspersed with periods of very rapid waves called (4)_____. During the very deep sleep of stage 4, large,

(5)_____ waves appear. At this time body temperature and blood pressure

(6)_____, the rate of breathing becomes more (7)_____,

and the sleeper becomes generally harder to awaken. After about one hour of sleep the individual goes

through these stages (8)_____. When he or she reaches an EEG pattern like

stage 1, (9)_____ occur. This (10)_____-minute

cycle from stage-1-REM through the various other NREM stages recurs over the sleep period. The first

REM period may be very brief, while a later one may last for (11)_____.

During REM sleep, the subject is harder to awaken, body muscles become very relaxed, reflexes are difficult

to elicit, and (12)_____ takes place. Two sub-REM stages have been

suggested: in (13)_____ REM sleep, the EEG and other physiological

measures are relatively stable, while during (14)_____ REM sleep, REM

activity is quite prominent and much muscular activity within the (15)_____

may occur. Dreams in which visual or auditory imagery and movement are prominent occur in

(16)_____ REM, while conceptual dreams occur in

(17)_____ REM sleep. REM sleep (18)_____

over a lifetime, with stage-1-REM taking up about (19)_____ of the sleeping

time of a newborn infant, and even more for a premature infant, and only (20)_____

of the sleeping time of an adult. REM sleep is also widespread among mammals and perhaps birds as well.

The waking state is dependent upon activity of the (21)_____ in the brain

stem, which produces a state of (22)_____ in the cerebral cortex and in a

region in the posterior part of the (23)_____, that contributes to arousal,

keeps muscles ready, and causes activity in the autonomic nervous system. The NREM sleep area

includes a (24)_____ system involving nuclei in the thalamus and anterior

hypothalamus. Lesions here may produce (25)_____, and electrical stimulation

may produce (26)_____. In addition, there is a brain-stem system involving

(27)_____ neurons, which use (28)_____ as a

transmitter substance. When this transmitter is increased or decreased experimentally,

(29)_____ increases or decreases accordingly. This system controls sleep by

sending (30)_____ impulses to the reticular formation. For REM sleep,

the crucial neurons are in the (31)_____ in the lower part of the pons. Increase

in the neurotransmitter (32)_____ and inhibition of

(33)_____ seem to increase REM sleep.

The sleep-waking cycle is one of many rhythms of body change, called (34)_____

rhythms, which last about 24 hours. There are also daily rhythms of body temperature, production of

certain hormones, and other activities, all under (35)_____ timing control.

This is shown by the disruptions that occur in ''jet lag'' and in laboratory studies in which no information about (36)_____ is provided and subjects are allowed to wake and sleep as

they wish. In the latter case, the subjects show somewhat (37)_____ cycles than

the 24-hour rhythm. There seem to be no neural systems that are completely

(38)_____ during sleep, and some even fire more frequently during sleep.

There is no proof that sleep loss has a (39)_____ physiological effect on the

nervous system or any other body mechanism. However, persons deprived of sleep, and especially stage-4

sleep, do feel "sleepy" and become distressed and somewhat less (40)_____.

It has been suggested that sleep and inactivity should be considered in terms of their overall effect on

the (41)_____ of the individual and the species rather than in terms of

the physiological recuperative effect they have. Sleep patterns may have developed in various species

to keep the individual inactive during the period of greatest (42)_____.

The somatic nervous system is concerned primarily with sensory input from the external world and with

the control of body movement by (43)_____ muscles. The autonomic nervous

system receives input from external sensory sources via pain and pressure receptors in the

(44)_____. On the motor side, it is divided into the sympathetic nervous

system and the parasympathetic nervous system, and they control the (45)_____

muscles of the intenal organs and glands. The sympathetic nervous system is built to facilitate a widespread

discharge, including dilation of the pupils, increases in heart rate and blood pressure, and rerouting of the

(46)_____. These reactions prepare the organism for

(47)_____ action. The parasympathetic nervous system is constructed to be

more (48)_____ in its influence upon the visceral organs. It operates in

a generally (49)_____ way to the sympathetic nervous system by returning

the system to normal and conserving (50)_____. The neural transmitter in

the sympathetic nervous system is (51)_____, while that for the parasympa-

thetic nervous system is (52)_____.

The endocrine system consists of a number of glands, each producing chemical products called

(53)_____, that are discharged directly into the bloodstream. The posterior

pituitary gland is controlled by the (54)_____. It secretes the

(55)_____ hormone that controls the rate and volume of urine production.

The anterior pituitary gland produces many hormones that control the amount of hormones secreted by

other (56)_____. Other anterior pituitary hormones influence body

(57)_____. The pituitary gland is partly under the control of the

(58)_____ and the autonomic nervous system and partly under the control

of other hormones. The secretion of adrenal steroids by the (59)_____ is

controlled by an anterior pituitary hormone known as (60)_____. The

amount of this hormone and other steroids increases as a function of physical and psychological

(61)_____, and they change the body's reaction to injury and increase the amount of energy available to the cells. This hormone also has specific effects on (62)_____ and behavior. Epinephrine and norepinephrine are produced by the (63)_____, which supports the actions of the sympathetic nervous system. The anterior pituitary gland also produces (64)_____ hormone, which controls the hormone secreted by the thyroid gland. Emotional excitement leads to increased secretion. The thyroid hormone tends to increase the speed of cellular (65)_____. In hyperthyroidism, there is an excess of this hormone, which causes the person to feel (66)_____. Undersecretion, or hypothyroidism, before or soon after birth results in (67)_____, with retardation in mental and physical growth.

The bodily responses accompanying emotional experience are under the control of the autonomic nervous system and the (68)_____. With emotional stress, the electrical resistance of the skin drops and the skin becomes a better (69)_____ of electricity. This electrodermal response is often called the (70)_____, and it is a function of the activity of the (71)_____. Also during emotional stress, there is an (72)_____ in blood pressure, rate of heartbeat, blood volume in various parts of the body, respiration, size of the pupils, and the chemical composition of various body fluids.

The James-Lange theory of emotion asserts that when an emotion-provoking stimulus is presented, we first react with the (73)_____ responses typical of emotion and appropriate to the situation. When the feedback from these responses arrives at the (74)_____, we experience the emotion. A second theory suggests that the emotion-provoking stimuli trigger the (75)_____, which in turn sends impulses to the cortex for emotional experience and to the muscles and glands for emotional responses. Another theory, called the (76)_____ theory of emotion, proposes that the reticular formation, with the help of the hypothalamus, controls the cortical areas important for emotional experience and the system responsible for emotional responses. Still another theory emphasizes the role of the (77)_____ system.

Evidence indicates clearly the role of the (78)_____ in emotion, especially for such responses as stalking behavior, alarm, flight, and rage. The (79)_____ is similarly involved, since arousal is necessary for emotion. Parts of the (80)_____ have also been shown to be involved in emotion, since lesions and electrical stimulation in this system cause changes in many kinds of motivated behavior and emotional responses. It has been suggested that this system contains the neuronal network for behavioral dispositions, and it has been shown to be involved in normal (81)_____.

Theories relating to the production of psychosis have centered on (82)_____ mechanisms and suggest that an excess or deficiency of a particular (83)_____ underlies a given abnormal condition. A psychotic depression is a deep and unjustified sadness accompanied by a withdrawal from (84)_____ and by insomnia, loss of appetite, and a reduction in the sex drive. The catecholamine theory of depression proposes that it is partly determined by a deficiency of the transmitters (85)_____ and (86)_____. Transmitter substances produced in a nerve cell may be (87)_____ before it leaves the axon or it may be (88)_____ by the axon terminal. Either way, there is (89)_____ transmitter to stimulate the next neuron. Antidepressant drugs in use today include (90)_____, which increases the amount of transmitter available by preventing an enzyme from destroying the catecholamines within the axon, and the (91)_____ drugs, which increase the amount of transmitter by blocking resorption of it by the axon that released it. Another transmitter substance, (92)_____, has been proposed to operate in a way similar to the catecholamines. Manic attacks sometimes accompany depression, and chemicals containing (93)_____ have been used in their treatment. It has been hypothesized that manic attacks result from an excess of (94)_____ and possibly other transmitters, and that lithium reduces them. The most common form of psychosis, (95)_____, is characterized by disorders of thought and emotion, often leading to hallucinations and delusions. One current theory is that this disorder is due to an excess of (96)_____. Normal mood swings may be due to changes in synaptic transmitters or to other causes, and many (97)_____ drugs have similar effects on both "normal" people and patients. The causes of psychoses may still be (98)_____ in nature, and the biochemical factors may simply tell us how the experiences have their effect on the brain and thus on behavior.

One effect of prolonged food deprivation is a reduction of (99)_____ in the blood. According to the (100)_____ theory of food intake, a decrease in the amount of glucose being used by the cells serves as an internal stimulus for hunger. The (101)_____ theory says that our hunger or eating mechanism is aware of the amount of (102)_____ stored in the body. Blood sugar and fat storage changes do not occur as (103)_____ as eating stops and hunger disappears, so other changes must be occurring in the body. Recent evidence suggests that a hormone, (104)_____, is released by the (105)_____ when food is present there, and this may signal turning off of further food intake. The (106)_____ and (107)_____ nuclei of the hypothalamus have been thought of as the feeding and satiation centers controlling hunger and food intake, respectively. While these centers are undoubtedly important in the hunger-feeding process, higher structures in both the cortex and the (108)_____ are also involved.

In addition to dry mouth, bodily conditions that seem able to produce thirst are (109)_____, or reduction of total blood volume, and (110)_____. With hypovolemia, the kidneys release a hormone that is transformed in the blood into (111)_____, which causes the kidneys to reduce (112)_____; when carried to the brain, this substance probably inaugurates drinking and stimulates thirst. The brain structures involved in these processes are probably in the (113)_____.

In the normally developed adult human being, visual, auditory, and olfactory stimuli play a major role in the sex motive, largely on a (114)_____ basis. Tactual stimulation of primary and secondary sex areas influences the sex motive on an (115)_____ basis. These stimuli trigger the (116)_____, which produces the congestion of the blood vessels, heart-rate and blood-pressure increases, deep breathing, and increased perspiration associated with sexual behavior. Sexual behavior is partly under the control of the gonads, the (117)_____ in the male, and the (118)_____ in the female. The anterior pituitary gland produces (119)_____ hormones which regulate the production of the sex hormones. The testes produce (120)_____, the male hormone, and (121)_____, the female hormone. The ovaries produce (122)_____, as well as (123)_____, which helps prepare the uterus for pregnancy. Testosterone and estrogen are responsible for the growth of (124)_____ and the development of secondary sex characteristics. Hormones are critical for the development of both sexual structures and normal (125)_____. In humans, once this development takes place, hormones play a relatively (126)_____ role. There is some evidence to suggest that the brain of a fetus or infant of either sex is organized to produce (127)_____ sexual behavior and that only when the (128)_____ is present in early development does normal male sexual behavior appear in later life. However, there is reason to believe that (129)_____ neuronal systems exist in every infant for both male and female types of behavior; furthermore, genetic factors, experience, and hormone balance throughout life probably determine how much of each kind of behavior will be shown later. Parts of the (130)_____ are also involved in the sex motive.

4. THOUGHT QUESTIONS

a. Stage-1-REM occupies at least half of the sleeping time of an infant, drops to about 25 percent in the adult years, and drops even further in old age. What do you think is the function of this type of sleep, and why should it drop over an individual's lifespan?

b. The "lie" detector is usually a polygraph, which measures such autonomically controlled body responses as the galvanic skin response. What is the basis for its being called a lie detector? What does it actually measure and how is it used?

c. Drugs influencing the increase or decrease of neural transmitters have been used in the treatment of psychosis. Their relative effectiveness has encouraged the notion that nature rather than nurture underlies such disorders. Do these chemical findings contribute at all to resolving the issue of nature and nurture in the etiology of psychosis?

d. Sex hormones are critical in the human for the development of sex organs and normal sexual behavior. However, they appear to be unimportant for the maintenance of sexual behavior in the adult. Why do you think this is so? What does such evidence indicate about the role of learning in adult sexual behavior?

5. EVALUATION (SELF-TESTS)

Correct answers and text page references are given at the end of the unit.

a. Fill-in-the-blanks Items

Write the word(s) that best complete(s) the sentence in the space provided.

1. Very deep sleep is characterized by large, _____ *slow* _____ EEG waves.

2. Tonic EEG sleep is characterized by _____ *conceptual* _____ dreams.

3. Increase in the neurotransmitter _____ *Ach* _____ is associated with an increase in REM sleep.

4. Circadian rhythms are those of about _____ *24* _____ hours in duration.

5. The reactions of the sympathetic nervous system prepare the organism for _____ *emergency* _____ action.

6. Body growth is influenced by hormones produced by the _____ *thyroid gland* _____.

7. The galvanic skin response is now called the _____ *electrodermal* _____ response.

8. Lesions and electrical stimulation of the _____ *lembic system* _____ cause changes in many kinds of motivated behavior.

9. The catecholamine theory of depression proposes that there is a _____ *decrease/ deficiency* _____ of specific neurotransmitters.

10. Gonadotropic hormones that regulate the production of the sex hormones are produced by the _____ *anterior pituitary* _____ gland.

b. Matching Items

Write the number of the correct item from the right column in front of the matching item in the left column.

_5_	stage-1-REM sleep	1. produces the antidiuretic hormone
_8_	waking state	2. locus coeruleus
_2_	REM sleep system	3. antidepressant drug
_1_	posterior pituitary gland	4. reduction of total blood volume
_6_	ACTH	5. occurs every 90 minutes
_9_	cretinism	6. increases with stress
_3_	MAO inhibitors	7. antimanic drug
_7_	lithium	8. reticular activity
_10_	glucostatic theory	9. hypothyroidism
_4_	hypovolemia	10. blood sugar changes underlie hunger

c. Multiple-choice Items

Circle the letter in front of the answer that best completes the stem.

1. While the first REM period may be rather short, a later period may be as long as:
   a. 15 minutes
   b. 30 minutes
   c. 45 minutes
   d. 60 minutes

2. The waking state is dependent on activity of the:
   a. locus coeruleus
   b. hypothalamus
   c. reticular formation
   d. limbic system

3. Sleep increases or decreases as which of the following transmitters is increased or decreased?
   a. epinephrine
   b. norepinephrine
   c. serotonin
   d. acetylcholine

4. The neural transmitter in the sympathetic nervous system is:
   a. epinephrine
   b. norepinephrine
   c. serotonin
   d. acetylcholine

5. The neural transmitter for the parasympathetic nervous system is:
   a. epinephrine
   b. norepinephrine
   c. serotonin
   d. acetylcholine

6. Which of the following glands secretes the antidiuretic hormone?
   a. anterior pituitary
   b. posterior pituitary
   c. adrenal cortex
   d. adrenal medulla

7. The speed of cellular metabolism is increased by:
   a. the thyroid hormone
   b. the adrenal steroids
   c. acetylcholine
   d. ACTH

8. Which brain structure is most intimately involved in emotion?
   a. hypothalamus
   b. reticular formation
   c. pons
   d. limbic system

9. The catecholamine theory of depression proposes that it arises partly as a result of a deficiency of:
   a. epinephrine and serotonin
   b. serotonin and norepinephrine
   c. norepinephrine and dopamine
   d. dopamine and epinephrine

10. In addition to dry mouth, bodily conditions that seem able to produce thirst are:
    a. cholecystokinin and hypovolemia
    b. hypovolemia and cellular dehydration
    c. cellular dehydration and the antidiuretic hormone
    d. the antidiuretic hormone and cholecystokinin

d. Short-answer Items

Answer the following questions with short, concise statements. Reference pages for the material are given at the end of the unit.

1. Contrast stage-1-REM sleep with stage-4 sleep in terms of EEG pattern, rapid eye movements, difficulty of awakening, and occurrence of dreams.

2. Contrast the functions of the sympathetic nervous system with those of the parasympathetic nervous system.

3. What is the likely action of MAO inhibitors on neural transmitters in the treatment of depression?

4. What are the roles of hormones in the development of sex organs and in the development and maintenance of normal sexual behavior?

ANSWER KEY FOR UNIT 21

Unit Review

1. 8 to 12
2. higher
3. regular
4. sleep spindles
5. slow
6. decline
7. regular
8. in reverse
9. rapid eye movements (REM)
10. 90
11. one hour
12. dreaming
13. tonic
14. phasic
15. middle ear
16. phasic
17. tonic
18. decreases
19. half/50 percent
20. 25 percent
21. reticular formation
22. arousal
23. hypothalamus
24. forebrain
25. insomnia
26. sleep
27. raphé
28. serotonin
29. sleep
30. inhibitory
31. locus coeruleus
32. acetylcholine
33. norepinephrine
34. circadian
35. internal

36. time of day
37. longer
38. inactive
39. deleterious
40. efficient
41. survival
42. danger
43. skeletal
44. viscera
45. nonskeletal
46. blood
47. emergency
48. specific
49. opposite
50. body resources
51. norepinephrine
52. acetylcholine
53. hormones
54. hypothalamus
55. antidiuretic
56. endocrine glands
57. growth
58. hypothalamus
59. adrenal cortex
60. adrenocorticotropic hormone (ACTH)
61. stress
62. learning
63. adrenal medulla
64. thyrotropic
65. metabolism
66. excited/irritable
67. cretinism
68. endocrine system
69. conductor
70. galvanic skin response (GSR)

71. sweat glands
72. increase
73. muscular-glandular
74. cerebral cortex
75. hypothalamus
76. activation
77. limbic
78. hypothalamus
79. reticular formation
80. limbic system
81. learning and memory
82. synaptic
83. transmitter
84. normal activity
85. norepinephrine
86. dopamine
87. destroyed
88. reabsorbed
89. less
90. monoamine oxidase (MAO) inhibitors
91. tricyclic
92. serotonin
93. lithium
94. norepinephrine
95. schizophrenia
96. dopamine
97. antipsychotic
98. environmental
99. sugar
100. glucostatic

101. lipostatic
102. fat
103. quickly
104. cholecystokinin
105. small intestine
106. lateral
107. ventromedial
108. limbic system
109. hypovolemia
110. cellular dehydration
111. angiotensin
112. urine flow
113. hypothalamus
114. learned
115. unlearned
116. autonomic nervous system
117. testes
118. ovaries
119. gonadotropic
120. testosterone
121. estrogen
122. estrogen
123. progesterone
124. sex organs
125. sexual behavior
126. unimportant
127. female
128. male hormone
129. separate
130. hypothalamus

Evaluation (Self-tests)

a.   **Fill-in-the-blanks Items**

1. slow (p. 494)
2. conceptual (p. 495)
3. acetylcholine (p. 496)
4. 24 (p. 496)
5. emergency (p. 499)
6. anterior pituitary gland (p. 500)
7. electrodermal (p. 503)
8. limbic system (pp. 505–507)
9. deficiency (p. 507)
10. anterior pituitary (p. 515)

b.   **Matching Items: Correct order and page references are:**

5 (p. 494); 8 (p. 495); 2 (p. 496); 1 (p. 500); 6 (p. 500);
9 (pp. 502–503); 3 (p. 509); 7 (p. 510); 10 (pp. 511–512); 4 (p. 514).

c.   **Multiple-choice Items: Correct answers and page references are:**

1—d (p. 494); 2—c (p. 495); 3—c (p. 496); 4—b (p. 500); 5—d (p. 500);
6—b (p. 500); 7—a (p. 502); 8—a (p. 505); 9—c (p. 507); 10—b (p. 514).

d.   **Short-answer Items: Page references for answer material are:**

1. pp. 494–495; 2. pp. 497–500; 3. pp. 507–509; 4. pp. 514–516.

Unit 22

PERSONALITY: DEFINITION AND MEASUREMENT

1. INTRODUCTION TO STUDY OF THIS UNIT

Concern for aspects of personality has been with us for many years. In ancient Roman theater, actors would use masks, which they would hold in front of them to indicate the kind of person they were portraying or the way that the character felt at the time. The term personality was derived from the Latin term *persona*, since the word refers to one aspect of personality as it is viewed today — the way that we appear to other persons. Personality means more than this now, and it is a difficult concept to define, as you will read in the text.

Systematic attempts to describe personality date back to at least early in the present century. Cesare Lombroso was a noted Italian criminologist who, around 1910, suggested that there were strong relationships between physiognomy and behavior. Specifically, he proposed that criminals had particular body configurations and that body type contributed to the behavior that ensued. He felt that certain facial characteristics were especially important. The criminal, for example, had a narrow forehead and usually displayed asymmetry of parts of the face (e.g., one ear larger than the other or one eye drooping more than the other). These characteristics resulted from a greater degree of sensory development than of cognitive development. It was some years later that Kretschmer presented his body typology system, partly described in the text, and still later that William Sheldon outlined a much more elaborate physiogmetric scheme.

Measurement of important personality characteristics has a much longer history. The Chinese developed a testing program around 2000 B.C. to select those eligible for public office and occasionally used independent scorers to reduce grading bias. This effort developed over the centuries to a systematic testing program to select Chinese civil-service officials. Around the time of Christ, an oral examination was required every three years of the civil servant who wished to retain his position, and in the Han Dynasty (around 1000 A.D.), batteries of tests were employed for such selection purposes. In the Ming Dynasty (around 1500 A.D.), different levels of examinations were used to select civil servants. Candidates were put through days of examinations at local and regional centers before becoming eligible for their final examinations in the capital. Western missionaries and diplomats observed these methods in the nineteenth century, and their observations influenced the development of the civil-servant selection program in England and in the United States.

World War I and World War II had an important influence on personality test development in this country. We have said in a prior study unit that development of Binet's IQ test for use in this country was stimulated by the necessity of screening candidates for the military in World War I. The period from that war to the end of World War II saw the importation to this country of the Rorschach test, developed earlier in Switzerland, and the development here of the TAT in 1935 and the MMPI in 1943. Since then, there has been great growth in personality measurement associated with the amazing growth of clinical psychology in the past 35 years.

2. ISSUES AND CONCEPTS

The unit begins by defining personality, noting that newer definitions emphasize the complexity and uniqueness of personality organization. A good definition focuses on the integration within each individual of abilities, attitudes, habits, and other characteristics and includes the two-way interaction between the individual and the environment.

You should learn next what a personality measure is and how measures of personality are related to personality theory. Also be able to state what generalizability and validity of personality measurement refer to.

The unit turns next to ratings and rating scales, including the adjective checklist. Be able to distinguish ipsative rating (an example is the Q-sort) from other, normative rating approaches. In addition, be able to describe what an interview is and distinguish a structured interview from an open-ended one. Learn what a situational test is, how this type of measure has been used, and the chief difficulty with this approach.

It is important to know as well what self-ratings or self-reports are and what the differences between self-reports and reports by others may be due to. Be able to describe the personality inventory approach and the two principal methods for designing such inventories, the *a priori* and the empirical. Also, you should be able to state how response bias influences inventories and how this affects the validity of instruments.

Concerning projective personality measurement techniques, learn what they are and how they relate to Freudian theory. Be able to discuss the basic procedures for the Rorschach test, why much skill is necessary to interpret this test, and why this method has been vigorously criticized. In addition, become familiar with the basic procedures of the Thematic Apperception Test and how this device is scored.

More recent personality appraisal, called personality assessment, makes use of multiple measures and you should learn how this operates. Be able to cite two criticisms of this approach as it has been used in commercial organizations.

Finally, learn the two major strategies for translating data into predictions about individual personality and be able to differentiate these two approaches. As you read, recognize that the relative worth of these two approaches has not yet been evaluated.

3. UNIT REVIEW

Correct answers are given at the end of the unit.

One of the earliest definitions of personality emphasizes the (1)_____ aspect of the individual. The word personality itself is derived from the Latin word *persona*, which was the (2)_____ in the early Roman theater. There have been many definitions of personality proposed in more recent times, each emphasizing different characteristics of the individual. Most newer definitions, however, emphasize the complexity and uniqueness of personality (3)_____ and that personality is not merely an assortment of specific (4)_____. Rather, the focus is on the (5)_____ within each individual of abilities, beliefs, values, motives, and habits and includes (6)_____ influences upon the developing personality and the effects of the individual's behavior on the social environment.

There is no best way to (7)_____ a given personality characteristic. The choice of a measurement instrument depends largely on the (8)_____ of personality used. A personality measure is only a (9)_____ of trait-related behavior. To be useful, it must have (10)_____, which refers to a test's applicability to a wide series of situations and to whether different raters or tests agree on the scores they assign to individuals; the test must also have (11)_____, that is, it must actually measure what is desired to be measured.

Perhaps the most frequently used personality measurement is the (12)_____, which typically evaluates behavior observed in relatively (13)_____ settings. It involves assigning an observed subject to a point on a (14)_____. The adjective (15)_____ is a simple scale which says that a subject either has this characteristic or does not. Most ratings scales have from (16)_____ points, the number of such points depending on the adequacy of information on which the rating is based and on how clearly the scale points are (17)_____. The (18)_____ is a type of rating in which a set of personality-descriptive items are placed in (19) _____ less and more characteristic of the individual being rated. The number of categories is (20)_____, as is (usually) the number of items permitted to be assigned to each category. This method of ordering traits within an individual is called (21) _____ rating, in contrast to (22)_____ rating, in which different persons are rated on a single scale. Whenever possible, ratings should be administered (23) _____ by several different raters so that degree of (24)_____can be evaluated.

One source of rating data is the (25)_____, which is a conversation between the subject and the data collector, who may follow a schedule to obtain responses to specific questions. The interviewee may reply freely to the questions in (26)_____ interviews, or he or she may be restricted to predetermined response categories.

Another approach to personality measurement is to record the response of the subject in a standard test situation that is a replica of a (27)_____ situation. This is called a (28)_____ test, and it assumes that behavior in the test situation will reflect the individual's behavioral (29)_____. One problem with such tests is their (30)_____. Whenever possible, it is best to observe a person's behavior in the setting in which the behavior actually occurs, but here there is the risk of the observer (31)_____ the "natural" situation. This has led to the development of (32)_____ measures.

The most commonly used information in the study of personality comes from (33)_____. Such measures may differ markedly from ratings made by (34)_____ observers, but they may still provide measures of how an individual views himself or herself. The (35)_____ is an organized and enduring perception in the individual's experience, unique to that person and constituting a central part of his or her personality (36)_____. Discrepancies between self-reports and those of others may reflect a (37)_____ between the public self and the private self (the "real me").

Another important approach to personality measurement is through personality (38)_____ aimed at discerning many traits. Each of these consists of a large number of statements or questions, to be responded to in one of several specified (39) _____. Different items may constitute a trait (40) _____, and there may be several of these on a single inventory. There are two main approaches to designing such inventories: the (41)_____ method, in which the items in the inventory are obviously related to the traits being measured; and the (42)_____ method, where the connection between the item and the trait, though statistically demonstrable, may not be at all apparent to the respondent. The Minnesota Multiphasic Personality Inventory (MMPI) and the California Psychological Inventory (CPI) are examples of (43)_____ derived inventories.

Subjects may develop (44)_____ with personality inventories so that the traits being measured are fairly apparent. For example, subjects tend to agree with (45)_____ items apart from their actual beliefs about them. The (46)_____ of the instrument would thereby be lessened, and personality inventories have been attacked for this difficulty. Response sets themselves have been measured as part of personality (47)_____.

Projective techniques are based on (48)_____ theory. In them, an (49)_____ stimulus pattern is presented to the subject, and he or she is asked to tell what is seen or to make up a story about it. The response is interpreted in terms of the (50)_____ processes at work in projection, or which involves protecting the conscious part of personality. Examples are the Rorschach inkblots and the (51) _____ pictures.

In the Rorschach test, (52)_____ inkblots, some black and white and others colored, are presented in turn to the subject, who is asked to describe what he or she sees. Responses are scored for location, stimulus characteristic, content, and (53)_____. The scores and their (54)_____ are taken to be diagnostic of specific tendencies. Interpretation requires a (55)_____ tester, since (56)_____ plays a large role. Validation studies show (57)_____ results, and the method has been widely criticized.

The TAT attempts to measure the 20 psychological (58)_____ in Murray's theory of personality. The subject is asked to tell a story about twenty pictures, each depicting a simple scene of (59)_____ meaning; he or she indicates what is happening, how it came about, and what will happen next. The nature of the plots, recurrent themes, types of heroes, and so on in the stories are analyzed to reveal important aspects of the person's (60)_____ and other characteristics.

No single technique for the measurement of personality has sufficient (61) _____ for useful predictive purposes, and individuals are occasionally (62)_____ on the basis of single tests. The typical procedure today is to do personality (63) _____, in which a (64)_____ of diverse measuring techniques is used. These measures are (65)_____ to yield a comprehensive personality description or a prediction of a specific performance. The approach is increasingly being used in corporate settings for personnel (66)_____. One criticism of this approach is that (67)_____ takes place: advancement in the firm is based on assessment profile, thereby "validating" the assessment. Another criticism is that selection may be based on (68)_____ expectations and lead to rejection of promising individuals.

Two major strategies for translating data into explicit predictions about individual personalities are the (69)_____ approach, making use of all available data, and the (70)_____ approach, in which such data are combined statistically to yield quantitative prediction. The two approaches have not been evaluated under entirely comparable conditions, and a (71)_____ verdict as to their relative worth is not yet possible.

4. THOUGHT QUESTIONS

a. One of the serious problems in the use of personality inventories is that respondents may adopt response sets, and their answers will tend to agree with socially desirable patterns. If you were developing such a measure, what would you do about this problem?

b. It has been found in some commercial and military situations that the reliability of ratings increases with the distance of the raters from the person being rated. For example, top management might agree more closely than two more immediate supervisors. Why do you think this might be so, and what does this phenomenon indicate about the usefulness of some ratings?

c. During World War II, the OSS (the precursor of the CIA) used elaborate situational tests to help select agents for foreign operations. Do you think that such tests were good techniques for these purposes? What kinds of difficulties do you suppose the OSS faced in this selection program? Could they have been avoided? If so, how?

d. Suppose that you devised a new projective personality measuring test that has the subject responding to different ambiguous patterns of mud droppings. You call your test the Multiple Estimate Symbolic Schedule (MESS). How would you go about doing validation studies on your MESS? Would it bother you that persons from different cultures saw different things or told different stories about your patterns? Explain.

5. EVALUATION (SELF-TESTS)

Correct answers and text page references are given at the end of the unit.

a. Fill-in-the-blanks Items

Write the word(s) that best complete(s) the sentence in the space provided.

1. Most definitions of personality emphasize the uniqueness and _____
   of personality organization.

2. The central part of the personality structure of a person is called the _____.

3. The most frequently used personality measurement device is the _____.

4. The method of ordering traits within an individual is called _____
   rating.

5. A personality measure must be applicable to a wide variety of situations, a characteristic
   called _____.

6. The adjective checklist is an example of a _____.

7. The Q-sort is an example of an _____ rating.

8. The MMPI is an example of a personality _____.

9. The TAT is an example of a _____ method.

10. Personality assessment makes use of a _____ of diverse
    measuring techniques.

b. Matching Items

Write the number of the correct item from the right column in front of the matching item in the left
column.

_____ generalizability	1. integration of all available information
_____ Rorschach inkblots	2. interviewee can respond freely
_____ locus of control	3. projective technique
_____ normative	4. applicability to many situations
_____ persona	5. actor's mask
_____ validity	6. internality or externality
_____ open-ended interview	7. agreeing with socially desirable items
_____ situational test	8. usual method of rating
_____ response set	9. measures what it is supposed to
_____ intuitive approach	10. replica of a real-life situation

c. Multiple-choice Items

Circle the letter in front of the answer that best completes the stem.
1. Most recent definitions of personality emphasize which characteristics of personality?
   a. complexity and uniqueness
   b. uniqueness and organization
   c. organization and habits
   d. habits and complexity

2. The rating method which orders traits within an individual is called:
   a. normative
   b. ipsative
   c. an adjective checklist
   d. projective

3. An example of an empirically derived personality inventory is the:
   a. TAT
   b. Rorschach
   c. MMPI
   d. adjective checklist

4. The most frequently used personality measurement is the:
   a. rating
   b. interview
   c. inventory
   d. projective

5. The personality measure that involves mainly conversation is the:
   a. rating
   b. interview
   c. inventory
   d. projective test

6. The personality measure aimed at discerning many traits is the:
   a. rating
   b. interview
   c. inventory
   d. projective test

7. The personality measure that makes use of ambiguous stimulus patterns is the:
   a. rating
   b. interview
   c. inventory
   d. projective test

8. The approach to designing personality inventories that uses items obviously related to the traits being measured is called the:
   a. intuitive approach
   b. quantitative approach
   c. empirical method
   d. *a priori* method

9. The strategy for translating personality data into explicit predictions that makes use of all available data is called the:
   a. intuitive approach
   b. quantitative approach
   c. empirical method
   d. *a priori* method

10. Projective techniques are based on the theory of:
    a. Jung
    b. Freud
    c. Kretschmer
    d. Murray

d. Short-answer Items

Answer the following questions with short, concise statements. Reference pages for the material are given at the end of the unit.

1. Describe what is meant by "unobtrusive" personality measurement, and indicate what problem such measures have been designed to help solve.

2. Contrast the *a priori* and the empirical approaches to personality inventory design.

3. Briefly describe the generalizability and validity requirements of any personality measurement.

4. Contrast the two most commonly used projective measuring techniques — the Rorschach test and the TAT.

ANSWER KEY FOR UNIT 22

Unit Review

1. outward
2. actor's mask
3. organization
4. traits
5. integration
6. environmental
7. measure
8. definition
9. sample
10. generalizability
11. validity
12. rating
13. natural
14. scale
15. checklist
16. 5 to 10
17. specified
18. Q-sort
19. categories
20. predetermined
21. ipsative
22. normative
23. independently
24. agreement
25. interview
26. open-ended
27. real-life
28. situational
29. traits
30. validity
31. changing
32. unobtrusive
33. self-reports
34. objective
35. self
36. structure
37. duality
38. inventories
39. categories
40. scale
41. *a priori*
42. empirical
43. empirically
44. response sets
45. socially desirable
46. validity
47. assessment
48. Freudian
49. ambiguous
50. unconscious
51. Thematic Apperception Test (TAT)
52. 10
53. originality
54. ratios
55. skilled
56. intuition
57. inconsistent
58. needs
59. ambiguous
60. needs
61. validity
62. misclassified
63. assessment
64. battery
65. combined
66. decision making
67. criterion contamination
68. stereotyped
69. intuitive
70. quantitative
71. valid

Evaluation (Self-tests)

a. Fill-in-the-blanks Items

1. complexity (p. 525)
2. self (p. 530)
3. rating (p. 526)
4. ipsative (p. 528)
5. generalizability (p. 526)

6. rating (p. 527)
7. ipsative (p. 528)
8. inventory (p. 532)
9. projective (pp. 534–535)
10. battery (p. 535)

b. Matching Items: Correct order and page references are:

4 (p. 526); 3 (p. 533); 6 (p. 531); 8 (p. 528); 5 (p. 525);
9 (p. 526); 2 (p. 529); 10 (p. 529); 7 (p. 532); 1 (p. 538).

c. Multiple-choice Items: Correct answers and page references are:

1—a (p. 525); 2—b (p. 528); 3—c (p. 532); 4—a (p. 526); 5—b (p. 528);
6—c (p. 530); 7—d (p. 533); 8—d (p. 530); 9—a (p. 538); 10—b (p. 533).

d. Short-answer Items: Page references for answer material are:

1. pp. 529–530; 2. pp. 530–532; 3. p. 526; 4. pp. 533–535.

Unit 23

THEORIES OF PERSONALITY

1. INTRODUCTION TO STUDY OF THIS UNIT

This unit reviews three general theoretical approaches to personality — the psychoanalytic, the behavioristic, and the phenomenological/humanistic. Of these three, certainly the psychoanalytic approach has had the most substantial influence on shaping the way that we think about personality, and many of its concepts and terms have become a part of our everyday language. The founder of this movement, Sigmund Freud, was born in Moravia, spent most of his life in Vienna, and lived out his last year or so in England, having escaped in 1939 from the Nazis, who had taken control of Austria.

Freud went to medical school at the University of Vienna to become a research scientist. Instead, having been married in the meantime and facing the expense of raising a family, he entered private practice. At the time, there were not many opportunities in academia for Jews in Austria. After deciding to deal with nervous disorders, Freud studied for a year with Charcot in France and learned the technique of hypnosis in the treatment of disorders. Back in Vienna, he formed an alliance with Joseph Breuer, who had already been using free association in treating symptoms of neurosis. He broke with Breuer over the importance of sexual motivation, but continued to use free association and developed dream analysis as a supplementary method.

His theory changed a good deal over the years. Initially, the model was very biologically oriented, and he spoke about the three levels of consciousness. Later he added the structure of the personality, describing the id, ego, and superego levels. Still later he framed the structure of personality as developing over the important psychosexual developmental stages. All along, he spoke about repression and the other ego defense mechanisms. Indeed, over time he developed over 30 somewhat different views of the concept of identification.

Freud was criticized vigorously for the unscientific nature of his inquiries. This is especially interesting since it is clear that Freud had a deep scientific interest and equally clear that he thought his enterprise was most scientific. Unfortunately, subjecting many of the psychoanalytic notions to objective scientific examination has been virtually impossible. In addition, Freud was never able to describe exactly how he came by most of his notions, so the process was not repeatable.

Another interesting feature of Freud, the person, was the difficulty he continued to have maintaining long-term associations, especially with the most outstanding of his colleagues. We mentioned above that he broke with Breuer over the importance of sexual motivation. A similar controversy was involved in his break with Alfred Adler. Adler preferred to emphasize social motivation, and this was not tolerable to Freud. Some of Freud's letters suggest that there were other disagreements between him and Adler, mainly interpersonal. The most important break for Freud, perhaps, was that with Carl Jung. Jung was his heir apparent, but their theoretical concepts began to diverge. Over a long correspondence between the two, Freud seemed to be maintaining some patience as an encouragement for rapprochement, but Jung's continued heresy led to Freud's final letter. In it he proposed the abandonment of their personal relations entirely. Jung replied, accepting the break with the classic phrase, ''The rest is silence.''

2. ISSUES AND CONCEPTS

Personality theorists strive for global understanding of the whole person. Of the three theoretical approaches which you will study in this unit (psychoanalytic, behavioristic, and phenomenological), the psychoanalytic theory of Freud comes closest. In this theory, learn the structure of personality with its three levels of id, ego, and superego, and how the three interrelate. Learn, too, the four psychosexual development stages, and the latency period, as well. Be able to describe how pleasure is obtained in each stage and how trauma and thwarting can lead to a twisting of personality. Be able to define the Oedipus and the Electra complexes, and to discuss how these contribute to identification and role processes. Definitions of repression and of the other defense mechanisms should also be learned, along with how they function to protect the ego. Since all of these processes are unconscious, they can be examined only by a trained analyst employing free association and dream analysis techniques. Be able to describe those methods. Finally, become familiar with how Freud went about developing his theory, the criticisms that have been made of it, and its current influence in psychotherapy and education.

Concerning other psychoanalytic theories, learn what the major emphases are in Jung's analytic theory, the difference between the personal and the collective unconscious, and how the archetype operates in the latter. Be able to differentiate his two basic attitudes of extroversion and introversion, and how these combine with the four basic functions of personality. Specifically, be able to distinguish the views of Freud from those of Jung.

Learn what the major emphases are in Adler's social-interest theory. Become familiar with his notions of upward striving for superiority, the role of real or fancied inferiority, and what consequences stress and failure have for adjustment.

Be able to describe how the neo-Freudians modified Freud by putting increased stress on the relative importance of interpersonal relationships. Learn why the popularity of psychoanalytic models has lessened greatly in recent years, at least in this country.

For the behaviorists, personality is simply a set of response dispositions, or habits. Learn how Neal Miller and John Dollard attempted to look at several of the psychoanalytic concepts in terms of conditioning principles, and the difficulties of this approach. Be able to cite the connection between the behavioral approaches and behavior therapy.

There are other learning approaches to personality that emphasize the role of cognition. Be able to differentiate the models of Julian Rotter and Albert Bandura in terms of the learning variables and cognitive variables emphasized by each.

Within the phenomenological/humanistic approaches, know what full development of the individual entails in Abraham Maslow's theory. Learn the hierarchical structure of needs and how individuals proceed through the structure. Learn, too, some characteristics of the actualized person, according to Maslow. Be able to differentiate the theory of Carl Rogers from that of Maslow in terms of drive emphasis and how growth occurs, and describe Roger's "healthy personality."

Finally, after reading the unit, you should be able to compare the three major theoretical approaches to personality in terms of the function of unconscious motivation, the role of needs and drives, the goals of change, and the approach to therapy of each.

3. UNIT REVIEW

Correct answers are given at the end of the unit.

Personality theorists strive for (1)_____ understanding of the whole person. This direction was most strongly shaped by (2)_____, whose theory was first presented at the end of the nineteenth century and came to dominate the field of personality. He asserted that humans are driven by unconscious (3)_____ urges, an idea not very compatible with Victorian notions of (4)_____ and high-mindedness.

For Freud, there was an (5)_____ mental life containing a world of motives and ideas that are kept hidden in order to avoid the (6)_____ that would occur if they were allowed to become (7)_____. These motives are analogous to the suggestions of the (8)_____ that govern behavior without the subject's apparent awareness. In Freud's time, such ideas received a (9)_____ reaction.

Freud was trained as a (10)_____ and became a research scientist and a determinist. He came to believe as a practicing neurologist that emotional problems, or (11)_____, reflected the hidden sexual concerns of his patients. He described metaphorically the structure of personality as composed of three systems, the id, the ego, and the (12)_____. The id is the (13)_____ part of personality out of which the other two parts grow. It is the reservoir of psychic energy, called the (14) _____, and of innate instinctual forces, largely (15) _____. The id wants immediate gratification, which Freud called the (16)_____. The ego is the (17)_____ part of the personality, and it behaves in accordance with the (18)_____ principle, taking consequences into account. It operates as a (19)_____ between the id and the superego. The superego is shaped by (20)_____ training and incorporates society's values, reflecting our identification with a (21)_____, usually of the same sex. It represents our striving toward some (22)_____ since it reflects our interjection of (23)_____ into of our own personality.

The personality develops by undergoing a series of potentially stressful periods, called (24)_____ stages. For Freud, personality can become stuck, or (25)_____, at one or another of these stages, resulting in characteristic forms of personal maladjustment. In early infancy the (26)_____ stage occurs, during which gratification is obtained from (27)_____ stimulation. If such pleasure is thwarted, the individual may become fixated at this stage and later release sexual or (28)_____ energy from mouth activities. As adults, such persons may continue to obtain (29)_____ by talking a lot, smoking, arguing, or waiting to be fed. In the second year of life, the (30)_____ period occurs when (31)_____ of the child takes place. People who become fixated at this stage may in later years be stingy (or (32)" _____") or extravagant (33)(_____). Fixation may occur because of toilet-training trauma and may result in obsession later with (34)_____. In the third to fifth years, the (35)_____ stage occurs, in which the child's interest turns to its own (36)_____. The young male seeks sole possession of his (37)_____ but is terrified of his (38)_____. This culmination of infantile sexuality is called the

(39)_____, wherein the child actually is or imagines being threatened with (40)_____. Female children go through a somewhat analogous state, called the (41)_____. Role learning and (42)_____ occur in this stage. After a brief latency period, most people around the time of (43)_____ enter the genital stage, at which point adult sexual interactions can take place.

We don't ordinarily remember these stages or associated traumas because of an active process of self-protection called (44)_____, wherein anxiety-provoking material is pushed into the (45)_____. Other defense mechanisms include (46)_____, which refers to the systematic shifting of sources of gratification away from an original object toward a less anxiety-provoking one; (47)_____, in which individuals explain their behaviors and feelings in conflict situations in such a way that self-esteem is maintained and anxiety avoided; (48)_____, in which the person entertains two logically incompatible concepts side by side without awareness of the obvious discrepancy; (49)_____, in which the person offsets anxiety arising from failure or guilt by projecting blame onto someone else; and (50)_____, in which strong anxiety-provoking impulses are accompanied by a counteracting tendency exactly opposite to the repressed tendencies.

Freud's theory is based on the free associations and reports of (51)_____ of his neurotic patients and on his own (52)_____. He assumed that the release of (53)_____ material through psychoanalysis can have beneficial effects. His notions have influenced other psychotherapies treating neurosis and concerned with child-rearing and (54)_____ practices. While that influence has been substantial, the theory has also been criticized vigorously because it is not subject to (55)_____.

In the analytic approach of Jung, the emphasis is on (56)_____ and on the innate human aspiration toward (57)_____ and wholeness. The total personality is called the (58)_____, which includes the conscious aspect of mind, or ego, and unconscious processes that conflict with ego. Jung broke down the latter into the personal unconscious (as in Freud's concept), and the (59)_____ unconscious, which reflects the (60)_____ of humankind and is not available to conscious thought, although it does affect behavior. Components of this aspect are called (61) _____, which are emotion-laden, universal thoughts or ideas. Art, myth, dreams, visions, hallucinations, and spiritual experiences contain many archetypal (62)_____. Jung differed from Freud in emphasizing the collective unconscious over the personal unconscious and in not emphasizing the (63)_____ drives that Freud did. Jung proposed that individuals have two basic attitudes: (64)_____, which reflects an orientation toward the external, objective world; and (65)_____, an orientation toward the inner subjective world. While each of us has both orientations, one usually predominates in consciousness and combines with the four basic functions of the personality: thinking, feeling, sensing, and (66)_____. The goal of selfhood is to achieve (67) _____ among these functions. The prime mover in this system is (68)_____, which operates according to (69)_____, or conservation of energy, and (70)_____, or balance. Whereas Freud emphasized the early stages of development, Jung emphasized the (71)_____ of life.

In Adler's theory, (72)_____ (rather than biological) determinants and the concept of the eternally (73)_____ of the self are emphasized. The prime source of human motivation is the innate striving for (74)_____. This striving is in compensation for the individual's feelings of real or fancied (75)_____, and these feelings are essential requirements for psychological (76)_____. Excessive stress or failures may have detrimental consequences for further (77)_____. Each individual is (78)_____ in the direction he or she takes to achieve superiority, and these strivings take socially constructive forms.

Like Adler, neo-Freudians stress the continuing search for emotional security in (79)_____, beginning with the family. However, neither the Freudian nor the neo-Freudian models enjoy today the (80)_____ they had 20 to 30 years ago.

In the behavioristic tradition, the views of Freud, Jung, and others are thought of as too (81)_____ to be accepted uncritically. For the behaviorist, personality is simply a set of (82)_____—that is, tendencies to respond in specific ways under particular physical conditions. Dollard and Miller tried to analyze personality as a set of habits acquired by (83)_____. While this approach suffered from the lack of (84)_____, just as psychoanalysis had, it has, along with other behavioral approaches to personality, stimulated promising approaches to psychotherapy, called (85)_____.

Other learning approaches to personality emphasize (86)_____ in the acquisition of expectations and symbolic constructions that serve as guides to behavior. Rotter's social-learning theory suggests that we learn how to behave in (87)_____ and that the satisfaction of our needs is governed by (88)_____. He combines reinforcement and (89)_____ to predict how the individual will behave in complex social situations. Expectancy is the subjective likelihood that a specific behavior will lead to (90)_____. Situational contexts and current (91) _____ are very important. Rotter has also postulated a (92)_____ continuum, on which individuals at one end have a generalized expectancy that reinforcement is brought about by their (93)_____ (i.e., they believe in (94)_____ control), while individuals at the other end credit reinforcement to (95)_____ control.

Bandura's social-learning theory emphasizes primarily the role of the social environment in the development of personality, in the form of individuals' (96)_____ their behavior after those they admire or those who are more powerful. An individual's characteristic way of behaving, which is personality, is determined by (97)_____ learning.

The approach called phenomenology opposes both psychoanalysis and (98)_____. It emphasizes the importance of (99)_____, unanalyzed experience as the given of personality. For example, Maslow asserted that humans have a unique psychological nature whose structure includes inherent needs, capacities, and (100)_____. Full development of the individual involves (101)_____ of this structure, while blocking of the structure results in psychopathology. Needs are arranged in a (102) _____ pattern, with needs generated by physiological and psychological deficiencies at the (103)_____. An individual has to satisfy lower needs before higher needs are (104)_____. When all of these basic needs have been satisfied well enough, the eventual actualization of a person's (105)_____ can take place through the pursuit of (106)_____ needs and goals, including goodness, justice, and so on. In interview studies, Maslow found that self-actualized persons were realistic, private, creative nonconformists who had a good sense of humor and had (107)_____ experiences.

Rogers developed his (108)_____ model of personality within his practice of psychotherapy. He feels that the client is not driven by unspeakably terrorizing instinctual forces, as Freud thought, but by a healthy drive toward (109)_____. Healthy personalities are in close contact with their own (110)_____ and values and are easygoing, natural, and as accepting of others as they are of themselves. Aggression and hostility are (111)_____ in such persons, who are relaxed and "laid back." Growth occurs through (112)_____.

Comparison of the three major approaches to personality reveals fundamental differences in their views of (113)_____. Basic biological urges that force much material into the unconscious, thus determining the conscious aspects of personality, are emphasized by (114)_____. A rejection of both consciousness and unconsciousness and an emphasis on a variety of drives and reinforcement that determine the learning of habits that constitute personality are basic to the approach of (115)_____. Seeing the individual as health seeking and capable of achieving high levels of fulfillment of aspirations is the view of the (116)_____ school. Each of these approaches has developed therapeutic techniques for changing personality, but none can be viewed as achieving the status of a general (117)_____.

4. THOUGHT QUESTIONS

a. Freud developed his theory on the basis of his own self-analysis and the analysis of his patients. If you wished to test the scientific merit of this model, how would you set about doing so? Can you think of any experimental analog of just one of the concepts — say, repression?

b. Jot down five characteristic behaviors of an adult friend that you know very well. Then, think how each can be traced back to one or another of Freud's psychosexual developmental stages in terms of being a fixation, reaction formation, or other defensive reaction to events of the stage. What does this little ''game'' tell you about Freud's theory?

c. Miller and Dollard attempt to portray basic psychoanalytic concepts in behavioral terms. Try to think of ways of conceptualizing psychoanalysis in the terms of phenomenology. Difficult? Of course. Perhaps you will have more luck if you try to conceptualize the approach of Maslow or Rogers in behavioral terms. Easier? Surely. What does this tell you about the three kinds of models?

d. Think about the three theoretical approaches to personality described in the text — the psychoanalytical, behavioristic, and phenomenological models. Be inventive and try to integrate the basic notions of each into a single model, a sort of analytic phenomenal behaviorism. What concepts did you have the greatest difficulty integrating into your single theory? Are these concepts of fundamental importance in their own theory?

5. EVALUATION (SELF-TESTS)

Correct answers and text page references are given at the end of the unit.

a. Fill-in-the-blanks Items

Write the word(s) that best complete(s) the sentence in the space provided.

1. For Freud, the primitive part of personality is the _____.

2. According to Freud, trauma in the _____ psychosexual stage can lead to stinginess in the adult.

3. Blaming someone else to offset your own anxiety is an example of the defense mechanism called _____.

4. Freud's theory is based on his analysis of the dreams and _____ of himself and of his patients.

5. In Jung's theory, the total personality is called the _____.

6. For Jung, emotion-laden, universal thoughts and ideas are called _____.

7. Adler asserted that the prime source of human motivation is the innate striving for

_____.

8. In the behavioristic view, personality is simply a collection of _____.

9. The social learning theorists emphasize learning and _____ in the development of personality.

10. For Rogers, the ultimate drive is for _____.

b. Matching Items

Write the number of the correct item from the right column in front of the matching item in the left column.

_____ superego	1.	adultlike sexual interactions
_____ phallic stage	2.	Adler's basic motivation
_____ Oedipus complex	3.	Bandura's theory
_____ genital stage	4.	emphasis on one's own sexual organs
_____ striving for superiority	5.	Rogers' theory
_____ response dispositions	6.	castration theory
_____ reinforcement and expectancy	7.	Maslow's theory
_____ observational learning	8.	ideal orientation
_____ self-actualization	9.	Rotter's theory
_____ self-esteem	10.	personality for the behaviorist

c. Multiple-choice Items

Circle the letter in front of the answer that best completes the stem.

1. The pleasure principle is most closely associated with which level of personality for Freud?
    a. id
    b. ego
    c. superego
    d. repression

2. The reality principle is most closely associated with which level of personality for Freud?
    a. id
    b. ego
    c. superego
    d. repression

3. The ideal orientation is most closely associated with which level of personality for Freud?
    a. id
    b. ego
    c. superego
    d. repression

4. In Freud's theory, the Electra complex occurs in which psychosexual stage?
    a. oral
    b. anal
    c. phallic
    d. genital

5. We don't ordinarily remember the psychosexual stages nor their associated trauma because of:
    a. rationalization
    b. projection
    c. reaction formation
    d. repression

6. The defense mechanism in which anxiety impulses are accompanied by an opposite counteracting tendency is called:
    a. rationalization
    b. projection
    c. reaction formation
    d. repression

7. In Jung's theory, primary emphasis is on:
   a. self-actualization
   b. personal unconscious
   c. social interest
   d. expectancy

8. In Adler's theory, primary emphasis is on:
   a. self-actualization
   b. personal unconscious
   c. social interest
   d. expectancy

9. Which one of the following is *not* one of the characteristics of the self-actualized person, according to Maslow?
   a. is realistic
   b. has a lot of friends
   c. is creative
   d. is a nonconformist

10. For Rogers, personality growth occurs through:
    a. biological drives
    b. self-actualization
    c. expectancy development
    d. self-knowledge

d. Short-answer Items

Answer the following questions with short, concise statements. Reference pages for the material are given at the end of the unit.

1. Describe briefly the oral, anal, and phallic psychosexual developmental stages of Freud in terms of central focus, possible trauma, and possible resolutions.

2. List three of Freud's defense mechanisms, and describe how each is supposed to operate.

3. Contrast the psychoanalytic theories of Jung and Adler in terms of basic instincts or motives.

4. Contrast the social-learning approach with the phenomenological-humanistic approach to personality.

ANSWER KEY FOR UNIT 23

Unit Review

1. global
2. Freud
3. sexual
4. rationality
5. unconscious
6. anxiety
7. conscious
8. hypnotist
9. hostile
10. neurophysiologist
11. neuroses
12. superego
13. primitive
14. libido
15. sexual
16. pleasure principle
17. rational
18. reality
19. control mechanism
20. moral
21. parent
22. ideal
23. social values
24. psychosexual
25. fixated
26. oral
27. mouth
28. aggressive
29. primary gratification
30. anal
31. toilet training
32. "anal retentive"
33. "anal expulsive"
34. neatness
35. phallic
36. sexual organs
37. mother
38. father
39. Oedipus complex
40. castration
41. Electra complex
42. identification
43. puberty
44. repression
45. unconscious
46. displacement
47. rationalization
48. insulation
49. projection
50. reaction formation
51. dreams
52. self-analysis
53. repressed
54. educational
55. testability
56. self-actualization
57. selfhood
58. psyche
59. collective
60. accumulated experiences
61. archetypes
62. images
63. biological/sexual
64. extroversion
65. introversion
66. intuition
67. balance
68. psychic energy
69. equivalence
70. entropy
71. last half
72. social

73. upward drive
74. superiority
75. inferiority
76. growth
77. adjustment
78. unique
79. interpersonal relationships
80. popularity
81. mentalistic
82. response dispositions
83. conditioning
84. testability
85. behavior therapy
86. cognition
87. social situations
88. other people
89. expectancy
90. reinforcement
91. life situation
92. locus of control
93. own efforts
94. internal
95. external

96. modeling
97. observational
98. behaviorism
99. immediate
100. growth potentials
101. self-actualization
102. hierarchical
103. base
104. considered
105. full potential
106. meta
107. peak
108. humanistic
109. self-esteem
110. feelings
111. subdued
112. self-knowledge
113. human nature
114. psychoanalysis
115. behaviorism
116. phenomenological/humanist
117. scientific theory

Evaluation (Self-tests)

a. Fill-in-the-blanks Items

1. id (p. 544)
2. anal (p. 545)
3. projection (p. 547)
4. free associations (p. 549)
5. psyche (p. 551)

6. archetypes (p. 551)
7. superiority (p. 553)
8. response dispositions/habits (p. 555)
9. cognition (p. 557)
10. self-esteem (p. 560)

b. Matching Items: Correct order and page references are:

8 (pp. 544–545); 4 (p. 545); 6 (pp. 545–546); 1 (p. 546); 2 (p. 553);
10 (p. 555); 9 (p. 557); 3 (p. 558); 7 (p. 559); 5 (p. 560).

c. Multiple-choice Items: Correct answers and page references are:

1—a (p. 544); 2—b (p. 545); 3—c (pp. 544–545); 4—c (p. 546); 5—d (p. 546);
6—c (pp. 547–548); 7—b (p. 551); 8—c (p. 553); 9—b (p. 559); 10—d (p. 560).

d. Short-answer Items: Page references for answer material are:

1. pp. 545–546; 2. pp. 546–549; 3. pp. 551–554; 4. pp. 557–560.

Unit 24

SOME DETERMINANTS OF PERSONALITY DEVELOPMENT

1. INTRODUCTION TO STUDY OF THIS UNIT

This unit devotes considerable attention to the concept of attachment, providing a life-span case history of the notion. Attachment refers to the critical human relationship that an infant normally develops early in life with the primary caregiver, usually the mother. Some of the earliest experimentation related to this variable was conducted by Konrad Lorenz, a German zoologist. He reported the initial studies in 1935. In them, he described how he hatched a number of gosling eggs and made certain that he was the first object to which they were exposed shortly after hatching. He found that they responded to him as though he were their "mother." That is, they followed him about the grounds, swam after him if he rowed a boat in a small pond there, and got very "excited" if he was not available to them. Given the opportunity to choose an adult female goose or Lorenz, they chose Lorenz even, in some cases, over their own "Mother Goose."

The year 1935 was not a good year for disseminating research reports, especially those emanating from Germany. Thus, the scientific world did not catch up with this phenomenon until World War II was over, and then the concept of imprinting caught fire, exciting much research on both sides of the Atlantic. The discovery was felt to be especially significant because it permitted the previously discarded notion of instinct to be reintroduced into psychology in this country. Why? Because essentially Lorenz had shown that the goslings' following behavior, which all had thought to be instinctually based, clearly had an experiential component. In effect, instinct is learned, at least in part. (Since the time of the discovery, most psychologists have accepted the obverse as well, that is, what is learned is instinctual, at least in part.)

After Lorenz's earliest reports, hundreds of related studies were undertaken to refine the relationships involved in the imprinting phenomenon. Lorenz himself had found that he had to bend over to be an effective stimulus for his goslings' following behavior. There appear to be limits on what will effectively imprint. Colorful, moving stimuli seem to be most effective, and the stimuli do not have to be human, lower-animal, or even animate. This kind of attachment, then, may be viewed as a potential set of behaviors, requiring some form of environmental stimulation and resulting in reasonably predictable forms of behavior. The environmental stimulus system, as we now know, allows for a great deal of latitude in both the specific stimulus characteristics and in the timing.

Lorenz was awarded the Nobel Prize for his many contributions to science. His imprinting studies led to the development of the field of ethology, which occupies a strong position in contemporary science.

2. ISSUES AND CONCEPTS

There are many determinants of personality, and as you read this unit, be aware that if any one factor is operating to an extreme degree, the influence of others will likely be somewhat limited. Learn the definition of attachment, a process that may involve learning and something more. Study the possible contribution of imprinting studies, stranger anxiety, and separation anxiety to the attachment process. Be able to discuss how bonding and its important characteristics relate to attachment and how attachment is presumed to influence behavior throughout an individual's life span.

The role of heredity is the next topic. Learn the evidence, including various twin studies, for the role of genetic constitution in the determination of individual differences in intelligence and in personality characteristics. Be able to cite specific personality characteristics that appear to be largely genetically determined. Know the results of studies of twins reared apart, and attend to results indicating that those reared apart may be more similar than those reared together, and why.

Somatic factors are also important, and you should learn when somatic factors contributing to personality begin to operate, and how psychosomatic disorders are thought to develop. Become familiar with proposals for the relationships between body build and personality, though be aware that the nature of these relationships is unclear. Be able to discuss how variations in the rate of development for boys and girls during adolescence relate to personality characteristics in adolescence and during adulthood.

Child-rearing practices vary greatly over time, and objective data do not suggest clear recommendations for any aspect of child rearing. Under these circumstances, evaluate what parents probably should do. Learn what the "best" pattern of feeding is, and what patterns of parental discipline behaviors appear to be related to socially acceptable behavior in children.

Be able to describe the apparent personality characteristics of firstborn children and how other factors may be involved in producing these characteristics. You should be able to cite as well several factors that have been identified in sex-role learning and to discuss how these vary by sex of child.

The influence of early experience cannot be regarded as irrevocable or irreversible, and the social and cultural contexts in which such experiences occur determine very importantly the influence that they have. One such influence is social class. Become familiar with the techniques that working- and middle-class parents have tended to use in rearing their children.

3. UNIT REVIEW

Correct answers are given at the end of the unit.

Personality is a process in constant (1)_____, and so to speak of its determinants is difficult, since there are so many forces that have demonstrable effects on personality development. To the extent that any one factor is operating to an extreme degree, it can set (2) _____ on possible influences by all other factors.

The critical human relationship that an infant normally develops with the primary caregiver, usually the mother, is called (3)_____. Research on monkeys suggests that this process is not simply a form of (4)_____ as a result of the caretaker providing satisfaction of biological needs; other factors such as contact (5)_____ are involved. Research on the phenomenon of (6)_____ suggests that for some animals attachment is due to distinctive moving (7)_____ cues. The fact that "critical" or (8)_____ periods exist for this phenomenon also suggests that

something more than (9)_____ may underlie attachment. Research on human

attachment shows wide variation in the time of appearance of that response to a familiar adult. Other research

has identified attachment behaviors in a "strange situation" and has found them to be related to the

(10)_____ ability of the mother and therefore the sense of effectance, or

(11)_____, that the child learns to expect from his or her

(12)_____. Attachment is increasingly seen as a two-way concept that has been

given the name (13)_____; the term implies a mutual relationship between

mother and child, a relationship that appears to begin immediately after (14)_____.

In addition to mothers and important others (15)_____ may also be involved in

bonding-attachment relationships, probably reflecting the particular qualities of (16) _____

between infant and target person. The infant's ability to form other attachment relationships allows for

(17)_____ from an early maladaptive experience. Attachment and separation

anxiety phenomena may be (18)_____ processes. The child begins to show

anxiety over separation from his or her mother generally at about (19)_____ of

age and can tolerate separation without great discomfort after about the age of (20) _____.

This may reflect the child's developing sense of being a (21)_____ person.

Attachment appears to be a critical process that has an influence throughout an individual's

(22)_____; many attachments develop during a lifetime, even with

(23)_____ objects. These attachments are a pervasive general process in

development affecting the growth of (24)_____.

　　Twin studies provide evidence that (25)_____ plays a role in determining

individual differences in intelligence. Little evidence exists for the genetic determination of the non-

intellective aspects of personality, except for (26)_____, a term that refers to

mood, reactivity, and energy level. Human studies of kin resemblance do not contribute to knowledge of

genetic determination of personality characteristics because (27)_____ simi-

larity usually accompanies genetic similarity. Twin studies do suggest an important genetic contribution

to personality, especially for the dimension of (28)_____ and for some

aspects of (29)_____. Studies examining twins reared in different homes sug-

gest that they are (30)_____ in many personality characteristics but also that

for some characteristics they are more alike when reared (31)_____ than when

reared (32)_____.

　　Somatic factors, consisting of the physical and physiological makeup of the individual, are important

contributors to personality. These factors begin to have an effect (33)_____,

as is shown by the influence of a mother's (34)_____ or level of

(35)_____. When psychological factors lead to chronic or long-lasting somatic

disturbances, we speak of (36)_____ disorders, such as stomach

(37) _____. Such disorders probably reflect an (38) _____

between a constitutional predisposition and personality factors. Relationships between body build and

personality have been found, but the relative contribution of heredity and environment to these relationships

is (39)_____. Variations in the (40)_____ of

individual maturation during adolescence affect personality development. An early maturing boy tends to

be rather poised and responsible in both adolescence and (41)_____, whereas a

late maturing boy is often restless, highly expressive, and socially (42)_____

in adolescence, but more self-reliant and tolerant in adulthood than the early maturer. For girls, the early

maturer seems to have difficulty in controlling her (43)_____ and tends to

be socially (44)_____ in adolescence, as compared with the late maturer. As an

adult, the early maturer is psychologically (45)_____ than the late maturer.

There are insufficient research data to suggest clear recommendations for any aspect of child

(46)_____, and what data there are do not permit simple and direct applica-

tions. Child-rearing practices are subject to (47)_____ swings but, regardless

of what is in fashion at the moment, parents should do that which most effectively fits their

(48)_____ and personality characteristics. The "best" pattern of early feeding

depends on the personality characteristics of the mother and the (49)_____ and

innate personality of the child. Studies indicate that parents of the most competent young children were

(50)_____ and rational but controlling and (51)_____,

characteristics labeled as (52)_____ parental behavior, in contrast to the

behavior of an (53)_____ parent, who is more punitive and restrictive.

Effective disciplining may be neither punitive nor permissive and may be associated with less

(54)_____ and more (55)_____ in the children

than would otherwise be the case.

There is evidence that firstborn children in Western cultures are more (56) _____

and conforming than their siblings, tend in later life to achieve greater (57)_____,

and especially in the case of boys, are less (58)_____. The factor of birth order

interacts significantly with other family variables, such as total number of children, number of boys and girls

in the family, and the (59)_____ of the children.

The process whereby we learn to behave as "proper" males and females in a given culture is called

(60)_____. Factors involved in this process include parental encouragement

to identify with the (61) _____ parent. The parents (62) _____

such "appropriate" behavior. Parents who are most effective in this program tend to be warm, nurturant, and (63)_____. For boys, greater (64)_____ and authority in the father facilitates learning of the traditional masculine role. The world at large, mainly through the (65)_____, contributes to these sex distinctions. Males are frequently portrayed as engaging in (66)_____ behaviors seen as more "masculine" activities. Such studies show that sex typing still exists, and it remains a critical (67)_____ for children.

With respect to the influence of early experience generally on personality development, no childhood experience can be regarded as irrevocably (68)_____, and no maladaptive adjustment to such an experience is forever (69)_____.

In considering the long-term effects of any childhood experience, the broader (70) _____ in which the event occurs must be considered. We must apply the criterion of cultural (71)_____, the notion that a given event must be interpreted within the values and norms of the particular culture in which the child is being reared. An important social influence that seems to cut across ethnic-group lines is (72)_____, especially as it affects child-rearing practices. Generally, (73)_____ parents have tended to train their children to stay out of trouble in order to avoid retaliation from the community, whereas (74)_____ parents place greater emphasis on self-control and inner standards. Child-rearing practices may be becoming increasingly (75)_____across social classes.

4. THOUGHT QUESTIONS

a. It has been suggested that the process of attachment may be relatively independent of those learned changes in behavior reflecting the application of reinforcement. What kinds of experiments would have to be done at the human level to test this possible influence? Do you think such experiments will ever be done? Why or why not?

b. Relationships between body build and personality characteristics have been investigated for quite a few years. There is, of course, a very serious chicken-and-egg problem in interpreting the results of these studies as favoring the position either of heredity or environment. What kinds of human experiments would have to be done to unravel these possible relationships?

c. Child-rearing practices have changed a great deal over the years, and child-rearing "experts" recommend quite different techniques from time to time. What do you think are the bases of their recommendations?

d. Sex-role learning has been reinforced systematically by social influences, especially the mass media. Changes have been taking place in recent years, and role distinctions are beginning to blur somewhat. What changes do you expect in 10 years? 25 years? Why?

5. EVALUATION (SELF-TESTS)

Correct answers and text page references are given at the end of the unit.

a. Fill-in-the-blanks Items

Write the word(s) that best complete(s) the sentence in the space provided.

1. Distinctive moving visual cues appear to be important in that form of attachment called

   _____.

2. Human attachment seems to be related to the communicative ability of the mother and the child's

   sense of _____.

3. The child can generally tolerate separation from his or her mother after the age of _____.

4. Twin studies suggest an important genetic contribution to the personality characteristics of emo-

   tionality and _____.

5. Somatic factors begin to exert their influence on personality during the _____ period.

6. A(n) _____ maturing boy tends to be poised and responsible as an

   adult.

7. A(n) _____ maturing boy tends to be more self-reliant and tolerant as

   an adult.

8. A(n) _____ maturing girl tends to be socially withdrawn in adolescence.

9. Warm and demanding parents tend to produce the _____ competent

   children.

10. Firstborn children are more affiliative and _____ than their siblings.

b. Matching Items

Write the number of the correct item from the right column in front of the matching item in the left
column.

_____ imprinting	1. mutual relationship between mother and child
_____ bonding	2. following the behavior of animals
_____ temperament	3. mother's nutrition
_____ somatic factors	4. trains children to stay out of trouble
_____ prenatal influence	5. emphasizes self-control
_____ authoritative parent	6. warm and supportive parents
_____ authoritarian parent	7. physical and physiological makeup
_____ facilitates sex-role learning	8. detached and controlling
_____ middle class	9. warm but demanding
_____ working class	10. mood, reactivity, and energy level

c. Multiple-choice Items

Circle the letter in front of the answer that best completes the stem.

1. An important factor in monkey attachment behavior was found to be:
   a. satisfaction of biological needs
   b. availability during illness
   c. the first moving stimulus seen
   d. contact comfort

2. An important factor in imprinting behavior was found to be:
   a. satisfaction of biological needs
   b. availability during illness
   c. the first moving stimulus seen
   d. contact comfort

3. When does a child begin to show anxiety over separation from his or her mother?
   a. 4 to 8 months
   b. 8 to 12 months
   c. 12 to 16 months
   d. 16 to 20 months

4. Temperament is a term that refers to:
   a. intelligence and mood
   b. mood and energy level
   c. energy level and sociability
   d. sociability and intelligence

5. Stomach ulcers may be an example of:
   a. psychosomatic disorders
   b. attachment failure
   c. imprinting difficulty
   d. prenatal influences

6. Those who tend to be more poised and responsible in both adolescence and adulthood are:
   a. early maturing girls
   b. late maturing girls
   c. early maturing boys
   d. late maturing boys

7. Those who tend to be socially withdrawn in adolescence are:
   a. early maturing girls
   b. late maturing girls
   c. early maturing boys
   d. late maturing boys

8. Those who tend to be highly expressive and restless in adolescence are:
   a. early maturing girls
   b. late maturing girls
   c. early maturing boys
   d. late maturing boys

9. Which one of the following has *not* been suggested as a characteristic of firstborn children as compared with their siblings?
   a. more affiliative
   b. more prominent in later life
   c. less conforming
   d. less aggressive

10. As compared with middle-class families, working-class families, in their child-rearing
    practices, tend to emphasize:
    a. self-control
    b. use of inner standards
    c. less affiliative behavior
    d. staying out of trouble

d. Short-answer Items

Answer the following questions with short, concise statements. Reference pages for the material are given at
the end of the unit.

1. Contrast what appears to be happening in the phenomenon called imprinting with that called
   bonding. How are they similar and how different?

2. Compare the important personality characteristics of early and late maturing boys and girls as
   they are during adolescence and in adulthood.

3. According to a number of studies, what are the personalities of firstborn children typically like
   and what family characteristics may be related to their development?

4. Specify three factors that appear to contribute importantly to sex-role learning.

ANSWER KEY FOR UNIT 24

Unit Review

1. flux
2. limits
3. attachment
4. conditioning
5. comfort
6. imprinting
7. visual
8. "sensitive"
9. learning
10. communicative
11. control
12. environment
13. bonding
14. birth
15. fathers
16. interaction
17. recovery
18. linked
19. 8 to 12 months
20. two
21. separate
22. life span
23. nonliving
24. personality
25. genetic constitution
26. temperament
27. environmental
28. introversion-extroversion
29. emotionality
30. still alike
31. apart
32. together
33. prenatally
34. nutrition
35. hormones
36. psychosomatic
37. ulcers
38. interaction

39. not clear
40. rate
41. adulthood
42. less successful
43. emotions
44. withdrawn
45. healthier
46. rearing
47. faddish
48. attitudes
49. sex
50. warm
51. demanding
52. authoritative
53. authoritarian
54. aggression
55. internal control
56. affiliative
57. prominence
58. aggressive
59. spacing ·
60. sex-role typing
61. same-sex
62. reward
63. supportive
64. dominance
65. mass media
66. socially desirable
67. early experience
68. damaging
69. irreversible
70. context
71. relativism
72. social class
73. working-class
74. middle-class
75. uniform

Evaluation (Self-tests)

a. Fill-in-the-blanks Items

1. imprinting (p. 568)
2. effectance/control (p. 569)
3. two years (p. 572)
4. introversion-extroversion (p. 576)
5. prenatal (p. 578)
6. early (p. 580)
7. late (pp. 580–581)
8. early (p. 582)
9. most (p. 585)
10. conforming (p. 586)

b. Matching Items: Correct order and page references are:

2 (p. 568); 1 (p. 569); 10 (p. 576); 7 (p. 577); 3 (p. 578);
9 (p. 585); 8 (p. 585); 6 (p. 588); 5 (p. 590); 4 (p. 590).

c. Multiple-choice Items: Correct answers and page references are:

1—d (p. 567); 2—c (p. 568); 3—b (p. 572); 4—b (p. 576); 5—a (p. 578);
6—c (p. 580); 7—a (p. 582); 8—d (p. 580); 9—c (p. 586); 10—d (p. 590).

d. Short-answer Items: Page references for answer material are:

1. pp. 568–572; 2. pp. 579–582; 3. pp. 586–587; 4. pp. 588–589.

Unit 25

MENTAL DISORDERS AND BEHAVIORAL PATHOLOGY

1. INTRODUCTION TO STUDY OF THIS UNIT

The major portion of this unit deals with the classification of mental disorders. The approach is psychodynamically based, and it follows the outlines of the last two diagnostic manuals offered by the American Psychiatric Association, which is committed to a medical model of mental disorder that assumes that many such disorders can be traced to neural and biochemical factors that are largely hereditary. This was not always the prevailing view, and we once more remind the reader of the importance of the Zeitgeist in determining quasi-scientific issues.

Early in the nineteenth century, the area of physical medicine was not highly developed, but people still suffered the effects of stress and displayed inappropriate behaviors (according to the values and norms of that day, of course). Their difficulties were not viewed as illness but rather as a response to the stresses of living. Therapy — it was called moral therapy — was applied and it seemed to have involved a retraining program in a social environment that was positive and sympathetic. In some cases, that environment was like those of the ''group home'' now being employed for readjustment and therapeutic purposes. This form of therapy was widely used in this country and in England for about a quarter of a century and studies indicate that it was a successful retraining model for about 80 percent of the clients. However, the entire movement was abandoned, quietly, about the time of the Civil War here and almost entirely forgotten after that. Why was this so?

The principal reason seems to be that physical medicine was developing rapidly around 1860, and the notion of physical illness was firmly established in the population. The types of procedures found to be effective in the treatment of physical illness, essentially the medical model, were proposed to be just as effective in the treatment of emotional disorder, which was then suggested to be mental illness. Thus, if moral therapy was supposed to be treatment for mental illness, this area should be the province of the medically trained. These notions probably sounded quite reasonable at the time, and the moral therapy movement disappeared.

So, what started out as social and psychological difficulties that were most often treated by nonmedical personnel employing psychosocial techniques were quite quickly changed to medical difficulties (mental illnesses), which were treatable within the medical model by medical techniques.

The Zeitgeist operates in curious ways. One wonders what might happen if some of those backing the movement that calls for the primary prevention of emotional disorder, and that points to sociopolitical and economic causative factors, win over the general population to this view. What will happen to the concept of mental illness or even that of emotional disorder?

2. ISSUES AND CONCEPTS

The text first presents various views of mental disorder, some emphasizing biological and others experiential events underlying such behaviors. Know that antisocial behavior is not necessarily "sick."

Be able to differentiate clearly the statistical, the cultural, and the personal-discomfort approaches to mental disorder. Similarly, be able to distinguish the medical, the psychodynamic, the behavioristic, the humanistic, and the social-oppression models as explanations of mental disorder. Become familiar with what epidemiology is, what the incidence of mental disorder appears to be, and the difficulties of making such estimates.

Study what is meant by referring to emotional disturbances as functional disorder. Be aware that *DSM-II* and *DSM-III* are classificatory schemes of mental disorders provided by the American Psychiatric Association and that these schemata are based on the psychodynamic model — a model that behaviorists, humanists, and others object to.

The various kinds of mental disorders are treated next. Learn a definition of anxiety and the relationship of this notion to neurosis. Be able to differentiate the various categories of neuroses: anxiety, hysterical neurosis (including conversion reaction, somatoform disorders, psychalgia, and psychosomatic disorders); dissociative neurosis, (including psychogenic amnesia, fugue, and multiple personality); and phobia, obsessive-compulsive, and existential neuroses.

Learn the distinctions between neurosis and personality disorder, and be able to differentiate the five subtypes of such disorders: obsessive-compulsive, hysterical, paranoid, cyclothymic and antisocial.

The category of psychosexual disorders is treated next. Learn to distinguish gender-identity disturbance, paraphilia, and psychosexual dysfunction. Be able to discuss the special circumstances under which homosexuality is now considered a disorder.

Under the topic of functional psychoses, study the general symptoms of affective psychosis. Learn the specific characteristics of depression and the distinction between exogenous and endogenous depression. Be able to discuss the four theoretical approaches to depression presented: the genetic, the psychodynamic, the hopelessness, and the learned-helplessness models. Be able, as well, to offer an explanation of the presumed increase of depression over recent years.

Learn the general symptoms of the most prevalent of psychoses — schizophrenia — and the subtypes of this psychosis: the catatonic, the paranoid, and the hebephrenic. The distinction between process and reactive subtypes should also be mastered, along with the distinction between the paranoid disturbance and the disorder called paranoia.

Be able to differentiate clearly between those psychoses that are called functional and those that are called organic.

Various factors may be involved in the origins of mental disorder. Be able to cite the evidence suggesting a genetic component to schizophrenia. Know what the terms schizophrenogenic and double bind mean.

The diagnosis of mental disorder is not highly reliable. Be able to cite some of the potential difficulties of applying disorder labels. Finally, be able to discuss recent attempts, such as the multiaxial classification system, to come up with clearer and more specific diagnostic schemes that may improve diagnosis.

3. UNIT REVIEW

Correct answers are given at the end of the unit.

Mental disorder, or psychopathology, occurs when an individual's ability to (1) _____

realistically and effectively with the challenges of daily life is no longer regarded as (2) _____.

While some believe that genetic, biochemical, and physiological factors underlie mental disorder, little

concrete evidence about such factors exists, and thus many current theories focus on

(3)_____ as the primary determinant of aberrant behavior. Such behavior

is likely to be interpreted as symptomatic of mental disorder when it violates current (4) _____

behavior. Antisocial behavior is not necessarily (5)_____ behavior.

In the statistical approach, psychological abnormality is defined as any substantial deviation from the

(6)_____ behavior of the group of which the individual is a member. A diffi-

culty with this definition is that it does not specify which statistically deviant behaviors are

(7)_____ and which are not; also it fails to acknowledge that the typical

behavior of an entire group may be (8)_____ to another group. According

to the cultural approach, normality is judged by the degree to which an individual (9) _____

to the behavioral standards deemed appropriate for someone of his or her standing in the society. Thus,

behavior may be called deviant when it simply reflects a clash in (10)_____.

The personal-discomfort approach suggests that subjectively reported unhappiness, guilt, depression, and

anxiety are the (11)_____ for judging disorder. Difficulties with the approach

include the possibility that some individuals may not feel (12)_____ with some

very unacceptable behavior, while others may feel so with routine problems.

The medical model regards abnormal behavior in a manner analogous to the way we analyze

(13)_____. Study of patterns of behavior can identify consistent groups of

symptoms that represent identifiable and discrete (14)_____ with specific

causes. When the causes are identified, particular (15)_____ or preventive

measures can then be developed. While this model recognizes psychosocial causes, the emphasis is on causa-

tion by (16)_____, biochemistry, and physical trauma. Accurate

(17)_____ is the cornerstone of the medical model, but this has been difficult

to achieve with mental disorder. The psychodynamic model views abnormal behavior as resulting from

(18)_____ between innate needs or desires, leading to impulses and socially

acquired (19)_____. When such impulses threaten to break through and achieve

expression, (20)_____ may result, and this constitutes a major source of disturbed

behavior. In this model, treatment is an attempt to allow the individual to gain (21) _____

of the underlying dynamics of his or her behavior and thus to achieve a more (22) _____

expression of impulses. The behavioristic model sees abnormal behavior as a product of

(23)_____ and therapy as a matter of dealing with the behavior as it now is.

Relearning of maladaptive responses that are associated with anxiety and (24)_____

must occur. The humanistic model suggests that humankind is inherently (25)_____

and that each of us has a drive for (26)_____. If social forces thwart this drive,

they can be the source of psychic pain and (27)_____. Therapy is directed at

getting the client to (28)_____ and to accept himself or herself more fully. The social-oppression model asserts that much of the observable deviance and personal discomfort is generated by (29)_____ forces external to the individual, such as oppression, poverty, and social disapproval. With respect to these several models, we should be cautious not to view all psychopathology from the perspective of a (30)_____, and we should be alert to the likelihood of multiple causation of mental disorders.

The study of the prevalence and variations of diseases over time and between populations to help infer causes and possible preventive measures is called (31)_____. The study of mental disorders is difficult because of inconsistencies in (32)_____. Acknowledging the difficulty of measurement, researchers have estimated that mental disorders affect between (33)_____ of the population, if disorder is defined as "being in need of help for psychological problems." Total admissions to mental hospitals have (34)_____ even though the average length of hospitalization has (35)_____ in recent years, reflecting the more general use of controlling (36)_____ and community-oriented mental-health facilities.

According to the *DSM-II* of the American Psychiatric Association, most emotional disturbances are (37)_____ disorders — that is, no specific (38)_____ basis for them has yet been discovered and the affected person's (39)_____ has played an important part. Functional disorders include psychoses, neuroses, and (40)_____. Psychoses involve a relatively high degree of psychological disorganization, with individuals at times showing severe (41)_____, emotional, and behavior aberrations. The psychotic may appear to have lost contact with (42)_____ and may experience delusions and (43)_____. Neuroses involve less severe disturbances but the neurotic usually experiences periods of acute pain and anxiety arising from no (44)_____. Personality disorders or character disorders refer to patterns of (45)_____ behavior that are usually illegal or maladaptive for the individual.

The classification scheme of abnormal behavior is largely based on the (46)_____ model. Behaviorists, humanists, and others feel that this kind of labeling (47)_____ our understanding and treatment of maladaptive behavior.

An essential feature of neurosis appears to be (48)_____ or its avoidance. This factor distorts experience and learning so that (49)_____ reactions cannot occur. The different ways in which (50)_____ is handled is at the core of distinctions among neuroses. These types include (51)_____ neurosis, in which the person suffers acute or chronic anxiety and may also experience insomnia, irritability, and even such physical symptons as ulcers and cardiovascular disturbances. A second type of neurosis is

(52)_____ neurosis, in which the anxiety may be expressed as or converted to physical sensory and motor disturbances (conversion hysteria). *DSM-III* discards this type and instead proposes the classification (53)_____ disorders, which includes conversion reactions, complaints of physical difficulties for which there are no (54)_____ bases, and (55)_____ (unwarranted chronic complaints of pain). Dissociative disorders include (56)_____, in which a person rather suddenly loses the ability to recall personal information; (57)_____, in which the amnesic person may even assume a new identity; and (58)_____, in which an individual develops two or more distinct personalities that often vary widely in character and style. Another neurosis is called (59)_____ and is characterized by excessive and irrational fear of objects, places, or situations. It includes the subtype called (60)_____, in which a person, more usually a female, develops an irrational fear of leaving home, and another possible subtype in students called (61)_____. In the (62)_____ neurosis, a person is subject to thoughts and actions that he or she finds undesirable but is unable to prevent.

Personality disorders consist of behaviors that are believed to be pervasive personality styles but are distinguishable from neuroses in that the behaviors are less (63)_____ and they are not seen by the individual as (64)_____. Disturbed sorts of personality include the (65)_____ personality of extremely neat, orderly, and conforming individuals; the (66)_____ personality of emotionally and behaviorally over-dramatic or histrionic individuals; the (67)_____ personality of hypersensitive, very suspicious, and jealous individuals; and the (68)_____ personality of individuals who manifest wide variations in mood. The antisocial reaction (previously called psychopathic personality) is characteristic of persons who show diffuse and chronic (69)_____ for persistent, ordered living. They act before they think, are unable to tolerate (70)_____, and are insensitive to the needs of others.

Emotional disturbances involving sexual behavior are called (71)_____ disorders in *DSM-III*. This classification includes (72)_____, which refers to the subjective feeling a person may have of residing in an anatomically inappropriate body; and (73)_____, which involves focusing on such behaviors as transvestism, fetishism, exhibitionism, voyeurism, pedophilia, sexual sadism, or masochism as the (74)_____ of sexual release. Homosexuality, while viewed in the past by most and in the present by many as indicating severe emotional disturbance, would be viewed in *DSM-III* as a disorder if the individual experiences a sustained pattern of homosexual arousal that he or she feels is a source of (75)_____. The classification psychosexual dysfunctions, or sexual (76)_____, refers to difficulties in the initiation or completion of the sexual cycle; many such difficulties may be due to anxiety over (77)_____.

The three main classes of functional psychoses are affective disorders, schizophrenia, and the
(78) _____ states. Each involves a significant (79) _____
in capacity to meet the ordinary demands of life. Affective disorders are characterized by exaggerations of
(80)_____, which sometimes fluctuate between extremes. The three most
commonly recognized types are the manic, the depressive, and the (81)_____
personality. In contrast to mood changes, which probably occur in each of us and sometimes to an extreme
degree, affective disorders may have little (82)_____ and the behavior may be
(83)_____ or may last too long. Depression, beyond being an affective
disorder, seems to be very (84)_____ within the general population. Symptoms
of depression include mood disturbance, sadness, feelings of low self-esteem, increased dependency,
suicidal thoughts or attempts, loss of appetite, loss of interest in (85)_____,
and insomnia. Depression can be (86)_____, or a response to an upsetting
event, or it can be (87)_____, originating from within the self. Susceptibility
to this latter type may be (88)_____. In addition to the psychodynamic and the
hopelessness approaches to depression, a recent model emphasizes (89)_____.
In it, the individual learns inappropriately that there is no way that he or she can control
(90)_____ in a situation. Depressives may tend to attribute failure to
(91)_____ factors, and nondepressives to (92)_____
factors. Therapy should involve attempts to increase the sense of personal (93) _____.
The increased incidence of depression over recent years may only reflect the fact that with an available drug
treatment for the difficulty, the frequency with which it is (94)_____ increases.

The majority of functional psychotics are diagnosed as suffering from (95) _____.
The symptoms are many and varied, but in general there appears to be distortion of emotion and
(96)_____. The individual may become very withdrawn and insensitive,
and may experience (97) _____. Subtypes include (98) _____
schizophrenia, characterized by agitated behavior or stuporous immobility; (99) _____
schizophrenia, characterized by suspiciousness and delusions of persecution or (100) _____;
and (101)_____ schizophrenia, characterized by extreme deterioration of
thought, emotion, and behavior The label (102)_____ schizophrenia is
given to persons who develop the condition gradually and have a (103)_____
prognosis for recovery; the label (104)_____ schizophrenia is given to persons
for whom the onset is quite sudden and who have a (105)_____ to recover.
Paranoid disorders are characterized by persistent (106)_____ of persecution
or jealousy, but these are not the thought and behavior disturbances of psychosis. A subtype called
(107)_____ involves the development of a long-lasting, often complex, but
internally logical delusional system.

Psychotic behavior frequently accompanies deterioration of the brain and nervous system due to accident, disease, or toxic agents, and these are often called (108)_____ disorders even though they are considered to be partly determined by the (109) _____ of the individual.

The origins of mental disorders may include current life crises, remote life experiences, subtle biochemical and neural disturbances, or (110)_____. Evidence based on twin and adoption studies argues for a genetic predisposition toward (111)_____ among some individuals; that predisposition renders them particularly vulnerable to certain environmental stresses. Schizophrenic-producing, or (112)_____, families may provide a (113)_____ situation in which distorted and often contradictory messages are given to family members.

Several studies indicate that diagnosis of mental disorder is not (114)_____ and the the application of diagnostic labels is strongly influenced by such factors as the (115)_____ of the person being diagnosed. Some have proposed that persons receiving these labels will begin to adopt behaviors in accordance with their (116) _____ of the ''sick'' role.

DSM-III and other recent systems are more (117)_____ and (118)_____ in terms of the criteria used to indicate the presence of a particular disorder. These systems may help to increase the (119)_____ of diagnoses, allowing for the possibility of an increase in the (120)_____ of these diagnoses and improvement in the effectiveness of (121)_____ selected on the basis of the diagnoses.

4. THOUGHT QUESTIONS

a. Why do you think that we have been unable to achieve an objective definition of abnormality that would be applicable cross-culturally? If we are ever able to do so, what will be the likely nature of this definition?

b. The labeling and classificatory scheme represented by *DSM-II* and *DSM-III* is largely based on a psychodynamic model of abnormal behavior. This approach is only one of several models of abnormal behavior. What would a *DSM-X* look like if it were produced by a group of behaviorists? by a group of humanists?

c. Homosexuality was once viewed by the American Psychiatric Association as an indication of severe emotional disturbance. The current view, as shown in *DSM-III*, is that such behavior is not abnormal unless it is accompanied by emotional stress. What does this important change in view over time tell us about labeling and classificatory schemes?

d. We have seen in other units how self-fulfilling prophecies influence behavior and the perception of behavior. In this unit it was suggested that if persons who are under some transient stress are told they are ''sick'' they might respond by acting ''sick.'' Do you think that persons of particular ages, educational backgrounds, occupations, and socioeconomic levels are more likely to receive this kind of ''message''? If so, why?

5. EVALUATION (SELF-TESTS)

Correct answers and text page references are given at the end of the unit.

a. Fill-in-the-blanks Items

Write the word(s) that best complete(s) the sentence in the space provided.

1. Psychological abnormality is defined as a substantial deviation from average behavior in the
_____ approach.

2. The psychodynamic model views abnormal behavior as a result of _____.

3. Epidemiology gathers information in order to infer _____ and
suggest possible preventive measures for diseases.

4. Functional disorders are those for which no _____ basis
has been discovered.

5. Hallucinations and delusions are characteristics of _____.

6. The essential characteristic of neurosis appears to be _____.

7. In personality disorders, the person typically does not view his or her behavior as
_____.

8. Exhibitionism is one of the behaviors expressed in _____.

9. Large mood swings are characteristic of the _____ disorders.

10. Persons who develop schizophrenia gradually have a _____
prognosis for recovery.

b. Matching Items

Write the number of the correct item from the right column in front of the matching item in the left
column.

_____ mental disorder	1. personal unhappiness
_____ cultural definition	2. silly speech
_____ discomfort definition	3. response to an upsetting event
_____ psychosis	4. antisocial behavior
_____ personality disorder	5. break with reality
_____ affective disorder	6. nonconformity to social standards
_____ exogenous depression	7. exaggerations of mood states
_____ catatonic schizophrenia	8. contradictory messages
_____ hebephrenic schizophrenia	9. agitated or stuporous behavior
_____ double bind	10. inadequate ability to cope

c. Multiple-choice Items

Circle the letter in front of the answer that best completes the stem.

1. Subjective reports of unhappiness and guilt are characteristics of which definition of mental disorder?
   a. statistical
   b. cultural
   c. personal-discomfort
   d. medical

2. Conformity to behavioral standards is the crux of which definition of mental disorder?
   a. statistical
   b. cultural
   c. personal-discomfort
   d. medical

3. Epidemiological studies of mental disorder are difficult to do because of the inconsistencies in:
   a. diagnosis
   b. the behavior of the psychotic
   c. the training of therapists
   d. cultural standards

4. Acute or chronic anxiety and sometimes insomnia are characteristic of those suffering from:
   a. anxiety neurosis
   b. hysterical neurosis
   c. agoraphobic neurosis
   d. psychogenic amnesia

5. An irrational fear of leaving home is characteristic of:
   a. anxiety neurosis
   b. hysterical neurosis
   c. agoraphobic neurosis
   d. psychogenic amnesia

6. The conversion of anxiety into physical sensory or motor disturbances is symptomatic of:
   a. anxiety neurosis
   b. hysterical neurosis
   c. agoraphobic neurosis
   d. psychogenic amnesia

7. The most frequent type of functional psychosis is:
   a. affective disorders
   b. paranoid states
   c. multiple personality
   d. schizophrenia

8. Silly speech is characteristic of those suffering from:
   a. reactive schizophrenia
   b. paranoid schizophrenia
   c. catatonic schizophrenia
   d. hebephrenic schizophrenia

9. Suspiciousness and delusions are symptomatic of:
   a. reactive schizophrenia
   b. paranoid schizophrenia
   c. catatonic schizophrenia
   d. hebephrenic schizophrenia

10. Stuporous immobility is characteristic of:
    a. reactive schizophrenia
    b. paranoid schizophrenia
    c. catatonic schizophrenia
    d. hebephrenic schizophrenia

d. Short-answer Items

Answer the following questions with short, concise statements. Reference pages for the material are given at the end of the unit.

1. Contrast the statistical approach with the cultural approach to the definition of abnormality. Specify the assets and liabilities of each.

2. Contrast neuroses and personality disorders in terms of their origins and the ease with which anxiety can be resolved.

3. Differentiate clearly but briefly between the functional psychoses called affective disorders, schizophrenia, and the paranoid states.

4. How can double-bind communications within a schizophrenogenic family contribute to emotional stress and mental disorder?

ANSWER KEY FOR UNIT 25

Unit Review

1. cope
2. adequate
3. experience/learning
4. socially approved
5. "sick"
6. average/typical
7. desirable
8. undesirable
9. conforms
10. values
11. criteria
12. discomfort
13. physical disease
14. diseases
15. treatments
16. heredity
17. diagnosis
18. unconscious conflicts
19. moral standards
20. anxiety/guilt
21. awareness
22. mature/balanced
23. learning
24. fear
25. good
26. self-actualization
27. aberrant behavior
28. express
29. cultural-social
30. single model
31. epidemiology
32. diagnosis
33. 10 and 30 percent
34. risen
35. decreased
36. medications
37. functional
38. organic
39. past experience
40. personality disorders
41. thinking
42. reality
43. hallucinations
44. apparent source
45. antisocial
46. psychodynamic

47. obscures
48. anxiety
49. appropriate
50. anxiety
51. anxiety
52. hysterical
53. somatoform
54. organic
55. psychalgia
56. psychogenic amnesia
57. psychogenic fugue
58. multiple personality
59. phobic
60. agoraphobia
61. text anxiety
62. obsessive-compulsive
63. bizarre
64. peculiar/troublesome
65. obsessive-compulsive
66. hysterical
67. paranoid
68. cyclothymic
69. incapacity
70. frustration
71. psychosexual
72. gender-identity disturbance
73. paraphilia
74. sole means
75. distress
76. inadequacy
77. performance capability
78. paranoid
79. impairment
80. mood states
81. manic-depressive
82. cause
83. excessive
84. widespread
85. sex
86. exogenous
87. endogenous
88. inherited
89. learned helplessness
90. reinforcement
91. internal
92. external

93. efficacy
94. diagnosed
95. schizophrenia
96. thought
97. hallucinations
98. catatonic
99. paranoid
100. grandeur
101. hebephrenic
102. process
103. poor
104. reactive
105. better chance
106. delusions
107. paranoia

108. organic
109. past experiences
110. all of these
111. schizophrenia
112. schizophrenogenic
113. double-bind
114. highly reliable
115. social class
116. expectations
117. clear
118. specific
119. reliability
120. validity
121. therapies

Evaluation (Self-tests)

a.   Fill-in-the-blanks Items

1. statistical (p. 595)
2. unconscious conflicts (p. 597)
3. causes (p. 598)
4. organic (p. 599)
5. psychosis (p. 599)

6. anxiety (p. 600)
7. peculiar (p. 607)
8. paraphilia (p. 609)
9. affective (p. 612)
10. poor (p. 615)

b.   Matching Items: Correct order and page references are:

10 (p. 594); 6 (p. 595); 1 (p. 595); 5 (p. 599); 4 (p. 600);
7 (p. 612); 3 (p. 613); 9 (p. 614); 2 (p. 615); 8 (p. 618).

c.   Multiple-choice Items: Correct answers and page references are:

1—c (p. 595); 2—b (p. 595); 3—a (p. 598); 4—a (p. 601); 5—c (p. 604);
6—b (p. 601); 7—d (p. 614); 8—d (p. 615); 9—b (pp. 614–615); 10—c (p. 614).

d.   Short-answer Items: Page references for answer material are:

1. p. 595; 2. pp. 600–608; 3. pp. 611–616; 4. pp. 617–618.

Unit 26

THE PSYCHOTHERAPIES

1. INTRODUCTION TO STUDY OF THIS UNIT

Many of the psychotherapies that you will read about in this unit are of recent origin. Psychoanalysis, of course, dates back to the work of Freud and others, early in this century. Some of the psychophysiological therapies, including psychosurgery and some of the shock and drug therapies, date back to the 1930s. But many of the therapies described were introduced only after World War II. Before this time, psychotherapy was largely the province of the physician, and the therapies a physician chose seem to have matched his or her particular training. However, the emotional trauma of World War II resulted in the need to train additional personnel and to develop techniques to deal therapeutically with the hundreds of thousands of military personnel suffering emotional disorder. Consequently, the training of clinical psychologists was greatly expanded to help deal with these problems, many of the psychological therapies described in this unit were developed.

One of the therapies discussed in this unit is that of Masters and Johnson, who began an in-depth study of human sexual behavior and sexual dysfunctioning in 1954. Their laboratory research examined physiological functioning during sexual intercourse as well as psychological response to all aspects of sexual behavior. General inquiries into sexual dysfunctioning had occurred long before Masters and Johnson's study — for example, the clinical investigations of Freud. However, studies of the physiological correlates of the sex act had also been undertaken 35 years before Masters and Johnson began their work. The director of these studies was John B. Watson, the father of behaviorism. At Johns Hopkins University, he conducted an investigation very similar to the early work of Masters and Johnson, albeit with much cruder physiological measurement techniques. Apparently he collected data over a number of months. His wife, becoming informed of this unusual research activity, sued for divorce, won her case, and was awarded custody of all of the papers relating to the sex research. She promptly destroyed these materials, and science had to await a more favorable time to resume such research (remember the Zeitgeist!).

The Baltimore press gave extended coverage to the divorce action over the trial period, and the administration of Johns Hopkins University asked Watson to resign, which he did. He then went to New York City to live with a friend, who introduced him to employees of the J. Walter Thompson Company, an important advertising firm. This firm hired him on a trial basis, and he soon found himself surveying the use of rubber boots by people living in several Southern states. He learned the business by working in several departments of J. Walter Thompson and even clerking for a short time at Macy's department store. He did very well in advertising, developed one of the early Lucky Strike cigarette slogans directed at getting females to smoke, and became vice-president of the company within four years. He continued his successful business career until his retirement, but he did very little else in his academic career save for the publication of two books summarizing his earlier work and a number of popular magazine articles having psychological themes.

2. ISSUES AND CONCEPTS

After reading this unit, you should, first of all, be able to describe how views of mental disorder have changed over the years as to the locus of causality of such disorders.

Next, for each of the principal therapy types described in the unit — psychoanalytic therapy, behavior therapies, phenomenological therapies, interpersonal therapies, and psychophysiological therapies — be able to discuss the view of deviant behavior held, the goals of therapy, the specific methods of therapy used, and criticisms made of the approach.

For behavior therapies, become familiar with the several specific techniques used, including systematic desensitization, implosive therapy, the direct application of reinforcement, biofeedback techniques, and self-observation and self-reinforcement. Similarly, for the phenomenological therapies, be able to describe the specifics of will therapy, client-centered therapy, and Gestalt therapy. And, for interpersonal therapies, familiarize yourself with Sullivan's approach, transactional analysis, group therapy, family therapy, Masters and Johnson's therapy for sexual dysfunctioning, brief therapy, and play therapy.

Learn that psychophysiological therapies are employed only by physicians and they are used either in conjunction with other forms of therapy or as the primary or only therapeutic intervention. For the three forms of this therapy — surgery, electroconvulsive shock, and drug therapy — be able to discuss the goals, specific procedures or drugs used, and results.

Know, finally, that the goals of therapy vary considerably with the approach used and that it is very difficult to conduct good evaluative research on therapeutic effectiveness.

3. UNIT REVIEW

Correct answers are given at the end of the unit.

For our primitive ancestors, the cause of abnormal behavior was thought to be (1) _____

the individual, such as possession by demons, and treatment took the form of (2) _____

of these evil spirits. Much later, the view developed that the cause was (3)_____

the individual, as in a medical illness, and therapy took the form of physical remedies. Today the causes

of deviant behavior are seen as both inside and outside the individual, and, as yet, no single "correct"

approach to understanding deviant behavior has been found nor is there any (4) _____

treatment.

In psychoanalytic theory, disturbed behavior is believed to be the result of (5) _____

conflicts that result from clashes among biological urges, the internalized demands of society, and the

demands of reality. These conflicts are reflected in (6)_____. The aim of

psychoanalysis is to bring unconscious processes to consciousness by eliminating resistance to conscious

awareness so that (7)_____ can bring about more effective functioning through

reasoning. This approach sees early experiences as having been repressed or distorted by defense mech-

anisms, and the techniques of (8)_____ and (9)_____

are used to gain access to the repressed material. Psychoanalysts use both techniques to reduce the person's

(10)_____ of his or her thought process. Today, a variant of psychoanalysis,

called psychoanalytically oriented psychotherapy, uses more (11)_____

interviews and only limited free association. The patient may develop very strong personal feelings toward the therapist, reflecting a process of (12)_____ of unconscious experiences and feelings toward key figures, particularly parents, from the individual's early childhood. The analyst helps the client to bring these feelings under (13)_____ control. The transference process is the (14)_____ of psychoanalytic therapy. A most important component of psychoanalytic therapy is the process of repetition and gradual emergence of new responses, called (15)_____, which is the reeducative aspect of this therapy. Psychoanalysis has been criticized in terms of its lengthy duration, high cost, lack of clearly demonstrated (16)_____, and apparent suitability for only a rather restricted group of individuals.

Behavior therapies reject the medical model and unconscious processes and view abnormal behavior as the direct result of poor or incorrect (17)_____; therapy is therefore thought of as a reeducative process to correct the mislearning. The symptoms *are* the (18)_____ that must be dealt with, and they have been learned through the direct association between an external stimulus and an observable behavioral response. Inner states and (19)_____ processes — for example, cognitive-symbolic processes of covert events — have been incorporated recently into behavior therapy. In reciprocal-inhibition therapy, the client's anxiety and its resultant behaviors are treated through (20)_____ and counterconditioning. The first process involves presenting stimuli, usually through imagery, that were previously anxiety provoking, while the client is under deep (21)_____. The anxiety response is inhibited from occurring and a new response, relaxation, is (22)_____ to the old anxiety-producing stimuli. In implosive therapy, the client is repeatedly and extensively exposed to the conditioned anxiety-producing stimuli in situations without (23)_____; where the client cannot avoid the stimuli and unpleasant consequences do not occur, the anxiety and anxiety-avoiding behavior, it is hoped, will eventually be (24)_____. Other forms of behavior therapy involve the direct application of primary and secondary positive and negative (25)_____ in the modification of unwanted behaviors; the client is thereby thought to effectively apply the principles of learning to his or her own behavior to achieve (26)_____. Biofeedback techniques and ''homework'' assignments in self-observation and self-reinforcement are also employed to enable individuals to (27)_____ their own behavior. Critics of behavior therapy say that symptom removal without treatment of (28)_____ pathology will result in symptom substitution, or the emergence of new symptoms. Beahvior therapists say that new symptoms are (29)_____ but that they too can be explained and treated in learning-theory terms. Behavior therapy has also been faulted on its claim to being scientific, since there are large (30)_____ between the techniques and the theory and experimental studies of learning upon which they are presumably based.

One of the phenomenological therapies is will therapy, which focuses on an individual's experience in the (31)_____ and which stresses his or her uniqueness as a self-determined, self-willed being. Phenomenological approaches reject the (32)_____ model of psychopathology as an illness. All psychological disorders are seen as emanating from conflict between a person's self-evaluation and the values of others, which leads to (33)_____. To avoid anxiety, individuals develop certain avoidance patterns, or (34)_____, that lead the person to seek therapy. The goal of will therapy is to help the individual to (35)_____. The goal of client-centered therapy is to help persons attain (36)_____ between their thoughts and feelings about themselves and their observations of their own behavior. This requires the individual in such therapy to develop a (37) _____ self-concept and to acknowledge more _____ of the self, which is done with the client's (39)_____ focus of reference guiding the course of therapy. The therapist helps the client to clarify the nature of personal problems by clearly (40)_____ what the client has expressed but not yet recognized and also by reflecting or (41)_____, aspects of the client's expressed feelings and emotions. The therapist does not propose (42)_____ but rather allows each client to find his or her own. In addition to being nondirective, the therapist must have (43)_____ positive regard for the client, empathic understanding, and genuineness in relation to the client. Technique and methods are (44)_____.

In Gestalt therapy, the individual is instructed to pay close attention to his or her (45)_____ feelings, thoughts, and wishes. The focus is on the (46)_____ and how the client blocks off experiencing a total awareness of his or her present self. Pathology is viewed as the (47)_____ of the individual from parts of himself or herself and experience. Therapy is directed to help the individual arrive at full (48)_____. Nonverbal behavior is frequently analyzed, but the therapist never (49)_____ for the client. A variety of part-playing techniques as well as work with dreams help the client reclaim those parts of the self that he or she tried to (50)_____. Among the criticisms of phenomenological therapies are that they are useful only with individuals who already have a (51)_____ personality structure, that they fail to deal with the roots of the client's difficulty in the (52)_____, and that the therapists avoid the necessary responsibilities of their role as therapists.

The interpersonal therapy model conceives of psychopathology as primarily an interpersonal rather than an (53)_____ problem. Maladaptive behavior is seen as developing out of disturbed relationships and disturbed (54)_____ among people, and treatment focuses on improving these features. In Sullivan's approach, the patient is believed to manifest his or her difficulties in the therapeutic situation, and the (55)_____ relationship is the main focus of therapeutic interpretation. The therapist helps to bring the client's

(56)_____ distortions to awareness so that the person can recognize the distortions of the past. Transactional analysis focuses on the various (57) _____ individuals play with one another. The personality is thought to be comprised of three "ego states": (58) _____, (59) _____, and (60) _____; the individual operates out of these various ego states in "transactions" with other people. Maladaptive (61)_____ patterns that underlie the interpersonal "games" and "life-scripts" of the client are analyzed so that the client can gain an understanding and therefore begin to change his or her relationships. In group therapy, the distortions in one's interpersonal relationships are acted out with, and responded to by, other (62)_____ in the group. Thus, an individual has the opportunity to learn (63)_____ of interacting within the context of real and varied interpersonal relations. A variant of group therapy is the T (training), or (64)_____, group, which has been used for improving communication in management and educational groups. In family therapy, interpersonal relationships are not merely the *source* of pathology but they *are* the (65)_____. The goal is to treat and change the family and its (66) _____ pattern. The (67) _____ patient is the acknowledged reason the family seeks therapy. The pathology of this person becomes part of the family (68)_____, and any change in his pathological behavior, even improvement, (69)_____ the family equilibrium. The family resists this change, but the therapist guides members to more effective (70)_____.

Masters and Johnson have provided therapy for sexual dysfunctioning on the premises that such difficulties are based on (71)_____ factors and the lack of (72) _____, not on deep-seated intrapsychic conflict or medical illness, and that the problem exists for both partners. Their co-therapy model provides that both partners train in specific (73)_____, gain information about sexual functioning, and explore their feelings, fantasies, desires, preferences, and emotional relationship. Development of more effective (74)_____ and a sense of support for each partner is important in this approach. Brief psychotherapy has more immediate, more limited, and more specific (75)_____ than open-ended or long-term treatment. Emphasis is often placed on the amelioration of specific symptoms, on emotional support, and on restoring the individual to the level of functioning achieved before the (76)_____.

In working with children, therapists frequently make use of (77)_____, in which toys, dolls, modeling clay, paints, and so on are used as projective techniques or means of behavioral observation for material that the child cannot (78)_____. Criticism of interpersonal therapies focuses on the generally high (79)_____ and activity of the therapist, on the fact that the therapies ignore intrapsychic pathologies, and on the unsystematic application of reinforcement.

Psychophysiological therapies, employed only by (80)_____, are frequently used in conjunction with psychotherapeutic approaches, although sometimes they are the primary and even the only form of therapy. These methods include psychosurgery, such as the prefrontal (81)_____, in which the nerve fibers connecting the frontal lobes and the (82)_____ are severed, even though there is no evidence of neural (83)_____. A more recent form of psychosurgery avoids lobotomies and focuses on the (84)_____. The objective of this therapy is to change the (85)_____ of the patient. Psychosurgery has been (86) _____ vigorously. Another psychophysiological method is shock therapy (electroconvulsive therapy or ECT); here electric current is used to produce brief convulsive seizures, which result in subsequent periods of (87)_____. It is not known why this treatment works, when it does work. Chemotherapy, or psychopharmacotherapy, is treatment by the use of chemicals or drugs and is probably the most (88)_____ form of treatment today either alone or in conjunction with other therapies. The major classes of psychotropic treatments are antipsychotic drugs, including the (89)_____; the antianxiety drugs, including Librium and (90)_____; and the antidepressant drugs, including tricyclic drugs such as Elavil or Tofranil and the (91)_____. Amphetamines have been used in the treatment of (92)_____ in children because they appear to produce a (93)_____ effect. Such treatment is not well understood and has been severely criticized.

The goals of therapy vary considerably with the general (94)_____ used. It is very difficult to conduct systematic (95)_____ of any of the forms of therapy because of complex methodological problems, so that reliable conclusions regarding therapeutic effectiveness are not yet available.

4. THOUGHT QUESTIONS

a. All of the psychotherapies involve reeducational processes for the client. Do you think systematic evaluation studies of the various forms of therapy can be made? Why or why not?

b. A major distinction among psychotherapies is that some emphasize the here and now and some emphasize the past, even very early experiences. Is this a real distinction or do all somehow have to attend to the here and now at some point during the therapeutic process?

c. Some view drug therapy not as an adjunct to other forms of therapy but as the sole therapeutic intervention. What kinds of evidence would be required to support this view?

d. Criticism of various psychophysiological therapies has suggested that such therapies could be easily abused to socially control behavior. How can we, as a culture, protect ourselves against this possible abuse?

5. EVALUATION (SELF-TESTS)

Correct answers and text page references are given at the end of the unit.

a. Fill-in-the-blanks Items

Write the word(s) that best complete(s) the sentence in the space provided.

1. Abnormal behavior is thought to have developed as an intrapsychic problem by _____ theory.

2. The process of transference reflects the client's feelings toward the _____.

3. Systematic desensitization involves presenting anxiety-provoking stimuli, usually through _____.

4. Implosive therapy involves the repeated presentation of anxiety-provoking stimuli without _____.

5. In client-centered therapy, the therapist does not propose _____ to the client.

6. In Gestalt therapy, the process is directed toward helping the client arrive at full _____.

7. In Sullivan's approach, the principal focus of therapy is on the _____ relationship.

8. In family therapy, the identified patient is the acknowledged reason that the family _____.

9. The goal of electroconvulsive shock therapy is to produce periods of _____.

10. Valium, one of the most widely used drugs today, is prescribed as a reducer of _____.

b. Matching Items

Write the number of the correct item from the right column in front of the matching item in the left column.

_____ working through	1. emergence of new symptoms after therapy
_____ reciprocal-inhibition therapy	2. games and life-scripts
_____ symptom substitution	3. hyperactivity in children
_____ client-centered therapy	4. reeducative aspect of analytic therapy
_____ transactional analysis	5. unconditional positive regard
_____ group therapy	6. stimulates anxiety when the client is relaxed
_____ brief psychotherapy	7. clients act as therapists
_____ phenothiazines	8. antidepressant drug
_____ Tofranil	9. crisis or trauma-oriented therapy
_____ amphetamines	10. antipsychotic drugs

c. Multiple-choice Items

Circle the letter in front of the answer that best completes the stem.

1. The form of therapy that views abnormal behavior as reflecting disturbed relations and communications is:
   a. psychoanalytic therapy
   b. behavior therapy
   c. phenomenological therapy
   d. interpersonal therapy

2. The form of therapy that views abnormal behavior as a form of poor learning is:
   a. psychoanalytic therapy
   b. behavior therapy
   c. phenomenological therapy
   d. interpersonal therapy

3. The form of therapy that views abnormal behavior as anxiety reflecting a poor self-view is:
   a. psychoanalytic therapy
   b. behavior therapy
   c. phenomenological therapy
   d. interpersonal therapy

4. The form of therapy that views abnormal behavior as the result of unconscious conflicts is:
   a. psychoanalytic therapy
   b. behavior therapy
   c. phenomenological therapy
   d. interpersonal therapy

5. Which form of therapy has been criticized as simply leading to symptom substitution?
   a. psychoanalytic therapy
   b. behavior therapy
   c. phenomenological therapy
   d. interpersonal therapy

6. Which form of therapy has been criticized as working only with clients who are in good psychological shape to begin with?
   a. psychoanalytic therapy
   b. behavior therapy
   c. phenomenological therapy
   d. interpersonal therapy

7. Which form of therapy has been criticized as being lengthy and costly?
   a. psychoanalytic therapy
   b. behavior therapy
   c. phenomenological therapy
   d. interpersonal therapy

8. Which form of therapy has been criticized for being too directive?
   a. psychoanalytic therapy
   b. behavior therapy
   c. phenomenological therapy
   d. interpersonal therapy

9. Amphetamines have been used in the treatment of:
   a. psychoses
   b. depressions
   c. hyperactivity
   d. anxiety

10. MAO inhibitors have been used in the treatment of:
    a. psychoses
    b. depressions
    c. hyperactivity
    d. anxiety

d. Short-answer Items

Answer the following questions with short, concise statements. Reference pages for the material are given at the end of the unit.

1. What are the principal differences between traditional psychoanalytic therapy and the more recent approaches called psychoanalytically oriented therapies?

2. Describe briefly the process of reciprocal-inhibition therapy, including the roles of relaxation and counterconditioning.

3. Contrast client-centered therapy with Gestalt therapy in terms of their philosophical origins and the techniques used.

4. List and describe briefly three different types of psychophysiological therapies.

ANSWER KEY FOR UNIT 26

Unit Review

1. outside
2. exorcism
3. inside
4. proven
5. unconscious
6. symptoms
7. insight
8. free association
9. dream analysis
10. censorship
11. focused
12. transference
13. conscious
14. core
15. working through
16. effectiveness
17. learning
18. pathology
19. covert
20. systematic desensitization
21. relaxation
22. counterconditioned
23. reinforcement
24. extinguished
25. reinforcers
26. self-regulation
27. control/modify
28. underlying
29. rare
30. gaps
31. present
32. medical
33. anxiety
34. symptoms
35. discover himself/herself
36. congruence
37. positive
38. parts
39. internal
40. summarizing
41. "bouncing back"
42. solutions
43. unconditional
44. deemphasized
45. current
46. now
47. alienation
48. self-awareness
49. interprets
50. disown
51. sound
52. past
53. intrapsychic
54. communications
55. patient-therapist
56. parataxic
57. roles
58. Parent
59. Adult
60. Child
61. communication
62. clients
63. new modes
64. encounter
65. pathology
66. interaction
67. identified
68. homeostasis
69. disturbs
70. communication
71. sociocultural
72. information
73. techniques
74. communication
75. goals
76. crisis/trauma
77. play therapy
78. verbally express
79. directedness
80. physicians
81. lobotomy
82. thalamus
83. pathology
84. limbic system
85. behavior
86. criticized
87. lucidity
88. popular
89. phenothiazines
90. Valium
91. MAO inhibitors
92. hyperactivity
93. quieting
94. approach
95. evaluation

Evaluation (Self-tests)

a.   Fill-in-the-blanks Items:

1. psychoanalytic (p. 625)
2. therapist (p. 627)
3. imagery (p. 631)
4. reinforcement (p. 632)
5. solutions (p. 635)
6. self-awareness (p. 636)
7. patient-therapist (p. 638)
8. seeks therapy (p. 640)
9. lucidity (p. 646)
10. anxiety (p. 648)

b.   Matching Items: Correct order and page references are:

4 (p. 629); 6 (p. 631); 1 (p. 633); 5 (p. 635); 2 (p. 638);
7 (p. 639); 9 (pp. 642–643); 10 (p. 647); 8 (p. 648); 3 (p. 649).

c.   Multiple-choice Items: Correct answers and page references are:

1—d (pp. 637–638); 2—b (p. 630); 3—c (pp. 634–636); 4—a (p. 625); 5—b (p. 633);
6—c (p. 637); 7—a (p. 629); 8—d (p. 645); 9—c (p. 649); 10—b (p. 648).

d.   Short-answer Items: Page references for answer material are:

1. pp. 626–627; 2. p. 631; 3. pp. 634–637; 4. pp. 645–649.

Unit 27

PROSOCIAL BEHAVIOR AND AGGRESSION

1. INTRODUCTION TO STUDY OF THIS UNIT

The principal topic in this unit is aggression, or antisocial behavior. Beyond the difficulties of defining this term, the most important problem associated with aggression is the determination of whether aggression in the human is innately based, completely a function of learning, or a product of both heredity and environment. The issue is not an easy one to resolve but it is important to attempt to do so. If we conclude that aggression is a strong innate drive in the human, then, since it is likely to be expressed by all, it would appear important for a culture to set up control mechanisms, individual protection systems, and means of allowing the drive to be expressed without harm. If we conclude that aggressive behavior is learned, then, since it is controllable, we should investigate mechanisms not only of control but of prevention.

What criteria do we use in attempting to decide if the aggressive drive is innate or learned? Some years ago, an important social psychologist suggested that in order to be considered primary or innate, drives ought to satisfy three criteria. They ought to be universal — that is, evidence for the drive ought to be found in all human beings. They ought to be found in lower animals as well, especially other primates and mammals (i.e., gorillas and chimps, and even cats, dogs, and rats). This second criterion is based on evolutionary notions of the inheritance of motivational states. Finally, they ought to have direct physiological bases in the organism. If we inherited a drive state, there should be some identifiable physiological substratum.

When we apply these criteria to the drive of aggression, they do not appear to be satisfied too well. While evidence for aggression in lower animals is common enough (and this is the chief basis for Lorenz's proposal that aggression is innate), there is much less evidence for the separate physiological basis of aggression. It appears, rather, that physiological changes associated with aggression exist because of the involvement of other intense drive states, such as the frustration of the hunger or the thirst drive. Finally, the evidence for universality is hardly overwhelming. There is as much evidence for prosocial behavior as for antisocial behavior in general, and there is evidence that some cultures have been quite cooperative and accepting, while others have been very aggressive.

On balance, then, without further specific information, the conclusion that aggression is learned and therefore controllable seems justifiable. It is possible that the evidence, while still unclear, allows for aggression as being innately based. If this is so, then aggression as an innate human drive must be a very weak one, because of the great variability in its expression. Also, in that case, aggressive behavior would be quite controllable.

2. ISSUES AND CONCEPTS

This unit explores both prosocial behavior and antisocial behavior. Become familiar first with a definition of prosocial behavior and the difficulties of accepting a single definition. Learn the principal argument for the proposition that prosocial behavior is innate and the slight evidence that exists to support this notion. A counterexplanation of prosocial behavior is that it is learned through socialization. Be able to cite the specific behaviors and the three general prosocial norms thought to be learned through reinforcement implementation, through direct instruction, and through imitation of social models.

Moral judgment shows a developmental process, and you should study the general stages of this process and the several dimensions of these stages. Be able to state how the younger and the older child differ in moral judgment. Learn that while moral judgment findings may be generalizable across some cultures, specific training experiences appear to be important for progress in developing a moral sense.

Become familiar with what is meant by the belief in the abstract concept of freedom to dissent. Since many persons do not apply the belief in specific situations, be able to discuss why this may be so.

Two definitions of aggression are presented next. Be able to state why neither is completely adequate. Learn the arguments for the innateness of aggressive behavior, especially those of Freud and Lorenz. Learn, too, what is meant by the socialization of aggression, what parental characteristics such socialization processes have been related to, and how role models may induce aggression. Be able to discuss the frustration-aggression hypothesis and the limited circumstances under which the notion appears meaningful. Know which other environmental circumstances induce aggression.

Finally, though the evidence is not strong, learn the possible roles of brain damage and chromosomal abnormality in aggressive behavior.

3. UNIT REVIEW

Correct answers are given at the end of the unit.

This unit, which deals with how the person functions in the social environment, explores both prosocial and antisocial behavior. A prosocial act may be defined as one that benefits another without the expectation of (1) _____. However, since we do not know the (2) _____ underlying most acts, it may be best to view prosocial acts behaviorally in terms only of their (3)_____ (do they aid or benefit another?).

Some scientists have proposed that prosocial behavior is innate and that more cooperative and social beings have better survived and, therefore, (4)_____. Sociobiologists suggest that members of species help to protect their gene pools and promote survival of the species by (5)_____. Other scientists question the innateness of prosocial behavior at the human level, pointing to the very large (6)_____ in such behavior.

Many psychologists argue that prosocial behavior is learned through (7) _____ because such behavior is necessary for harmonious relations. In addition to specific responses, general norms of prosocial behavior are acquired at an early age, including the norm of (8)_____ (helping those who have helped us and not those who have harmed us); the norm of (9) _____ (helping those in need who are dependent upon us); and the norm of (10)_____ (giving to people according to what they deserve). This latter norm does not rule out the possibility of (11)_____ but says that pressure exists for humans to favor and to seek equity for themselves and others. Persons may actually distort their perceptions of a victim's character or fate to preserve the belief that equity exists, as is evident in our blaming (12)_____ or their blaming (13)_____. Norms that prescribe prosocial behavior are learned through the active implementation of (14)_____ and direct (15)_____, as well as by observation of the behavior of occasional and recurrent (16) _____, including parents and (17) _____.

Moral judgment shows a (18)_____ process. The rate of its occurrence in children depends on their level of (19)_____, the society or culture in which they are raised, and the (20)_____ practices to which they are exposed. The sequence of developmental stages does not seem to vary, and dimensions of these stages include attending to (21)_____ rather than to consequences, judging relativistically rather than (22)_____, learning to disregard whether (23)_____ have or have not been applied in reaching a moral judgment, using reciprocity, using (24)_____ for restitution or reform, and viewing misfortune as punishment or as a (25)_____. In general, the young child focuses on specific (26)_____, obeying the letter more than the spirit of the law, because rules are seen as (27)_____. The older child begins to perceive that rules are made by people for the (28)_____ of all, that rules can be imperfect, and that each of us must decide which rules are generally (29)_____. While these findings are based on Western morality, they may be generalizable to other (30)_____. Progress in morality may be subject to specific (31)_____ experiences. Some research indicates that the moral-judgment level of college students is related to the presence and extent of prosocial helping behavior.

Belief in the abstract concept of freedom to dissent is a major social (32)_____ in America. This belief increases with age and is related to level of (33)_____, knowledge of American (34)_____, political involvement, exposure to television, and level on Maslow's (35)_____. For many persons, however, the abstract belief is not applied in specific instances, a difference that may be related to the intensity of (36)_____ perceived, the (37)_____ of the believer, and the manner in which the belief system was acquired. Some research indicates that prosocial behavior, morality, and tolerance of dissent may represent interrelated and (38)_____ human characteristics.

According to the behavioral definition, aggression is any behavior that (39)_____ another. A second definition defines aggression as any act that is (40)_____ to harm another. Neither definition is completely (41)_____.

Some, including Freud and Lorenz, believe that aggression is controlled by (42)_____. For Freud, it represents the externalization of (43)_____ impulses. For Lorenz, aggression serves important (44)_____ functions. Sincer there are many variations in aggressiveness across cultures and among individuals, it seems clear that this behavior can be modified and is influenced by (45)_____ conditions. The process of learning to control aggression or to express it in ways that are acceptable to one's own culture is called the (46)_____. This is related to the (47)_____ of parents (their willingness to allow the child to be aggressive) and to the (48) _____ of punishment (the extent of parental punishment of an aggressive act). Parents who are (49)_____ on both dimensions have children who express the least aggression, while parents (50)_____ on both dimensions have children who express the most aggression. The children of the remaining two groups of parents studied agree at an (51)_____ level. Children may learn to be aggressive from punitive parents, who operate as (52)_____. They may also be influenced by the media, especially (53)_____.

The frustration-aggression hypothesis proposes that aggression is always (54) _____ by frustration and that (55)_____ always leads to some form of aggression. While some research supports this hypothesis, much research indicates that the two factors are related only when the frustration is (56) _____ and is perceived as (57) _____. Other environmental conditions may induce aggression, including excessive (58) _____ or the presence of (59)_____.

Some evidence suggests that aggressive behavior may result from brain damage, especially in the (60)_____ area. Even with brain damage, however, provocation to aggression may still depend on aggressive (61)_____. Some evidence relates aggressiveness and criminality to the appearance of an extra (62)_____ chromosome in the sex cells of some males. This XYY pattern is referred to as the (63)_____ syndrome, which consists of mental retardation, excessive (64)_____, and occasional violence; the syndrome is reported to be much more common in (65) _____. Other evidence suggests that if the extra Y chromosome is related to aggression, the relationship is indirect, through a combination of (66)_____ and genetic factors.

4. THOUGHT QUESTIONS

a. Unjustified self-blame is prevalent in many groups, including the terminally ill and rape victims. What do you think is the role of self-blame in these persons? How did it come about?

b. In Western cultures, transitions from one moral stage to another seem to occur at roughly the same ages in most people. Do you think that such findings support the position that moral judgment is innately determined? Why or why not?

c. Why do you think that a strong belief in freedom to dissent may occur in individuals who will not tolerate the expression of dissent on some issues? Is this hypocrisy? Does it reflect conflicts in cultural values? Or is this simply another case of individual differences?

d. After what you have read in the text concerning the role of parents in bringing about certain levels of aggressive behavior in their children, what advice would you give to prospective parents about aggression training?

5. EVALUATION (SELF-TESTS)

Correct answers and text page references are given at the end of the unit.

a. Fill-in-the-blanks Items

Write the word(s) that best complete(s) the sentence in the space provided.

1. An act that benefits another without the expectation of reward is referred to as a

   _____ act.

2. Many suggest that prosocial behavior is learned through socialization and increases

   _____.

3. The norm of equity says that people should get _____.

4. Prosocial norms probably are learned on the basis of reinforcement, observation of role models, and direct _____.

5. Paying more attention to intentions than to consequences would be seen as a relatively

   _____ level of moral judgment.

6. Belief in the abstract concept of freedom to dissent is related to intelligence and it

   _____ with age.

7. For Freud, self-destructive impulses are frequently displayed as _____.

8. Parents who are very permissive and very punitive with respect to aggression in their children have children who tend to be _____ aggressive.

9. Parents who are not permissive and not punitive about aggression in their children have children who tend to be _____ aggressive.

10. Recent research on the frustration-aggression hypothesis suggests that frustration will result in aggression only if it is seen as arbitrary and it is _____.

b. Matching Items

Write the number of the correct item from the right column in front of the matching item in the left column.

_____ sharing	1. behavioral definition of aggression
_____ norm of equity	2. expressing aggression in a culturally
_____ attending to intentions	accepted manner
or consequences	3. parents who are high permissive and
_____ any behavior that harms	high punitive
another	4. prosocial behavior
_____ socialization of aggression	5. XYY chromosome
_____ least aggressive children	6. increased aggression in the presence of guns
_____ most aggressive children	7. environmental cue for an increase in
_____ weapons effect	aggressive behavior
_____ excessive heat	8. dimension of moral judgment
_____ ''supermale'' syndrome	9. people should get what they deserve
	10. parents who are low permissive and low punitive

c. Multiple-choice Items

Circle the letter in front of the answer that best completes the stem.

1. A prosocial act may be defined as one that benefits another without the expectation of:
   a. approval
   b. reward
   c. punishment
   d. reciprocation

2. Many psychologists argue against the innateness of prosocial behavior because of the occurrence of very large:
   a. genetic effects
   b. antisocial behaviors
   c. absences of helping behaviors
   d. individual differences

3. The prosocial norm of reciprocity states that:
   a. we should help those who help us
   b. we should help those in need
   c. people should get what they deserve
   d. people should get what they work for

4. The prosocial norm of social responsibility states that:
   a. we should help those who help us
   b. we should help those in need
   c. people should get what they deserve
   d. people should get what they work for

5. In contrast to younger children, older children perceive that rules are:
   a. perfect
   b. absolute
   c. made for the convenience of all
   d. made as a nuisance for all

6. Belief in the abstract concept of freedom to dissent is related
   to all but which of the following factors?
   a. knowledge of history
   b. intelligence
   c. age
   d. political involvement

7. Lorenz feels that aggression is innate because this behavior has:
   a. political acceptance
   b. been learned to solve important problems
   c. a high incidence in families across generations
   d. survival value

8. Children who tend to be lowest in aggression have parents who are:
   a. high in permissiveness, low in punitiveness
   b. low in permissiveness, high in punitiveness
   c. high in permissiveness, high in punitiveness
   d. low in permissiveness, low in punitiveness

9. Children who tend to be highest in aggression have parents who are:
   a. high in permissiveness, low in punitiveness
   b. low in permissiveness, high in punitiveness
   c. high in permissiveness, high in punitiveness
   d. low in permissiveness, low in punitiveness

10. More recent research on the frustration-aggression hypothesis suggests that frustration will result
    in aggression if it is:
    a. a friend who frustrates us
    b. an enemy who frustrates us
    c. high in magnitude
    d. low in magnitude

d. Short-answer Items

Answer the following questions with short, concise statements. Reference pages for the material are given at the end of the unit.

1. Describe briefly the evidence used to support the proposition that prosocial behavior is innate.

2. Specify three ways in which young children differ from older children in the dimensions of moral judgment.

3. Comment on the relationships found between the level of aggression in children and parents, and severity in punishing their children's aggressive behavior.

4. How has brain damage and chromosomal abnormality been related to level of aggressive behavior?

ANSWER KEY FOR UNIT 27

Unit Review

1. reward
2. motivation
3. consequences
4. reproduced
5. sacrificing themselves
6. individual differences
7. socialization
8. reciprocity
9. social responsibility
10. equity
11. selfish behavior
12. victims
13. themselves
14. reinforcement techniques
15. instruction
16. social models
17. the media
18. developmental
19. intelligence
20. child-rearing
21. intentions
22. absolutely
23. sanctions
24. punishment
25. natural event
26. rules
27. absolute
28. convenience
29. good
30. cultures
31. training
32. norm
33. intelligence
34. politics
35. need hierarchy
36. conflict
37. personality
38. durable
39. harms
40. intended
41. adequate
42. instinct
43. self-destructive
44. survival
45. environmental
46. socialization of aggression
47. permissive
48. severity
49. low.
50. high
51. intermediary
52. role models
53. television
54. preceded
55. frustration
56. high in amplitude
57. arbitrary/illegitimate
58. heat
59. weapons
60. limbic
61. environmental cues
62. Y
63. "supermale"
64. height
65. criminals
66. learning

Evaluation (Self-tests)

a. Fill-in-the-blanks Items:

1. prosocial (p. 661)
2. harmonious relations (p. 662)
3. what they deserve (p. 663)
4. instruction (p. 664)
5. high (p. 666)

6. increases (p. 667)
7. aggression (p. 670)
8. more (p. 671)
9. less (p. 671)
10. high in magnitude (p. 672)

b. Matching Items: Correct order and page references are:

4 (p. 661); 9 (p. 663); 8 (p. 666); 1 (p. 669); 2 (p. 670);
10 (p. 671); 3 (p. 671); 6 (pp. 672–673); 7 (p. 672); 5 (p. 674).

c. Multiple-choice Items: Correct answers and page references are:

1—b (p. 661); 2—d (p. 662); 3—a (p. 662); 4—b (pp. 662–663); 5—c (p. 666);
6—a (pp. 667-668); 7—d (p. 670); 8—d (p. 671); 9—c (p. 671); 10—c (p. 672).

d. Short-answer Items: Page references for answer material are:

1. pp. 661–662; 2. pp. 665–666; 3. pp. 670–671; 4. pp. 673–674.

Unit 28

ATTITUDES AND ATTITUDE CHANGES

1. INTRODUCTION TO STUDY OF THIS UNIT

The term attitude has two basic meanings. It is derived from the Latin word *aptus*, as in the term aptitude. Both referred to a mental state of readiness to behave. In various fields of art, including painting, attitude refers to the bodily position of a figure. The mental and motor aspects of attitudes were identified in the second half of the nineteenth century. Herbert Spencer described mental attitudes in 1862. L. Lange described motor attitudes in 1888 in a reaction time study. He found that subjects who were consciously prepared to press a key after receiving a signal responded faster than if they were simply awaiting the signal. This task attitude was called *Aufgabe* and was soon found to be important in all areas of psychological investigation. Thus, the importance of "preparedness" became universally recognized. In Germany, there developed a proliferation of preparedness-like concepts and terms, including that of *Einstellung* (set), which we met earlier in the discussion of problem solving. The multitude of similar concepts probably reflected the fact that there was not a general term such as attitude available at the time.

Toward the end of the nineteenth century, most of the major schools of psychology adopted the concept of attitude even though it did not offer a great deal of information in introspection studies. However, all psychologists began to feel that the notion was very important. It was Freud who invested the concept with vigor when he equated attitudes with dynamic unconscious processes.

Finally, in 1918, two sociologists named Thomas and Znaniecki gave attitude its central and systematic position. They reported an important study of Polish peasants in which they used value and attitude as explanatory concepts. For them, the study of attitudes was the field of social psychology. Refinements of the concept were made during the following 12 years or so. Since then, there have been many attempts to do away with the notion of attitude by learning theorists and others. The concept has survived, has been refined further, and has remained the central concept in the field of social psychology.

2. ISSUES AND CONCEPTS

First of all, learn the relationship between attitude and thinking, feeling, and behavior. Next, be able to define belief and belief system, and know what is meant by belief centrality. Learn the basic distinctions among the five types of beliefs described (Types *A, B, C, D,* and *E*) and the methods that may be used successfully to change those beliefs. Be able to distinguish vertical and horizontal belief structure.

A formal definition of attitude is presented, which should also be learned. Be able to describe how the emotional components of attitudes are learned and then revealed and how attitudes are related to past and future behaviors.

The various elements of the communication-persuasion approach to attitude change are presented next. Be able to discuss the roles of communicator creditability, target attention, communication acceptance, communication discrepancy, and target involvement. In addition, be able to describe an S-R approach to attitude change employing these variables.

Become familiar with Heider's balance theory and the bases on which this theory predicts attitude change. Be able to cite a definition of dissonance, how that concept is related to attitude-discrepant behavior, and how attitude change takes place within this model. Know how to differentiate this approach from a similar one that emphasizes self-perception. Know, as well, how attitude change is said to take place in self-perception theory.

Finally, be able to compare the S-R and the cognitive-balance approaches to attitude change in the communication and persuasion situation, and the cognitive-dissonance and self-perception theories to attitude change in the attitude-discrepant behavior situation.

3. UNIT REVIEW

Correct answers are given at the end of the unit.

Attitude typically defines some relationship between individuals and their (1)_____;
it suggests some quality inside people that influences their (2)_____. Attitude
implies thinking, feeling, and behaving in certain ways and is a very central concept in the field of
(3)_____. Attitudes are based on (4)_____,
involve our emotions, and influence our behavior.

Beliefs, also known as (5)_____, are an important component of attitude.
A belief system has been defined as the total universe of an individual's beliefs about the physical world,
the social world, and the (6)_____. The extent to which any one belief provides
a foundation for others defines its (7)_____ in the belief system. Central beliefs
are seen as factual and important and are (8)_____ to change. Type *A* primitive
beliefs are usually central beliefs and are not derived from other beliefs; they are reinforced, maintained (not
changed), and never controverted (they have (9)_____ percent consensus).
Type *B* primitive beliefs are identical with Type *A* beliefs except that their (10)_____
does not depend on their being shared, reinforced, or agreed upon by others. These beliefs are impervious
to arguments and include delusions, phobias, and ego-enhancing (*B* +) and ego-deflating (*B* –) beliefs arising
from (11)_____. They are learned via direct experience, and confusion about

them may underlie (12)_____. Type *C* beliefs are nonprimitive convictions

about who is an (13)_____ on what. Since these beliefs do not have the same

factual status as primitive beliefs, they can be changed by (14)_____ of the

reference group supporting the belief, by limiting the range of expertise of an individual's authorities,

or by attempting to (15)_____ his or her authorities directly. Type *D* beliefs

are derived and may vary according to the type of belief from which they emanate and according to their

(16)_____ structure, (the presence or absence of premises supporting the

belief). They are generally easier to change the more (17)_____ their under-

lying structure and the less (18)_____ the belief from which they derive. On

the other hand, they may be more difficult to change if their (19)_____

structure (the presence or absence of independent and parallel premises supporting the same belief) is well

developed. Type *D* beliefs are maintained because they derive from (20)_____

beliefs (Types *A, B,* and *C*), are supported by others who agree with these beliefs, and are bolstered by

(21)_____. They may be changed by (22)_____

any of these supports. Type *E* beliefs represent rather arbitrary preferences or tastes and are

(23)_____ because they have few if any connections with other beliefs. They

are learned from (24)_____ with the belief object. They do not require social

support to be maintained, may or may not be intensely held, and may change when new

(25)_____ experiences are encountered.

Attitudes often involve (26)_____, both positive and negative, toward

the different individuals, objects, and situations that we encounter. These components may be learned

directly through experience, indirectly from the reactions of other people, or even from mere

(27)_____ with the attitude object. The emotional component of an attitude

is often revealed when the attitude is (28) _____ or (29) _____,

and it is likely to be stronger for an attitude that is intensely held and/or based on

(30)_____. Our present attitudes result, in part, from our past behavior and

in turn influence our (31)_____. That is, behaving in certain ways leads to

the development of attitudes that (32)_____ the behavior, and holding a

particular attitude leads to behaving in ways that (33)_____ the attitude. A

more formal definition of attitude is that it is a relatively enduring set of (34) _____

and associated feelings about an object or situation that (35)_____ an

individual to behave in a particular way toward the object or situation.

In the communication-persuasion approach to attitude change, a communicator typically presents a

communication containing a new (36)_____. Communicators produce more

attitude change to the extent that they are seen as both expert and trustworthy, referred to as communicator

(37)_____. Communication can influence how a person thinks and feels about an issue and how he or she behaves. It does this by keeping the target's (38)_____ or by increasing communicator credibility, in these ways increasing (39)_____ of the communication. The difference between the target's initial attitude and the attitude advocated in the communication is called communication (40)_____. In general, the greater this is, the greater the attitude change, but the lower the credibility of the communicator, the more likely that greater attitude change will result from (41)_____ discrepancy and, overall, the (42)_____ will be the attitude change produced. People with more education are more influenced by (43)_____ arguments while those with less education are more affected by (44)_____ messages. Attempts to change attitudes are successful *only* when targets are relatively (45)_____ or not committed to that attitude (target involvement). The S-R approach to attitude change suggests that the target has to (46)_____ to the new attitude by articulating it, usually implicitly; then *acceptance* of the new attitude has to be (47)_____.

Heider's balance theory involves affective relationships among (48)_____ people and the attitude object. These relationships should be (49)_____. For example, if person *A* likes person *B*, who has a positive attitude toward *C*, then *A* should have a (50)_____ attitude toward *C*. However, if *A* dislikes *B*, who has a positive attitude toward *C*, then *A* should (51)_____ *C*. Both relationships (triangles) are in balance. This theory predicts that most attitude change will occur when the triangle is (52)_____, there is (53)_____ communicator credibility, the communicator delivers a (54)_____ discrepant message, and the target is (55)_____. Attitude change, then, is a matter of creating maximum (56)_____; balance is (57)_____ when the attitude is changed.

Dissonance is defined as an unpleasant psychological (58)_____ felt whenever one cognition follows from the opposite of the other cognition, leading to (59)_____ behavior. The tension should lead to an attempt to (60)_____ the dissonance. Attitude change will occur whenever individuals engage in behaviors that are discrepant with their (61)_____, the amount of change being proportional to the (62)_____ of cognitive dissonance. In addition, the less the magnitude of induced forces operating on attitude-discrepant behavior and the greater the magnitude of the attitude-discrepant behavior, the (63)_____ the attitude change.

An alternative to the dissonance-reduction approach to attitude change emphasizes

(64)_____. We come to know our attitudes by inferring them from observations

of our own (65)_____ and the circumstances in which this occurs. If we know

our "attitude" (i.e., have a strong initial attitude), we will not use our behavior to infer a

(66)_____. However, if we do not know our attitude, we will rely on these

(67)_____ cues (self-perception) to infer our attitude.

In summary, in the communication and persuasion situation, both S-R theory and cognitive-balance

theory assume that attitude change (68)_____ behavior change and that if

we can get someone to attend to and accept a new attitude, then behavior change will follow. In the

attitude-discrepant behavior situation, both the cognitive-dissonance and the self-perception theories agree

that behavior change (69)_____ attitude change. All social psychology

theories of attitude change agree about where attitudes come from and what their effects are and about

their (70)_____ for understanding individual and group behavior.

4. THOUGHT QUESTIONS

a. What do you think would be the most effective program to assemble in order to "brainwash" a person politically? What kinds of beliefs are political beliefs? What kinds of programs of change would be most effective?

b. Review in your mind the five types of beliefs described in the text. Think of specific attitudes that *you* have held, associated with each of these types of belief. Review changes that have or have not occurred in these attitudes over the years to evaluate which types of beliefs are more susceptible to change and the circumstances (methods of attack) associated with these changes.

c. Think about the cognitive-dissonance and the self-perception models of attitude change. Are they really different theoretical models, or can they be brought together quite easily into a single framework? What would be the nature of that framework?

d. Knowing what you now know about various theories of attitude change, how would you go about changing attitudes and behaviors relating to an important content? Assume that you are the surgeon general of the United States and you wish to begin a new antismoking advertising campaign. What would be the nature of this campaign? Why do you think that it would be more effective than the present campaign?

5. EVALUATION (SELF-TESTS)

Correct answers and text page references are given at the end of the unit.

a. Fill-in-the-blanks Items

Write the word(s) that best complete(s) the sentence in the space provided.

1. Attitude implies thinking, feeling, and _____ in certain ways.

2. The centrality of a belief is the extent to which it provides a foundation for

   _____

3. A delusion would be an example of a Type _____ belief.

4. Of the five types of beliefs discussed, the one that would probably be the easiest to change is the

   Type _____ belief.

5. The emotional components of attitudes may be learned from the reactions of other people, mere

   association, or through _____.

6. Communicator credibility refers to the perception of the communicator as both expert

   and _____.

7. Communication discrepancy is the difference between the communication's attitude and the

   target's _____ attitude.

8. One-sided arguments influence more attitude change in people who are _____

   educated.

9. According to balance theory, balance is restored when the attitude is _____.

10. According to cognitive-dissonance theory, attitude change occurs when people's attitudes are

    discrepant with their _____.

b. Matching Items

Write the number of the correct item from the right column in front of the matching item in the left column.

_____ veridicality	1. phobia
_____ centrality	2. attitude change in cognitive-balance theory
_____ Type *A* belief	3. correspondence to reality
_____ Type *B* belief	4. inconsequential belief
_____ Type *C* belief	5. "parents know everything"
_____ Type *E* belief	6. faith in our senses
_____ target involvement	7. external cues are important for attitude change
_____ maximum imbalance	8. initial attitudes and behavior are discrepant
_____ cognitive-dissonance theory	9. one belief providing the basis for others
_____ self-perception theory	10. commitment to an attitude

c. Multiple-choice Items

Circle the letter in front of the answer that best completes the stem.

1. Attitude implies _____, _____, and _____ in certain ways.
   a. thinking, willing, and behaving
   b. perceiving, behaving, and sensing
   c. sensing, thinking, and behaving
   d. thinking, feeling, and behaving

2. A delusion is an example of a:
   a. Type *A* belief
   b. Type *B* belief
   c. Type *C* belief
   d. Type *D* belief

3. Thinking that parents know everything is an example of a:
   a. Type *A* belief
   b. Type *B* belief
   c. Type *C* belief
   d. Type *D* belief

4. Having faith in our own senses is an example of a:
   a. Type *A* belief
   b. Type *B* belief
   c. Type *C* belief
   d. Type *D* belief

5. A belief based on other beliefs is a:
   a. Type *A* belief
   b. Type *B* belief
   c. Type *C* belief
   d. Type *D* belief

6. In the communication-persuasion approach, attitude change is dependent upon:
   a. target attention
   b. communicator credibility
   c. communication discrepancy
   d. all of the above

7. In balance theory, attitude change is dependent upon creating:
   a. maximum balance
   b. maximum imbalance
   c. maximum balance or imbalance, depending on the circumstances
   d. maximum balance or imbalance, depending on initial attitudes

8. According to self-perception theory, we come to know our attitudes from:
   a. communicator messages
   b. target attention
   c. our own behavior
   d. our own intuition

9. Both S-R theory and cognitive-balance theory assume that attitude change leads to:
   a. behavior change
   b. feeling change
   c. thinking change
   d. communication change

10. Both cognitive-dissonance and self-perception theory agree that behavior change leads to:
    a. communication change
    b. attitude change
    c. emotional change
    d. attitude discrepancy

d. Short-answer Items

Answer the following questions with short, concise statements. Reference pages for the material are given at the end of the unit.

1. Differentiate clearly between Type *A* and Type *B* primitive beliefs.

2. List the three methods suggested for attempting to change Type *C* beliefs, and indicate which would probably be the least successful and why.

3. Contrast the S-R explanation with the cognitive-balance explanation of attitude change accomplished within the communication and persuasion format.

4. Contrast attitude change in the communication and persuasion model and in the attitude-discrepant model.

ANSWER KEY FOR UNIT 28

Unit Review

1. environment
2. behavior
3. social psychology
4. beliefs
5. cognitions
6. self
7. centrality
8. difficult
9. 100
10. stability
11. early experiences
12. emotional disturbance
13. authority
14. criticism
15. discredit
16. vertical
17. complex
18. central
19. horizontal
20. more basic
21. logical arguments
22. attacking
23. inconsequential
24. direct experience
25. contradictory
26. feelings
27. association
28. attacked
29. supported
30. central beliefs
31. future behavior
32. agree with
33. agree with
34. beliefs
35. predisposes

36. attitude
37. credibility
38. attention
39. acceptance
40. discrepancy
41. lesser
42. less
43. two-sided
44. one-sided
45. uninvolved
46. attend
47. reinforced
48. two
49. balanced
50. positive
51. dislike
52. unbalanced
53. high
54. highly
55. uninvolved
56. imbalance
57. restored
58. tension
59. attitude-discrepant
60. reduce
61. initial attitudes
62. magnitude
63. greater
64. self-perception
65. overt behavior
66. new attitude
67. external
68. leads to
69. leads to
70. importance

Evaluation (Self-tests)

a. **Fill-in-the-blanks Items:**

1. behaving (p. 677)
2. other beliefs (p. 679)
3. *B* (p. 682)
4. *E* (p. 685)
5. direct experience (pp. 686–687)

6. trustworthy (p. 688)
7. initial (p. 689)
8. less (p. 690)
9. changed (pp. 690–691)
10. behaviors (pp. 694–695)

b. **Matching Items: Correct order and page references are:**

3 (p. 679); 9 (p. 679); 6 (p. 680); 1 (p. 682); 5 (pp. 682–683);
4 (p. 685); 10 (p. 690); 2 (p. 691); 8 (p. 693); 7 (p. 695).

c. **Multiple-choice Items: Correct answers and page references are:**

1—d (p. 677); 2—b (p. 682); 3—c (pp. 682–683); 4—a (p. 680); 5—d (p. 685);
6—d (pp. 688–690); 7—b (p. 691); 8—c (p. 695); 9—a (p. 696); 10—b (p. 696).

d. **Short-answer Items: Page references for answer material are:**

1. pp. 679–682; 2. pp. 682–683; 3. pp. 688–692; 4. pp. 688–696.

Unit 29

PERSON PERCEPTION

1. INTRODUCTION TO STUDY OF THIS UNIT

One of the areas emphasized in this unit is impression formation. How we form impressions of another person has been of interest for hundreds of years, and much speculation about the process has occurred. We are all familiar with the influence of such impressions on our preconceived notions of the importance of certain characteristics; and how a person looks, talks, and dresses affects impressions. Actual research on the issue began with the work of Abraham Luchins in 1942. Luchins developed short paragraphs of material, each describing a series of behaviors of a person. The sentences were arranged so that the first several might suggest that the person was an extrovert and the remaining ones might suggest that the person was an introvert. With such materials, he discovered the order effect in impression formation. He found that the information presented earlier was more important than later information. In the example given, the person would be seen as an extrovert. To confirm this order effect, Luchins reversed the sentences and found that the person was viewed as an introvert. In each case, the later conflicting information was explained away and integrated and not seen as modifying the first impression. Later research has replicated this primacy effect but has also found that under other circumstances late information is very important in determining impressions (recency effect). Research has also indicated that certain powerful traits, such as warm/cold, differentially influence impressions and that other variables, such as prior expectations of a person's characteristics, have an important influence on the sequential effect.

First impressions stick. They persist in real life as well as in research situations and even in the face of much conflicting information. Since first impressions are not necessarily accurate, it would seem important, perhaps, to delay the formation of person impressions, at least somewhat, in order to increase their reliability and meaningfulness and to ''give the other person a break.''

2. ISSUES AND CONCEPTS

Begin by learning a definition of and the four basic principles of person perception. Remember that person perception has historically involved many other processes than perception, and that now it is concerned with the acquisition, processing, organization, and utilization of information about people.

Study the early research in the area, in which people formed impressions from photographs or from descriptive statements. Know Darwin's view about emotional expression and the results of research on emotion recognition. Learn the difference between emotion expression and emotion recognition, the evidence for the innateness of each, and the specific emotions that children can recognize at different ages.

All perceivers are inaccurate judges of persons. Be able to discuss the five types of judgmental errors that they tend to make. Study the research on nonverbal behaviors as they contribute to or detract from our impressions of others.

You should also have a good idea of what is meant by impression formation and implicit theories of personality, and how the latter may be formed. Be able to state three explanations for the permanence of first impressions in person perception.

Learn Heider's explanation of why we are able to understand the behavior of others and ourselves as well. Be able to explain what attribution theory is and the essence of the attribution process, including the differences between environmental and personal attributions and cues to the beginning and ending of this process.

Learn the four conditions that facilitate personal attributions and how these factors influence one another. Finally, be able to describe two biases that influence the attribution process.

3. UNIT REVIEW

Correct answers are given at the end of the unit.

Person perception may be defined generally as the study of what we understand about

(1)_____, and how we come to achieve such understanding. Our

(2)_____ with other individuals reveals four of the basic principles of person

perception. The first is that person perception involves, at the outset, a basic "gut-level" reaction to another

person that leaves us with a somewhat (3) _____ or (4) _____

feeling about the person. The second is that we tend to both pay attention to and seek more information about

(5)_____ behavior or persons. The third is that person perception involves

relationships between behaviors and (6)_____'. The fourth is that what we

"know" about a person is our (7)_____, which is a unified cluster of

personality traits. Person perception has historically involved not only perception but also observation,

recognition, memory, impression formation, cognition, inference, and (8)_____.

More recently it is concerned with the acquisition, processing, organization, and (9) _____

of information about people.

Historically, person perception was thought to be equivalent to (10)_____

perception, and research was directed to finding out what characteristics people use in

(11)_____ from photographs or from brief descriptive personal statements.

Darwin felt that we could recognize emotions from facial expressions because such expressions reflected

(12)_____ physiological habits. Further study concluded that recognition

of emotions from facial expressions alone was exceedingly difficult and that emotional expressions were not

(13)_____ within a given culture. However, more recent research, carefully

done to avoid the methodological flaws of earlier studies, suggests that there are at least six recognizable

emotions: happiness, sadness, anger, fear, surprise, and (14)_____; other

research reveals two more: interest and (15)_____. These emotions are

recognized from facial expression only and quite accurately across cultures, better by

(16)_____ cultures than by (17)_____ cultures.

Expression of emotion appears to be (18)_____, while the recognition of

emotions is (19)_____ to some extent. By age three, children can recognize

(20)_____, and they generally add the recognition of the other emotions by

age (21)_____. Recognition of (22)_____

is the most difficult.

The results of many studies done to find the personality characteristics of more accurate person

perceivers have been (23)_____. While it was found that all perceivers

were (34)_____ judges, the kinds of errors made were consistent for all

subjects and five judgmental errors were identified: the halo effect (giving similar ratings on several traits

based on (24)_____ impression of the judged person); logical error (assuming

that certain traits (26)_____); the (27)_____

(rating others high on desirable traits and low on undesirable traits); assumed similarity (attributing to

others traits that you would assign to (28)_____); and

(29)_____ (assigning to people characteristics of the typical member of the

group to which they are thought to belong).

Research on nonverbal (30)_____ behaviors has increased a great deal

in recent years. Touching behaviors, (31)_____, and other nonverbal

behaviors may be important cues in person perception. However, psychologists at this time are unable

to say that any particular nonverbal behavior will always reveal the same (32) _____

or to suggest precisely how nonverbal behaviors contribute to or detract from our impressions of

other people.

Asch was convinced that we experience persons as unified (33)_____,

a Gestalt position. His research demonstrated this point and also the facts that some traits are more

central to (34)_____ and that initial (35)_____

information influences the impression. Thus, impressions are determined more by what is

(36)_____ of the perceiver than by the stimuli presented. Our own private

views of relations among visible descriptive features or traits of people, which determine the unified impressions we form of others, are referred to as an (37)_____. This apparently consists of a particular set of descriptive categories and assumptions about which (38)_____ go with which others. Such a theory may be formed by our learning perceived relationships among traits, by employing evaluative, potency, and activity dimensions in forming impressions, or by our making (39)_____.

In combining information about another person, (40)_____ are important, and they resist change. One explanation for their performance is the (41)_____ hypothesis, which suggests that the initial information we have about a person provides meaning (directional set) to the additional information we receive about the person. A second explanation is that we (42)_____ more to what came first as opposed to later. A third explanation, called (43)_____, suggests that we do not apply to our impression any information that appears later and contradicts our earlier ''knowledge.''

Heider suggested that we are able to understand the behavior of others because we see behaviors and persons as connected by (44)_____ relationships, that is, we see people as (45)_____ their own behavior on the basis of their own traits. We also infer our own traits from our (46)_____. One person perception principle is that we tend to notice and want to know more about (47)_____ behavior and people; such behavior initiates the (48)_____ process. The theory underlying this process attempts to bridge the gap between perception and (49)_____. The essence of this process is the decision about the (50)_____ of a behavior that we have observed. An (51)_____ attribution entails a decision that some external force accounts for an observed behavior. A (52)_____ attribution entails a decision that something about the observed person(s) accounts for the behavior. The attribution process starts with observation of the (53)_____ behavior of a person in a situation. It ends when we make an attribution and believe that we (54)_____ what we have observed.

Conditions that facilitate personal attributions include (55)_____ (meaning that the more we believe a person attempts to perform a certain behavior, the more likely we are to attribute a personal cause; both effort cues and (56)_____ cues increase the degree of personal attribution); ability (which means the more we believe a person has the ability to perform a behavior, the more likely we are to attribute a (57)_____ cause); low consensus (which means much the same as (58)_____); and low distinctiveness (meaning that the lower the distinctiveness of the observed behavior, the (59)_____ likely we are to attribute a personal cause). These factors are not (60)_____, and frequently information from one source is used to infer another source. Biases in the attribution process include (61)_____ (when our own wishes or needs determine the attribution; the more involved we are, the more likely we are to be biased and the more pervasive the effects of our bias will be); and a self-other bias (with self-perceivers biased in favor of (62)_____ causes and other-perceivers biased because of (63)_____ causes).

4. THOUGHT QUESTIONS

a. By age three children can recognize happiness from facial expression. By age fourteen several other emotions can be so recognized. What do such findings suggest regarding the innate or learned nature of emotional expression or recognition of emotion?

b. The first impressions we form of people are very important. However, they are not always more correct than later ones. What specific advice would you give to your friends about forming impressions of others? Specifically, what would you suggest they do about holding off an impression until more complete information is obtained? How would you suggest they do this?

c. It has been suggested that public figures, whose abilities are often evaluated as high, sometimes deliberately blunder in public view. If this is so, why do you think they do this? How are such blunders likely to be evaluated by the public?

d. Assume that you are in an elevator, facing forward toward the door. Another person enters, faces the rear, and sits on the floor. What kinds of attributions would this scene stimulate in you? How would you investigate both the environmental and personal attributions that you made?

5. EVALUATION (SELF-TESTS)

Correct answers and text page references are given at the end of the unit.

a. Fill-in-the-blanks Items

Write the word(s) that best complete(s) the sentence in the space provided.

1. The study of what we know about people and how we come to achieve such understanding is known as _____.

2. According to the principles of person perception, we pay more attention and seek more information about the _____.

3. Historically, object perception and _____ perception were thought to be basically the same.

4. The most difficult emotion for us to recognize is that of _____.

5. Expression of emotion appears to be _____.

6. The judgmental error in which we give similar ratings on several traits to a person based on our overall impression is called the _____.

7. An implicit theory of personality reflects our own private view of relations among _____.

8. The three explanations of the permanence of first impressions are change of meaning, discounting, and _____.

9. The essence of the attribution process is the decision about the _____ of a behavior that we have observed.

10. Conditions that facilitate personal attributions include trying, low consensus, low distinctiveness, and _____.

b. Matching Items

Write the number of the correct item from the right column in front of the matching item in the left column.

_____ phylogenetic habits	1. innate nonverbal expressive behaviors
_____ logical error	2. the situation is the cause
_____ stereotyping	3. later contradictory information is disregarded
_____ evaluative, potency, and activity	4. assigning group characteristics to an individual member
_____ change of meaning	5. influenced by our own wishes and needs
_____ discounting	6. independent dimensions used in forming impressions
_____ environmental attribution	7. unusual behavior
_____ trying	8. equals intention and effort
_____ low consensus	9. assumption that certain traits go together.
_____ egocentric attribution	10. early information provides a directional set

c. Multiple-choice Items

Circle the letter in front of the answer that best completes the stem.

1. Which of the following is *not* a basic principle of person perception?
   a. basic ''gut level'' reaction
   b. secondary impressions
   c. attending to the unusual
   d. relationships between behavior and traits

2. Which of the following is *not* one of the recent concerns of research involving information about person perception?
   a. acquisition
   b. processing
   c. unitization
   d. utilization

3. Which of the following emotions is facially recognized earliest by young children?
   a. happiness
   b. anger
   c. surprise
   d. disgust-contempt

4. Which of the following emotions is facially recognized latest by young children?
   a. happiness
   b. anger
   c. surprise
   d. disgust-contempt

5. Which of the following judgmental errors refers to giving of similar ratings on several traits to persons based on overall impressions?
   a. halo effect
   b. logical error
   c. assumed similarity
   d. stereotyping

6. Which of the following judgmental errors refers to attributing to others traits that you would assign to yourself?
   a. halo effect
   b. logical error
   c. assumed similarity
   d. stereotyping

7. Impressions of others are mostly influenced by:
   a. what exists in objective stimuli
   b. what is in the head of the perceiver
   c. our public views of trait relationship
   d. knowledge of cultural variation

8. Implicit theories of personality may be formed on the basis of all but which one of the following?
   a. learning perceived relationships among traits
   b. employing the evaluative dimensions in forming impressions
   c. using judgmental errors
   d. using explicit dimensions in forming impressions

9. The discounting explanation of the permanence of first impressions suggests that:
   a. initial information provides a directional set
   b. we pay more attention to initial information
   c. we disregard later information
   d. we reject what other people tell us

10. Conditions that facilitate personal attributions do *not* include which one of the following?
    a. trying
    b. inability
    c. low consensus
    d. low distinctiveness

d. Short-answer Items

Answer the following questions with short, concise statements. Reference pages for the material are given at the end of the unit.

1. Comment on evidence supporting the position that expression of emotion is innate.

2. Differentiate between the two judgmental errors called the halo effect and assumed similarity.

3. Contrast the three explanations of the importance of first impressions: the change-of-meaning hypothesis, the attention hypothesis, and the discounting hypothesis.

4. Contrast the two conditions that facilitate personal attributions: trying and low consensus.

ANSWER KEY FOR UNIT 29

Unit Review

1. people
2. experience
3. positive
4. negative
5. unusual
6. traits
7. impression
8. attribution
9. utilization
10. object
11. forming impressions
12. innate
13. universal
14. disgust-contempt
15. shame
16. "advanced"
17. primitive
18. innate
19. learned
20. happiness
21. 14
22. disgust-contempt
23. unimpressive
24. inaccurate
25. overall
26. go together
27. leniency effect
28. yourself
29. stereotyping
30. expressive
31. eye contact
32. feeling

33. wholes
34. impression formation
35. incomplete
36. "inside the head"
37. implicit theory of personality
38. characteristics
39. judgmental errors
40. first impressions
41. change-of-meaning
42. attend
43. discounting
44. causal
45. causing
46. behavior
47. unusual
48. attribution
49. impression
50. cause
51. environmental
52. personal
53. ongoing
54. understand
55. trying
56. intention
57. personal
58. unusual behavior
59. more
60. independent
61. egocentric attribution
62. environmental
63. personal

Evaluation (Self-tests)

a.   Fill-in-the-blanks Items:

1. person perception (p. 701)
2. unusual (p. 699)
3. person (p. 701)
4. disgust-contempt (p. 704)
5. innate (p. 703)

6. halo effect (p. 705)
7. traits (p. 709)
8. attention (p. 711)
9. cause (p. 713)
10. ability (p. 714)

b.   Matching Items: Correct order and page references are:

1 (p. 701); 9 (p. 705); 4 (p. 705); 6 (p. 710); 10 (p. 711);
3 (pp. 711–712); 2 (p. 713); 8 (p. 714); 7 (p. 714); 5 (p. 715).

c.   Multiple-choice Items: Correct answers and page references are:

1—b (pp. 699–700); 2—c (p. 701); 3—a (p. 704); 4—d (p. 704); 5—a (p. 705);
6—c (p. 705); 7—b (p. 709); 8—d (pp. 709–712); 9—c (pp. 711–712); 10—b (p. 714).

d.   Short-answer Items: Page references for answer material are:

1. pp. 701–704; 2. p. 705; 3. pp. 711–712; 4. p. 714.

Unit 30

THE INDIVIDUAL IN THE GROUP

1. INTRODUCTION TO STUDY OF THIS UNIT

One of the topics covered in this unit is personal space. Personal space is an important concept in the area of proxemics, or the study of the relationships between humankind and space. Personal space refers to that invisible bubble of space around each of us within which we resist intrusion. It is not necessarily symmetrical from side to side or front to back, and may change its shape, depending on environmental circumstances. If it is invisible, how do we know of it? In two ways. First, by observing the interpersonal distances of persons in natural settings. Second, by sending in experimental decoys to invade the personal space of unknowing subjects. In both circumstances, we can study the influence of such variables as sex, age, societal and cultural dimensions, and the like on interpersonal distances and resistance to intrusions.

We have learned much of personal space from such studies. It begins to be observed in the late preschool years and grows over the years until it achieves adult size at age 12 or 13. This suggests that much of personal space may be learned, although some believe that some aspects of it are innate. In Western cultures the adult female has a smaller personal space than the male, probably reflecting her stereotype of being more accessible and nurturant. Heterosexual couples, however, have a smaller collective personal space than two males and a bit smaller one, although not reliably so, than two females. There are large differences in the cultural expression of personal space. Northern European peoples, those in England, and those in the United States have large personal spaces. Peoples in Germany and the Netherlands have even larger personal spaces. Considerably smaller are the personal spaces of peoples in the Mediterranean countries, and males in Arabic countries have the smallest personal spaces of all.

There are some personality correlates to personal space. While studies of the personal space of deeply emotionally disturbed persons present contradictory results, there is more consistent evidence for persons labeled introverted to have larger personal spaces than those labeled extroverted.

What do all of these findings reflect? What is the role of personal space? There are several theoretical answers to these questions. One of the most intriguing is that personal space is a means for each of us to preserve our privacy and to identify and maintain the self. While this possibility is speculative, it does appear likely that personal space is intimately involved in patterns of interpersonal communication.

2. ISSUES AND CONCEPTS

This chapter begins with the information that virtually all human behavior occurs in a social group context, starting with the family in early life. Learn how groups may influence individual performance through social facilitation and through coaction, how these influences vary with well-practiced or new tasks, and the meaning of social loafing. Be able to describe the specific circumstances under which group performance may be more proficient than individual performance and those under which risky shift may occur. Become familiar with group think, why it takes place, its results, and how it can be avoided.

Learn next what conformity pressure is and the circumstances under which substantial conformity effects take place. Be aware of the difference between informational social influence and normative social influence, and how the latter is illustrated in obedience studies. Be able to discuss how a consistent minority may influence group decision.

Deindividuation is the next topic, and you should learn what kinds of behavior it may result in. Groups can behave irresponsibly through inaction as well as through action, and you should be able to discuss why this response probably takes place.

The definitions of territoriality and personal space are also important. Learn the differences between the two concepts and the behavioral and physiological correlates of personal space. Be able to discuss what the negative responses to crowding may be due to, especially under low density conditions.

Finally, become familiar with the internal and external environments of groups and how the internal group environment may be related to group versus individual problem-solving behavior. Leadership within groups is an important topic. Be able to cite some of the possible personality characteristics of leaders and to describe how leaders come to be leaders. Lastly, learn the differences between task leaders and socioemotional leaders, and between democratic and autocratic leaders, and familiarize yourself with the circumstances under which each functions best.

3. UNIT REVIEW

Correct answers are given at the end of the unit.

Groups constitute the immediate social environment of the individual and this social context influences virtually all (1)_____. Group influences, with the (2)_____ as the most relevant social group, are fundamental in the transformation of an infant into a (3)_____ adult.

Groups can affect individual performance through social facilitation, which can take place through (4)_____ effects (the effect on individual behavior of the presence of passive spectators) and through (5)_____ effects (the effects on individual behavior of other persons engaged in the same activity). The mere presence of others seems to have an arousing effect, perhaps, in part, because of the performer's concern that others may be (6)_____ his or her performance. In general, well-practiced performances (7)_____ from the group context, while new ones are (8)_____. Individual performance may also suffer in a group because people sometimes respond with less effort when they are part of a group (called social (9)_____).

Groups up to four or five members appear to work more proficiently than individuals when the problem to be solved has a (10)_____ that can be clearly recognized, once discovered. When the problem has no correct or incorrect solution, group performance may not necessarily be (11)_____ than individual performance. Of relevance here is the (12)_____ phenomenon, or the tendency to attempt higher-risk or less responsible solutions under some group circumstances. Research indicates that such shifts following group discussion are more likely to occur when the problem discussed is one in which there is a strong element of economic or social (13)_____, and less shift will occur when the problem discussed is one in which a person's (14)_____ is at stake.

When a group is composed of individuals with strong allegiances to one another and a commitment to group success, it is susceptible to (15)_____ processes, in which independent critical thinking is decreased. This seems to be due to feelings of false (16)_____, members' belief in the morality of other members, development and reinforcement of negatively stereotyped views of opposition (17)_____, individual suppression of doubts concerning the behavior of the group, and pressure on deviants to (18)_____ or leave, and protection of the group leader from (19)_____ opinion. Decisions reached by such groups are likely to be (20)_____, as evidenced by research and public records of international crises. Minimizing pressures toward group think can be effected by encouraging an (21)_____ style of leadership and possibly by having a different group member play the role of (22)_____ at each meeting.

In general, then, the relative efficacy of individual versus group problem solving depends on the nature of the (23)_____, the distribution of ability among group members, the arrangements for dividing and coordinating the activities of group members, and the scheme for combining individual efforts into a (24)_____.

The most widely observed and researched phenomenon in social psychology is (25) _____, in which pressure is used to modify what we say and do to get us to agree with what others say and do. Such effects of group pressure are very strong and depend on the size of the unanimous group consensus (up to (26)_____ confederates), whether any confederate made the (27)_____ response, and the perceptual difference between the correct and false responses.

A group can affect its members through (28)_____ social influence, that is, by providing information to increase cognitive clarity. The less information a member has, the (29)_____ the impact of the majority can be expected to be. Groups can also affect individual members through (30)_____ social influence, by promising rewards or approval or by threatening punishment, rejection, or embarrassment. A powerful form of this involves the request for (31)_____ by some authority, as in the Milgram studies. These studies demonstrate clearly the group's influence in supporting cruel treatment and also (32)_____ treatment of another human being. In both instances the individual goes along with the group, apparently irrespective of his or her (33)_____ inclinations.

Research has also indicated that a consistent (34)_____ can influence the majority. Such influence does not occur early in the process, and it tends to (35)_____ once one member of the majority shifts to the minority position. In addition, members of the minority tend to be (36)_____ by the majority, and majority members report that minority members made them think more about their positions than did (37)_____ members.

Being part of a group may produce a state of deindividuation due to a feeling of (38)_____. In this state, the individual loses a sense of (39)_____ and also normal restraints and standards, which then facilitates (40)_____ behavior; the individual also seems to be particularly susceptible to influence by (41)_____ cues (that is, the behavior of others). The increased behavior may be either antisocial or (42)_____.

Groups can behave irresponsibly through (43)_____ as well as through action. For example, persons are less likely to (44)_____ others when they are part of a group than when alone. This may be due to the (45)_____ of responsibility for helping in a group or to an information social influence of seeing other people (46)_____, leading to the conclusion that action is unnecessary.

Groups also affect the individual by the amount of (47)_____ they allow the individual to occupy. Persons have certain needs for spatial privacy; when these needs are not met, personal ineffectiveness and (48)_____ may occur. Our assumption that we have exclusive rights to certain geographical areas is labeled (49)_____. Personal space refers to the space surrounding our body that "moves" with us and that we try to prevent others from (50)_____. Personal space varies with circumstances. For example, pairs of acquaintances stand (51)_____ than pairs of strangers. Persons attempt to reduce the extent to which they are invaded in dense situations, such as in an elevator, by closing their (52)_____, standing back to back, looking down, or holding a newspaper at eye level. Physiological responses to personal space invasions include sweating, coldness of hands and feet, and increased (53)_____ and blood pressure. Maintenance of personal space and territoriality is usually regulated at a (54)_____ level.

The negative responses to crowding may not strictly depend on interpersonal

(55)_____ but may arise from the possibility that one's achieved

level of (56)_____ is less than a desired level. Experiments demonstrate

that crowding effects can occur in low-density conditions if privacy is (57)_____.

In addition, if the presence of others does not interfere with (58)_____

behavior, people tend not to perceive themselves as being crowded. Finally, a person's perceived

(59)_____ over the density conditions is important. Chronic density may lead

to the perception of having less control in one's home environment and may generate a feeling of

relative (60)_____.

Groups appear to have two environments and two corresponding sets of (61) _____.

The (62)_____ environment consists of whatever events and problems the

group has been organized to deal with. The (63)_____ environment consists

of the behavior of the group members toward one another. Management of this environment is a

(64)_____ task, one at which many groups fail. This may account for group

problem-solving behavior being far more (65)_____ than individual problem

solving; a group may accomplish more than could be achieved if individual efforts were merely summed

only if the (66)_____ environment is managed with great skill.

An important feature of group structure is that there are leaders and followers. A persistent debate

is whether leaders are born or are determined by the (67)_____. No

personality factors have been found to be consistently related to leadership ability, although frequently

associated characteristics are intelligence, dominance, and (68)_____. Simply

being (69)_____ a leadership role or having a person (70)_____

more than the other group members can produce leadership behavior. Emergence of leadership is probably

due to an (71)_____ between the person and the situation. Some leaders,

called (72)_____ leaders, are oriented to getting the job done, while others,

called (73)_____ leaders, attend to high morale and group member needs.

Each functions better as a leader depending on the task of the group and (74) _____

relations. Style of leadership, whether democratic or (75)_____, is also

important. On the one hand, authoritarian leadership may be associated with more

(76)_____ and discontent but also high production of lesser quality than

democratic leadership. When the situation is very ambiguous and (77)_____,

authoritarian leadership may be preferred. Effective leaders may actually become more

(78)_____ during stressful phases. At present it cannot be said that any

one type of leadership is better than another or that specific kinds of persons become the most compatible

group members. What type of leadership is to be preferred for a given group depends in part on the

(79)_____ of the individual group members.

4. THOUGHT QUESTIONS

a. It appears that "group think" may have contributed to the poor decisions to invade Cuba or to cover up the Watergate break-in. Why do you think that such important decisions could have been influenced by group think? How could a new U.S. president avoid such pressures?

b. If you were head of a public relations department and had to develop a new campaign for Beauty Odor Soap, how would you organize your 10-person unit to develop the best ideas for the program? Would you get suggestions individually or collectively? What would your role(s) be? Why?

c. Territoriality has been observed reliably in various lower-animal groups, where it appears to play a very important role in population control and in stabilizing social relations. Do you think that human territoriality exists? What possible examples of it can you suggest? What needs does it appear to satisfy?

d. Different styles of leadership are effective under different circumstances. If you were appointed the leader of your college's affirmative action student advisory committee, what style of leadership would you adopt? Why? What kinds of group factors do you think would be associated with this style of leadership?

5. EVALUATION (SELF-TESTS)

Correct answers and text page references are given at the end of the unit.

a. Fill-in-the-blanks Items

Write the word(s) that best complete(s) the sentence in the space provided.

1. The phenomenon known as audience effects is one means of producing _____.

2. Frequently a group context will benefit _____ performances.

3. When the problem to be solved has a single, clearly recognized answer, group performance will be _____ proficient than individual performance.

4. In group think, independent critical thinking is _____.

5. Informational social influence can be produced by providing information to increase _____.

6. If a consistent minority influence occurs, it typically takes place _____ in the process.

7. Anonymity of individuals within a group can produce a curious state called

_____.

8. We try to prevent others from entering an area around our body, which is called

_____.

9. The effects of crowding may not be due to density but rather to a disturbance of

_____.

10. Groups may not function as well as they might because of a poorly managed

_____ environment.

b. Matching Items

Write the number of the correct item from the right column in front of the matching item in the left column.

_____ audience effects	1. group influences less responsible decisions
_____ coaction effects	2. available space divided by people present
_____ risky shift	3. groups helping less than individuals do
_____ conformity pressure	4. influence of passive spectators
_____ bystander effect	5. oriented to group morale
_____ territoriality	6. influence of persons doing the same activity
_____ personal space	7. behavior of group members toward one another
_____ interpersonal density	8. "rights" to certain geographic areas
_____ internal environment	9. makes one agree with what others say and do
_____ socioemotional leader	10. space surrounding the body

c. Multiple-choice Items

Circle the letter in front of the answer that best completes the stem.

1. The influences on individual behavior of passive spectators are labeled:
   a. coaction effects
   b. evaluating social effects
   c. audience effects
   d. loafing effects

2. The group context is most likely to interfere with:
   a. emotional tasks
   b. new performances
   c. well-practiced performances
   d. interactive tasks

3. Which one of the following is *not* associated with the "group think" process?
   a. members' belief in the morality of other members
   b. negative views of opposition leaders
   c. feelings of unanimity
   d. feelings of anonymity

4. The relative efficacy of individual versus group problem solving is *not* dependent on which one of the following?
   a. the nature of the environment
   b. the nature of the task
   c. the scheme for coordinating group members
   d. the scheme for combining individual efforts

5. Conformity pressures are dependent on the size of the unanimous group consensus, up to how many confederates?
   a. three
   b. five
   c. seven
   d. nine

6. Which one of the following is *not* characteristic of the consistent minority effect?
   a. it occurs early in the process
   b. there usually is a snowball effect
   c. minority members are disliked by the majority
   d. majority members think more about their positions

7. Which one of the following is *not* characteristic of the deindividuation process?
    a. the individual loses a sense of self
    b. the effect of external cues is enhanced
    c. normal standards are enhanced
    d. irresponsible behavior takes place

8. Persons attempt to reduce the extent to which their personal space is invaded in an elevator by:
    a. maintaining eye contact with fellow passengers
    b. conversing with fellow passengrs
    c. singing songs
    d. closing their eyes

9. Which one of the following is *not* associated with producing crowding effects under low-density conditions?
    a. interference with privacy
    b. knowledge of other group members
    c. interference with goal-directed behavior
    d. control over density conditions

10. Which one of the following is *not* a personality characteristic frequently associated with leadership ability?
    a. intelligence
    b. sociability
    c. dominance
    d. extroversion

d. Short-answer Items

Answer the following questions with short, concise statements. Reference pages for the material are given at the end of the unit.

1. Differentiate clearly between the two types of social facilitation known as audience effects and coaction effects.

2. List three of the characteristics of "group think" groups and one way that has been demonstrated to minimize pressures for group think.

3. Differentiate clearly between informational social influence and normative social influence.

4. Contrast territoriality and personal space, and indicate two conditions under which crowding effects can take place.

ANSWER KEY FOR UNIT 30

Unit Review

1. human behavior
2. family
3. socialized
4. audience
5. coaction
6. evaluating
7. benefit
8. interfered with
9. loafing
10. single answer
11. better
12. risky-shift
13. competition
14. autonomy
15. group think
16. unanimity
17. leaders
18. keep quiet
19. dissenting
20. poor
21. "open"
22. devil's advocate
23. task
24. group solution
25. conformity pressure
26. three
27. correct
28. informational
29. greater
30. normative
31. obedience
32. more humane
33. true/own
34. minority
35. "snowball"
36. disliked
37. majority
38. anonymity
39. "self"
40. irresponsible
41. external
42. prosocial
43. inaction
44. help
45. diffusion
46. not acting
47. physical space
48. anxiety
49. territoriality
50. entering
51. closer
52. eyes
53. heart rate
54. subconscious
55. density
56. privacy
57. disturbed
58. goal-directed
59. control
60. powerlessness
61. functions
62. external
63. internal
64. difficult
65. complicated
66. internal
67. situation
68. extroversion
69. assigned
70. talk
71. interaction
72. task
73. socioemotional
74. leader-member
75. autocratic
76. aggression
77. stressful
78. authoritarian
79. needs

Evaluation (Self-tests)

a. **Fill-in-the-blanks Items:**

1. social facilitation (p. 722)
2. well-practiced (p. 722)
3. more (p. 722)
4. decreased (p. 726)
5. cognitive clarity (p. 727)

6. later (p. 732)
7. deindividuation (p. 732)
8. personal space (p. 735)
9. privacy (p. 736)
10. internal (p. 738)

b. **Matching Items: Correct order and page references are:**

4 (p. 721); 6 (pp. 721–722); 1 (pp. 723, 725); 9 (p. 726); 3 (p. 733);
8 (p. 734); 10 (p. 735); 2 (p. 736); 7 (p. 738); 5 (p. 740).

c. **Multiple-choice Items: Correct answers and page references are:**

1—c (p. 721); 2—b (p. 722); 3—d (pp. 723–724); 4—a (p. 726); 5—a (p. 727);
6—a (p. 732); 7—c (p. 732–733); 8—d (p. 735); 9—b (pp. 736–738); 10—b (p. 739).

d. **Short-answer Items: Page references for answer material are:**

1. pp. 721–722; 2. pp. 723–726; 3. pp. 727–732; 4. p. 734–738.

Statistical Appendix

MEASUREMENT, DESCRIPTION, AND GENERALIZATION

1. INTRODUCTION TO STUDY OF THIS UNIT

The mathematics of probability was the forerunner of psychological statistics, the topic treated in this unit. This type of mathematics was developed initially because of interest in games of chance. A pioneer in these developments was Karl Gauss (1777–1855), an astronomer and mathematician who pointed out the very practical value of what was to be called later the normal curve. For this reason, the curve is sometimes called the Gaussian curve. He developed techniques for computing the arithmetic mean, probable error, and standard error.

The initial application of statistics to social and biological data was done by Adolph Quetelet (1796–1874), a Belgian astronomer and mathematician. He applied the "law of deviation from an average" (the normal curve) to anthropometric measures of humans to show that they were distributed normally, and he spoke about "the average man."

Sir Francis Galton (1822–1911) was influenced by Quetelet's work on the normal curve and began to use the technique in his laboratory work on individual differences. He developed several statistical notions, including the median, standard score, order of merit scale, rating scale, scatter diagram, and correlation technique. He developed correlation after observing for some time the phenomenon of regression toward the mean. He needed a way to assess this regression; the technique was, of course, correlation, and the symbol for correlation — r — was named aftr the first letter of the word regression. Most modern techniques for estimating the reliability and validity of psychological measures are based on Galton's work, as are various factor analysis techniques.

Finally, the work of Karl Pearson (1857–1936) is of relevance here. Pearson was a junior colleague of Galton's and developed many techniques for the treatment of data. Specifically, he is responsbile for the present form of the product-moment correlation coefficient. Since he developed the mathematical procedures for this coefficient — r — it is frequently referred to as the Pearson r.

2. ISSUES AND CONCEPTS

The meaning of the term statistics and the general functions of various statistical techniques are the first topics you should become familiar with in this unit. Learn what a frequency table is, how to develop one, what the shape of a displayed frequency table (curve) can tell us, and what skewness means.

Be able to differentiate the three averages — the mean, median, and mode — and know how to calculate each. In addition, be able to discuss the advantages and disadvantages of each.

Learn next why we need a measure of dispersion or variability of scores in a distribution and how to calculate the two measures of dispersion described — the range and the standard deviation.

The scaling terms — absolute zero and equal units — are treated next. Be aware that psychological measures rarely possess these two characteristics. Know of and be able to calculate percentile scores and understand how they can be used, with caution, to compare performances. Be able to differentiate as well the two other scaling terms — nominal and interval measurement.

Be able to discuss what correlation tells us and the distinction between positive and negative correlation as well as what zero correlation means. Learn the meanings of correlation coefficient and how it measures both the sign (direction) and magnitude of relationship, and of rank-order correlation technique and how it measures relationship, as well as how to calculate a rank-order coefficient. Be able to describe the most commonly used method for calculating correlation coefficients — the product-moment technique (r), which makes use of the real scores, not ranks. Know that correlations tell us nothing about cause-and-effect relationships but may be useful in predicting scores. Be able to explain why.

Concerning reliability, learn what it is and the two methods described for estimating it — the repeated measures and split-half techniques. Be able to define validity as well, and know how it is frequently estimated and the differences involved. The general relationships between reliability and validity should also be studied.

The text discusses sampling errors in psychological studies next. Become familiar with the typical steps taken to avoid or reduce them. Learn the two kinds of information used to evaluate our trust in a sample mean, and how to do the evaluation. Know how this same logic is employed in comparing data obtained from two groups of subjects and in evaluating conclusions reached from such comparisons.

Finally, learn why it is hazardous to generalize beyond actual existing data and how statistical methods can act as guidelines by suggesting the probabilities of our conclusions being correct.

3. UNIT REVIEW

Correct answers are given at the end of the unit.

Statistics refers to techniques for enumerating, describing, and analyzing data. Such techniques permit us to (1)_____ beyond the collected data. When we have a great deal of data (numbers) to describe and analyze, we first order them in (2)_____ tables, which tell how frequently each value occurs. We may group individual values into equal (3)_____ and specify the number of cases falling within each. We may wish to display the frequency table data graphically by usine a frequency curve or a (4) _____.

The shape of the frequency curve can tell us whether the distribution is symmetrical or whether it is (5)_____. Almost all behavioral measures show the later type of curve.

Averages refer to measures of (6)_____ in a distribution. One average is the mean (X), or (7)_____ average. It is calculated by summing all of the scores in a distribution and dividing by the (8)_____. A second average is the mode, which is the score that occurs (9)_____ in a distribution. A third average is the median, which is the score that falls exactly in the (10)_____ of the distribution, or the (11)_____ percentile. Average may refer to any of these three measures, which frequently have (12)_____ values, advantages, and disadvantages. The arithmetic mean is strongly influenced by (13)_____ scores, whereas the median and mode are not.

  An average is not sufficient to describe a distribution of scores well. We must also have information on the degree of (14)_____ of the scores. The simplest numerical measure of variability is the (15)_____, or the distance between the highest and lowest scores. It is, however, easily influenced by a single (16)_____ value. A more commonly used measure of variability is the (17)_____. This statistic is frequently abbreviated as S.D. or *s* and is based on (18)_____ score in the distribution. To calculate S.D. we determine how each score deviates from the distribution (19)_____, we square each of these deviations, sum the squares, and divide by the (20)_____. We then take a (21)_____ of the result to obtain the S.D.

  In order to make certain kinds of quantitative comparative statements (for example, this is twice as long as that), we must have measuring instruments that have a real zero (22)_____, as in a ruler or a weight scale. These instruments have a real or (23)_____ zero. Psychological measures (24)_____ have a real zero starting point, and thus we cannot make ratios of our scores and say, for example, that Joe is 25 percent more intelligent than Bill. Physical measuring instruments also frequently have (25)_____ units; an inch on a ruler is the same distance regardless of which part of the ruler is sampled. Most psychological measures can (26)_____ assume equal units.

  A percentile score is a derived score that tells us a person's standing in relation to the rest of the group. For example, a percentile of 80 would indicate that (27)_____ percent of the group scored above it and (28)_____ percent below it. Percentile scores vary from 0 to 100, no matter what the range of the (29)_____. They can be used, with caution, to compare the performances of different people on different tests having different (30)_____ of measurement.

  If the instrument we are using has equal units, such as a temperature scale, it is said to provide (31)_____ measurement. Psychologists are sometimes willing to assume that a well-standardized test does provide that. In most cases, psychologists use scales that provide only (32)_____ measurement, in which higher scores mean more of whatever the test measures than lower scores do. A procedure, called (33)_____ measurement, allows us to classify a subject into one or more categories (for example, male or female). These three different types of measurement help to determine (34)_____ of statistical methods we can use in summarizing our findings and in generalizing to larger groups.

To compare two or more aspects of the same persons we may use (35)_____ statistics, which tell us the extent to which a change in one characteristic is associated with a change in another. Two sets of measures whose values go together will give us a (36)_____ correlation, and we can get some indication of this in a correlation plot. If high scores on one distribution tend to be associated with high scores on the second, low scores on one with low scores on the second, and so on, we expect a (37)_____ correlation. If high scores on one distribution are associated with low scores on the second, and vice versa, we expect a (38)_____ correlation. The sign of a correlation, whether positive or negative, tells us only the (39)_____ of the relationship of the scores on the two measures. If there is no particular relationship and the scores on the two distributions vary haphazardly, we expect (40)_____ correlation. The statistic that measures both the sign and magnitude of a relationship is the (41)_____. A perfect positive coefficient is (42) _____ and a perfect negative coefficient is (43) _____; a low positive might be around +0.18 and a high negative might be around −0.92, and so on. The simplest method for calculating a correlation coefficient is to use the (44)_____ technique. Here the scores in the two distributions for each of the subjects are rank ordered. The formula provided in the text calculates a coefficient based on a comparison of the ranks in the two distributions; if there is a high degree of correspondence — that is, few rank (45)_____ — we can expect a high (46)_____ coefficient. If there is haphazard correspondence, we can expect something close to a (47)_____ coefficient, and if there is a high degree of reversals, a high (48)_____ coefficient. The most commonly used correlation technique is the (49)_____ correlation coefficient (r), which makes use of the real scores of the subjects, and not ranks.

Correlation coefficients cannot specify which of the two correlated variables (50) _____ the other. Indeed, the relationship may reflect the influence of a third or other (51) _____ variable. We can use the coefficient, however, to (52)_____ a score on the second distribution from knowledge of a person's score on the first distribution.

Any measure contains some degree of error, and some measuring instruments give us larger errors than do others. The (53)_____ of a measuring device is defined as the degree to which repeated measurement of the same quantity with the instrument will give the same readings. We can correlate such repeated measures to provide a numerical index that expresses the degree of reliability of a test — for example, in a reliability (54)_____. To avoid repeated measures, we can (55)_____ the data collected for each of our subjects and correlate, across subjects, performance on one-half of the data (test or task scores) with performance on the other half. This (56)_____ reliability coefficient is frequently a reasonable estimate of the reliability of the instrument. Of course, a test may be highly reliable and still be a poor measuring instrument because it lacks (57)_____. This dimension is concerned with whether a test or other instrument measures what we (58)_____ it to measure. We usually estimate the validity of a measure by correlating scores on the measure with scores on an (59)_____ of the aspect being measured, through a validity (60)_____. It is frequently difficult to find such a (61) _____ with which to correlate test scores. A test, then, may have high reliability and (62) _____ validity. However, a test that has low reliability (63)_____ have high validity.

Often when we measure in psychology, we are interested not only in the subgroup or sample of people we measure, but in the larger group called the (64) _____. Since we rarely measure all persons in the population, we are liable to (65)_____ errors. To reduce such errors, we may draw for our study a (66)_____ sample, in which every member of the entire population has an equal chance to be included in the sample. Here, there is no systematic (67)_____ in favor of any kind of person or sample. There is no way that we can completely avoid sampling errors, but statistical analysis can help us to predict their probable (68)_____. Our trust in a sample mean is influenced by two kinds of information: the (69)_____ of the sample being used, and the (70)_____ of the scores in the group under study. The larger the sample and the smaller the variability in the sample scores, the more trust we have that the sample mean represents the (71)_____ mean.

In comparing two groups, the same sort of statistical logic is employed. That is, we compare the means of the two groups (frequently an experimental group and a control group), and the size of this difference is interpreted in terms of the (72)_____ of the two samples involved and the (73)_____ of scores in the two distributions. Using appropriate statistical tools, we may conclude that there is a reliable, or statistically (74)_____, difference between the means of the two groups, or not. This is done by estimating whether the difference found in the two samples would still exist if we were able to measure (75)_____ in the two populations that the samples represent.

When we attempt to generalize beyond the actual data on hand, it is impossible for us to be completely confident about being (76)_____. Statistical methods cannot prove (77)_____ but they serve as a guide to conclusions and provide information about how probable it is that we will be correct.

4. THOUGHT QUESTIONS

a. What do you think would be the shapes of the following frequency curves, and why? (1) the heights or weights of every male student on your campus; (2) the final grades of all of the students in your psychology course; and (3) the final grades in an advanced undergraduate course in psychology.

b. In a completely normal distribution, what should be the relationship between the mean, median, and mode? If the distribution is skewed toward high (better) scores, what will the relationship of these three averages be now?

c. Why do you think it is that data in psychological experimentation are never ratio and rarely interval, but rather, most likely ordinal or even nominal? What is there about our measuring devices that results in these kinds of scales?

d. It is said that we can lie with statistics. Try to think of at least two specific ways that we could manipulate data statistically to give false impressions. (You might think of economic inflation data or grade inflation information, for example).

5. EVALUATION (SELF-TESTS)

Correct answers and text page references are given at the end of the unit.

a. Fill-in-the-blanks Items

Write the word(s) that best complete(s) the sentence in the space provided.

1. Frequency table data are often displayed graphically in histograms or ___frequency curve___.

2. The average that is always the 50th percentile in a distribution is the ___median___.

3. The most common measure of variability of scores in a distribution is the ___standard deviation___

4. Physical measures frequently have a real zero starting point and ___equal___ units.

5. A percentile score of 60 would indicate that ___40___ percent of the group scored higher.

6. A correlation coefficient measures both the sign (direction) and ___magnitude___ of a relationship.

7. Cause-and-effect relationships are ___not___ specified by correlation coefficients.

8. A reliability coefficient specifies the degree to which ___repeated___ measures give the same readings.

9. If a measuring instrument measures what we want it to measure, we say that it is ___valid___.

10. A random sample is one in which every member of the entire population has an ___equal chance___ to be included in the sample.

b. Matching Items

Write the number of the correct item from the right column in front of the matching item in the left column.

__4__	class interval	1. scatter of scores in a distribution
__9__	mean	2. inverse relationship
__5__	mode	3. repeatability estimate
__1__	variability	4. range of values treated as one group
__8__	range	5. most frequent value
__2__	negative correlation	6. lack of representativeness of a sample
__3__	reliability coefficient	7. categorizing every subject
__7__	nominal measurement	8. difference between highest and lowest scores
__10__	ordinal measurement	9. most commonly used average
__6__	sampling error	10. rank order of a set of subjects

c. Multiple-choice Items

Circle the letter in front of the answer that best completes the stem.

1. The most frequently appearing score in a distribution is called the:
   a. mean
   b. median
   c. mode
   d. range

2. Which of the following averages is most influenced by skewness in the distribution?
   a. mean
   b. median
   c. mode
   d. range

3. Which of the following is *not* a measure of dispersion in a distribution?
   a. s
   b. standard deviation
   c. sampling error
   d. range

4. Which of the following scales does *not* have a real zero starting point?
   a. a ruler
   b. the IQ test
   c. a weight scale
   d. a tape measure

5. If 30 percent of the group scores above a particular score, what would its percentile score be?
   a. 10
   b. 30
   c. 50
   d. 70

6. Which of the following correlational coefficients would we expect if the scores on the two distributions vary quite haphazardly?
   a. 0.15
   b. 0.40
   c. 0.65
   d. 0.90

7. The sign of a correlation coefficient tells us what about a relationship?
   a. magnitude
   b. direction
   c. magnitude and direction
   d. goodness

8. The repeatability of a measuring device is indicated in a:
   a. sampling error
   b. scaling measure
   c. validity coefficient
   d. reliability coefficient

9. To reduce sampling errors, we frequently:
   a. test the entire population
   b. use split-half techniques
   c. use a random sample
   d. decrease the size of our sample

10. Our trust in a sample mean is *not* influenced greatly by the:
    a. size of the sample
    b. variability of the scores
    c. number of scores in the distribution
    d. sampling error of the population

d. Short-answer Items

Answer the following questions with short, concise statements. Reference pages for the material are given at the end of the unit.

1. Define the three statistical averages and indicate the advantages and disadvantages of each.

2. Define variability as it pertains to a distribution, and indicate two ways of estimating it.

3. Differentiate clearly between nominal, ordinal, and interval measures.

4. Define reliability and validity, and indicate what the relationships are between the two.

ANSWER KEY FOR APPENDIX

Unit Review

1. generalize
2. frequency
3. class intervals
4. histogram
5. skewed
6. central tendency
7. arithmetic
8. number of cases/scores
9. most frequently
10. middle
11. 50th
12. different
13. extreme
14. variability/dispersion
15. range
16. extreme
17. standard deviation
18. every
19. mean
20. number of cases
21. square root
22. starting point
23. absolute
24. rarely
25. equal
26. not
27. 20
28. 80
29. raw scores/distribution
30. raw units
31. interval
32. ordinal
33. nominal
34. what kinds
35. correlation
36. positive
37. positive/high positive
38. negative
39. direction

40. zero
41. correlation coefficient
42. +1.00
43. −1.00
44. rank-order
45. differences
46. positive
47. zero
48. negative
49. product-moment
50. causes
51. unmeasured
52. predict
53. reliability
54. coefficient
55. halve
56. split-half
57. validity
58. want
59. independent index
60. coefficient
61. criterion
62. low
63. cannot
64. population
65. sampling
66. random
67. bias
68. size
69. size
70. variability
71. population
72. size
73. variability
74. significant
75. every person
76. correct
77. certainty

Evaluation (Self-tests)

a. **Fill-in-the-blanks Items:**

1. frequency curves (p. 745)	6. magnitude (p. 752)
2. median (p. 745)	7. not (p. 753)
3. standard deviation (p. 748)	8. repeated (p. 754)
4. equal (pp. 749–750)	9. valid (p. 755)
5. 40 (p. 750)	10. equal chance (p. 756)

b. **Matching Items: Correct order and page references are:**

4 (p. 744); 9 (p. 745); 5 (p. 745); 1 (p. 747); 8 (p. 748);
2 (pp. 752–753); 3 (p. 754); 7 (p. 750); 10 (p. 750); 6 (p. 757).

c. **Multiple-choice Items: Correct answers and page references are:**

1—c (p. 745); 2—a (p. 746); 3—c (pp. 747–748); 4—b (p. 749); 5—d (p. 750);
6—a (p. 752); 7—b (pp. 751–752); 8—d (p. 754); 9—c (pp. 756–757); 10—d (pp. 757–758).

d. **Short-answer Items: Page references for answer material are:**

1. pp. 745–746; 2. pp. 747–748; 3. p. 750; 4. p. 754–756.